INNOVATION U.: NEW UNIVERSITY ROLES IN A KNOWLEDGE ECONOMY

Louis G. Tornatzky, Ph.D.
Senior Fellow, Southern Technology Council
Senior Principal Associate, Battelle Memorial Institute
Senior Scholar, Tomás Rivera Policy Institute

Paul G. Waugaman
Senior Fellow, Southern Technology Council
Principal, Technology Commercialization Group LLC

Denis O. Gray, Ph.D.
Professor, Psychology in the Public Interest Program
North Carolina State University

Copyright 2002, Southern Growth Policies Board
All Right Reserved

A publication of the Southern Technology Council and Southern Growth Policies Board.
Copyright 2002, Southern Growth Policies Board
All Right Reserved

ISBN 0-927364-25-5

TABLE OF CONTENTS

Preface 5

Acknowledgments 7

Foreword 9

Introduction 13

Georgia Tech 27

N.C. State University 43

Ohio State University 55

Pennsylvania State University 67

Purdue University 79

Texas A&M University 91

University of Wisconsin 105

Virginia Tech 115

University of California at San Diego 129

University of Utah 137

Carnegie Mellon University 145

Stanford University 157

Summary and Recommendations 169

PREFACE

Southern Growth Policies Board and the Southern Technology Council (STC—our standing advisory body for technology and innovation issues) are pleased to present *Innovation U.*, an important tool for policymakers, politicians, and university practitioners. To rewrite Tom Wolfe, "No knowledge, no knowledge economy." And for most states and regions, universities are a primary source of that knowledge. Here then are case studies on 12 universities that are doing a particularly good job of building alliances with industry and playing active roles in the economic development of their regions. As lead author Louis G. Tornatzky notes in the Introduction, these are not the only universities doing a good job, but they are excellent examples of the kinds of behavior that will pay economic dividends. We applaud their efforts as well as those of many other universities playing leadership roles in stimulating regional and state economies.

Of course, building a strong regional or state economy is neither easy nor simple. Southern Growth's 2001 Report on the Future of the South, *Invented Here: Transforming the Southern Economy*, calls for the development of a culture of learning, a commitment to innovation and entrepreneurship, and an understanding that quality of life issues are inseparable from economic development issues. Whenever we are tempted to oversimplify the daunting challenges of economic development, we invoke H.L. Mencken, who said, "For every complex problem, there is a solution that is simple, neat, and wrong." The best university with the greatest commitment to innovation cannot, on its own, transform an economy. Indeed, some of the institutions profiled here are located in communities that would not make a list of the top technology regions in the country. In every case, however, the universities are making substantial and inventive contributions to local and state economies. In each case, the economy would be substantially worse except for the university's contribution.

The release of this report extends our long-term commitment to exploring the workings of innovation in economic development. Since the creation of the STC in 1986, and particularly since the publication of *Turning to Technology* in 1989, Southern Growth has led the regional conversation for innovation-based development. We have published work on technology in the classroom, advanced transportation systems, industrial networks, regional strategies, workforce toolkits, the migration of science and engineering graduates, and, last year, the groundbreaking *Invented Here*.

Meeting three to four times a year for the past 15-plus years, the STC has created an ongoing conversation on technology and the future of the South. With the publication of *Invented Here*, southern states are creating technology-driven strategic plans and making long-term commitments to benchmark targets. The STC will soon publish the first *Southern Innovation Index*, which will chronicle the progress of southern states towards these objectives on an annual basis. Many if not most of the goals and objectives put forward in *Invented Here* can be met only with the full involvement of research universities operating in strategic harmony with both government and the private sector.

The Southern Growth Policies Board was created 30 years ago on the premise that states have more to gain than lose by cooperating and collaborating with each other. Except in the area of industrial recruitment, the sharing of experience, knowledge, and information only helps us build stronger states. As committed as we are to building a stronger southern economy, we also know that we have only to gain by working with our colleagues outside the region. For that reason, we are particularly thankful to the National Science Foundation for its financial support to this project and to those institutions within and outside of our region that cooperated so generously in providing the information presented here. Finally, we thank the members of Southern Growth Policies Board and the STC for their ongoing support and contributions.

Jim Clinton
Executive Director, Southern Growth Policies Board
Director, Southern Technology Council

ACKNOWLEDGMENTS

This book was made possible by the support and active participation on the part of a number of individuals and organizations.

First of all, since 1993 the members of the Southern Technology Council have supported the program of benchmarking research on new university partnerships. This support has been both financial and substantive. The topics and issues addressed – including those that were the foci of this book – were significantly steered by the wisdom of many Council members. John Ahlen, William Todd, William Schwieri, Lari Murray, and Bill Eads were particularly helpful in this regard.

Second, through a series of project awards the National Science Foundation has enabled a longitudinal program of research that provided much of the intellectual background and empirical research results that have significantly informed this book. NSF grant EPS-98 19351 provided direct support for the research and writing. In addition, Richard Anderson and James Hoehn, senior managers at the Foundation, provided substantive advice throughout the course of the project.

Third, as described in the introductory chapter of the book, our case study approach demanded the active assistance of the institutions being studied. To this end, each of the universities identified a liaison to the project that in turn enabled our knowledge of and access to informants, reports, internal data, Web sites, and various forms of fugitive literature. In addition, since a major task of the project was to condense voluminous information about each institution into a succinct chapter, our university liaisons also provided good advice of a more editorial nature. This book would not have been possible without the help of the following individuals who performed these roles: David Allen, Lynne Chronister, Jeanne Garon, Art Heim, Gary Isom, Kathy Ku, William Perry, Steven Price, Donald Smith, John Toon, Mary Walshok, and David Winwood.

Finally, the administration and leadership of Southern Growth Policies Board, in the form of Jim Clinton, was essential for the successful completion of the project and the book. Everything was much more complex, took longer, and was more expensive than was anticipated when we started this effort. The project team has appreciated the patience, forbearance, and guidance.

> Louis G. Tornatzky
> Paul G. Waugaman
> Denis Gray
>
> March, 2002

FOREWORD

Innovation U.: New University Roles in a Knowledge Economy, written by Louis Tornatzky, Paul Waugaman, and Denis Gray, is an important work for scholars, practitioners, and others interested in the role of higher education and regional economic development. The American university has set a world-class standard for fundamental, basic research. Less well known is that in the past 10 to 15 years a new model for the American university, as a partner in its regional and state economy, has also emerged. This publication lays out a series of case studies as to how America's best universities in business-higher education partnerships have undertaken these tasks and identifies the multiple ways these partnerships continue to unfold. The universities selected through a nomination process are among those that systematically understand and are comprehensively addressing their role in regional economic development, not piecemeal with one or another exceptional program, but in a myriad of functions and roles.

Business-higher education partnerships have emerged from the "grass roots," as opposed to being discovered in Washington and imposed as a top-down, one-size-fits-all uniform formula. The most successful American higher education institutions in business-higher education partnerships have demonstrated a very pluralistic and individually tailored approach to the evolution of their practice of partnering. There are common practices but no one model or approach is being followed by all. Each university discussed in this publication necessarily takes into account varying external and internal cultures, customs, and experience in developing its approach to contributing to its regional economy.

Each of the case studies focuses the discussion to varying degree on examining three general areas: (1) mechanisms and facilitators for partnerships; (2) spanning structures and systems; institutional enablers; and (3) boundary-spanning structures and systems. This discussion is further broken into 10 specific areas including:

- Industry research partnerships
- Technology transfer
- Industrial extension and technical assistance0
- Entrepreneurial development
- Industry education and training partnerships
- Career services and placement
- Formal partnerships with economic development organizations
- Industry/university advisory boards and councils
- Faculty culture and rewards
- Leadership/structures, policies, and institutionalization

A concluding chapter provides a summary of these case studies as well as suggestions by the authors regarding the future of higher education-business partnerships.

Interestingly, most of the 12 American universities spotlighted in this publication come from regions and states either dominated by traditional heavy manufacturing (with the exceptions of Stanford and the University of California-San Diego) or from more resource intensive, agriculture dominated areas represented by Georgia Tech, Virginia Tech, and Utah. But institutions such as Carnegie Mellon, North Carolina State, Ohio State, Penn State, Purdue, Texas A & M, and Wisconsin are midwestern or southern, predominantly land grant institutions that have "gotten it" regarding the transition of the American economy to one that is increasingly knowledge-driven. Only two of these dozen institutions are private — Carnegie Mellon and Stanford. Except for N.C. State, UCSD, and

Stanford, none of these institutions is located within a regional economy that has completed its transition from durable commodity manufacturing to a more technology-driven one.

It may well be, as we will further examine, that American universities that excel in contributions to regional economic development are stimulated by adverse state or regional economies affecting their state financial support and revenue, although the Stanford example argues to the contrary. And perhaps while stagnating or transitional economies contribute to increased support and/or demand for institutions to respond, my experience in one of the states with one of the selected universities found that firms outside of that state were more positive about its partnering than firms within that state.

THE EVOLUTION OF STATE AND LOCAL ECONOMIC DEVELOPMENT PRACTICE

State and local economic development practice for much of the post-World War II era focused on manufacturing and the needs and interests of the American manufacturer. Consequently, the "tool kit" of state and local economic development emphasized "bricks and mortar" assistance, ranging from local and state grants for site improvements, financing of buildings and equipment to reduction of personal property, inventory and other business taxes, and other costs of doing business. Financing programs revolved around debt or loan support backed by the collateral of buildings and equipment.

Notably absent from this list of state and local economic development tools were any of what are now recognized as elements of the knowledge economy: workforce and education programs, technical assistance and advice from faculty and university labs, or sponsored research. The prevailing culture of economic development practice was reinforced by a manufacturing culture of secrecy, fierce domestic competition, and long lag times in introducing changes in manufacturing practice or product development and differentiation. If groups of manufacturers did get together, they focused almost exclusively on "stopping" the public sector from doing something perceived as adverse; rarely did these groups organize to ask the public sector or higher education institutions for anything in the way of a positive, systemic solution.

Higher education at most was a tax burden to these manufacturers; certainly college graduates might make up a small part of their managerial and technical workforce, but these were "commodities" in oversupply. As to research, either that was left to larger firms with immense internal research and development operations or ignored completely.

The emergence of the digital revolution beginning in the '80s and then the biotech revolution of the '90s are fundamentally changing the dynamics of regional economies. Only slowly are economic development practitioners adapting to these changes or are higher education leaders leading the response.

Firms do not stay in place so long, nor do products, or careers for that matter. Change is a constant of firms, products and careers, and regions going through a transitioning may be even more aware of this as they try to rebuild their economies. The need for knowledge workers with skills to develop and produce value-added products dramatically changes labor and talent requirements. Workers can no longer be considered commodities that are easy to find and replace. Business capital involves fewer loan and debt instruments, and more equity, including seed and venture capital sources. Collaboration across and within sectors — private, public, higher education, nonprofit — requires more networking and relationship building. Hiding in a cocoon making the same thing the same way for a decade or more is more a recipe for bankruptcy than growth. And with these changing dynamics the role of higher education becomes much more critical for the growth and survival of all industries, not just technology-driven enterprises.

HIGHER EDUCATION IN THE 21ST CENTURY

The success of the American university in the post-World War II era in part has been the result of the emergence of the federal government as a major investor in the higher education research enterprise. Led by funds from the National Institutes of Health and National Science Foundation for basic research, supplemented by more mission-oriented financial support from other federal agencies, particularly the Department of Defense and Department of Energy, the American research university has become the world's leader in basic research. The legacy of this research support and investment is that we have a nationwide university innovation system, albeit haphazardly connected to where industry is located. Universities recruit and build strengths in various disciplines and fields based on existing strengths and interests of faculty, rarely with the involvement and participation of a state or regional set of industries. In some cases this can result in the emergence of whole new sets of industries, which has happened in regard to new technologies such as biosciences and information technologies. But in other fields whether it is energy, materials, or advanced manufacturing, there has been a disconnect between university strengths and regional industry strengths.

States in particular over the past two decades have attempted to address this disconnect by supporting and funding research and development, technology applications, and other programs that help create new emerging industries or build stronger relationships between existing industries and the region's higher education anchors. The experience has been mixed, in part because the federal research support engine and infrastructure dwarfs that of states and regions. For example, as public land grant institutions see a continued decline in their state financial support that has been ongoing for many years, a focus on regions may not bring much in the way of state government leverage. Nonetheless, while innovation is global, research converted to technology must be reduced to practice, produced and made in some locality. The future of regions is much more "man made." That is, it can be influenced by what a region's leadership does to address the key elements involved in creating a critical mass, like active higher education leadership engaged in regional economic development. This book shows what a dozen American universities are doing to help address their regions' futures.

The future American economy is going to need and rely on higher education even more than in the past, and not just for it role in educating the future workforce. All fields and careers will require at least some post-secondary education for entry. Higher education will need to play an ongoing lifelong education and learning role for much of the workforce. A key discriminating factor for future regional economies is likely to be the talent pool. Those that offer quality workers with the right generic skills and career experiences can differentiate themselves. No longer a commodity item, talent is something all regions can address, but it will require collaboration of their higher education institutions including community colleges as well as four-year colleges and research universities.

Globalization of the economy means that the only way that American firms can compete with lower paying economies worldwide is with technology and talent, both of which require active collaboration with higher education institutions, whether it be in education and training, research and applications, or other innovation roles, including new firms and new products. "Benign neglect" does not address and solve such issues; rather strong alliances of groups of firms and education institutions and their leadership are required.

While higher education is most organized and can provide most impact by its technology and talent roles, it can indirectly at least affect the issues of capital and entrepreneurship, which go hand in hand. University endowments can help invest in seed funds attuned to helping regional economies. Higher education board trustees can play leadership roles in not only addressing regional capital gaps but also helping find and provide solutions. And faculty and students can think about spinning their research into new firms and new products that remain in the region, provided they are not forced to move to where capital markets are dominant. While the U.S. is making improvements in capital distribution — venture capital going to Silicon Valley has decreased from its former dominating share — the fact remains that capital markets are disproportionately geographically concentrated.

The variety of partnerships and approaches taken by the dozen American universities featured in this publication show there is lots of room for experimentation and there is no lock on approaches to relationship building. Indeed, these case studies provide solid grounds for optimism as to an expanded higher education role in helping build regional economies in the future.

>					Walter H. Plosila, Ph.D.
>					Vice President, Battelle Memorial Institute
>					Cleveland, Ohio

AN INTRODUCTION

BACKGROUND

This book of case studies focuses on understanding how universities can play a larger and more effective role in bettering regional economies. The descriptive cases involve 12 undeniably excellent institutions, but ones that are additionally redefining themselves in terms of what constitutes the model research institution.

Innovation U. bloomed from a larger effort. It is the last project in a seven-year program of public policy analysis that was undertaken by a group of senior researchers associated with the Southern Technology Council (STC). That program addressed the growing involvement of research universities in industry partnerships, particularly those concerned with the commercialization of research findings and faculty inventions. The resultant series of projects and reports incorporated a benchmarking approach to understanding these phenomena and the format proved attractive to practitioners and policy makers alike. The approach included: (1) periodic *performance* benchmarking of more than 50 universities on indices of patenting, licensing, and commercialization; and (2) parallel *best practices* studies of smaller groups of institutions that were exemplary, or "best-in-class" in some performance domain (e.g., launching start-up companies based on university technology). The methodologies[1] and results[2] of each component of that program of research have been summarized elsewhere and will not be reviewed here. Suffice to say, however, most institutions tended to be effective and innovative in just a few areas of external partnering, and run of the mill in other domains. The exceptions to this generalization were what led to the study reported here.

The 12 Universities

Carnegie-Mellon University
Georgia Institute of Technology
North Carolina State University
Ohio State University
Pennsylvania State University
Purdue University
Stanford University
Texas A & M University
University of California - San Diego
University of Utah
University of Wisconsin
Virginia Tech

An Evolving Understanding

After conducting several of our more targeted performance and practice benchmarking studies, one unexpected finding became obvious: a small group of institutions were notably effective and innovative *across performance or practice domains*. We kept seeing the same universities among those that were best in class and engaging in novel practices or policies. We seemed to be observing the emergence of a new, 21st century model of the research university: one that aggressively partners with technology-based industry and regional economic development interests, exhibits and encourages entrepreneurial behavior, and champions these new directions in its public pronouncements and internal values.

> **The objectives of this book are:**
>
> - To describe how a small group of research universities are using their technological strenghts to engage industry and other external partners
>
> - To point out ways that external partnering can enhance regional, state-focused economic development

At the same time, others were reporting complementary analyses of the "engaged university,"[3] the "triple helix"[4] of industry-university-government interactions, or of the university as an engine of regional economic development.[5] It would be fair to say that during the late 1990s the U.S. research university began to be anointed – legitimately or not – as the poster child of the knowledge economy. As one analyst of regional technology growth stated it:

> *Research centers and institutions are indisputably the most important factor in incubating high-tech industries. A side effect of the technical capability and scientific research activities is the training and education of the skilled labor that will be critical to the expansion and reinforcement of regional high-tech industries.*[6]

Admittedly, there is some dispute in the literature about the extent of and ways in which universities can contribute to economic development.[7] For instance, some have argued that the most important way that universities contribute to regional economies is by producing highly skilled graduates,[8] rather than by commercializing their technology or working directly with industry. On the other hand, there is growing consensus that universities can play a significant and proactive role in regional economic development in a variety of other ways including strengthening an area's intellectual infrastructure and producing spillovers of knowledge.[9]

Although high-technology regional economies are almost always anchored by great research universities, not all great research universities are surrounded by a booming regional technology economy. Nor do those universities' graduates automatically stay in their universities' communities to help build technology enterprises. In fact, a growing literature[10] on interstate "brain drain" demonstrates that in the absence of the rudiments of a technology-based regional economy, the best and brightest most likely will leave.[11] We are convinced that aggressive, mission-driven research universities can counteract that trend and contribute to the building of regional knowledge economies.

A Survey of Stakeholders

A second impetus behind the project reported here came from the "stakeholders" themselves. To focus the program of university-industry benchmarking studies mentioned above, in 1998 our team conducted a survey of more than 250 regional leaders from a variety of sectors and points of view for guidance on where to focus our next round of performance and practice benchmarking studies.

The survey sample included individuals drawn from various constituencies of the research university. These included university officials (chief executive officers, chief academic officers, chief research officers, research administrators), economic development officials (both state and regional), government leaders (e.g., legislators, executive level staff) and business leaders, particularly those from high-growth, technology-based companies. The survey allowed respondents to indicate their relative preferences (using rating scales) among a menu of technology-focused performance and practice benchmarking research topics. After extensive follow-up, stakeholders in 28 states returned 126 questionnaires.

Respondents expressed strongest interest in a cluster of closely related "best practice" study topics that included: (1) the practices academic institutions use for attracting and organizing industry-sponsored research projects; (2) practices of universities interfacing with state and regional economic development activities; (3) practices for operating university-affiliated business incubators; and (4) practices concerning university involvement in early stage capitalization of spin-off companies. These topics defined a large portion of the intersection between general university-industry partnering and university involvement in local economic development. Respondents wanted to know if and how universities could play a role in enhancing their regional economic and technological environment.

The team decided that a national, institutional-level qualitative study could capture useful information on all of these issues and held the most promise for making a major contribution to the literature. This was particularly so given the accelerating interest in the policy community (and in the popular press) about technology-based economic development and what universities "ought" to be doing about it.

Why is This Topic Important?

There is abundant evidence that the world economy continues to go through dramatic changes in its basic characteristics, which are, in effect, changing the bases for wealth creation. These include:

- An increasing reliance on products and service with a high degree of knowledge content, often derived from relatively recent advances in science and technology;
- An economy that is global in nature, fueled by changes in trade agreements, transportation systems, and telecommunications;
- An increasing importance of entrepreneurial enterprises, and associated approaches to venture capitalization, as opposed to the traditional dominance of large firms;
- A critical reliance on the highly educated and highly skilled, with firms and regions scrambling to retain and attract the best and brightest.

It would seem *a priori* that universities might be uniquely positioned to make significant contributions to this new economic order. After all, colleges and universities do produce the lion's share of highly skilled workers at an entry level, as well as being a major source of cutting edge science and technology. They have also been early users of and advocates for new technology, such as the Internet and other telecommunications innovations.

In fact, as we will show, a significant body of literature documents the importance of university activities to the innovation process generally and, in turn, to technology-based industrial performance. What is less clear and more controversial is whether the university's role in economic development can be targeted geographically such that benefits will be realized primarily in its home state. While we agree with skeptics who argue this is not easily accomplished and that some universities and states appear to be looking for a quick fix, we believe that there is enough evidence to demonstrate that universities that are committed and thoughtful can impact their state or local economic environment in a number of ways. That stated, the project team took on the challenge of designing a study that would describe and prescribe how a university might become optimally positioned to have such an impact.

The objectives of the study are threefold:

- To describe and define, in broad categories, what constitutes university partnering or engagement in terms of technology-based economic development
- To objectively identify a small group of universities that are considered exemplary in those categories of partnering
- To describe what those universities are doing differently from their peers in terms of specific practices, policies, and programs

A Conceptual Framework

Before launching the study proper the research team had to create a conceptual schema that might frame the analysis. In effect, how can one more precisely subdivide the somewhat unwieldy notion of university-industry "partnering" into more manageable, and operational chunks? The partnering metaphor has wide currency in the research literature but it has been used to describe so many institutional behaviors that it is not very helpful.

After much discussion and reappraisal of the literature, the team identified 10 "domains" of institutional behavior that encompassed the range of specific external interactions that universities might have with industry and economic development interests, as well as underlying organizational characteristics and functions that enable those interactions. We assumed, for purposes of this study, that if an institution were doing anything in terms of partnering, it would be found in one of these categories.

These interactions, characteristics, and functions, in turn, were grouped into three broad groups of more specific domains: (1) **mechanisms and facilitators** of partnerships and economic development; (2) **institutional enablers,** which primarily pertain to organizational culture and rewards; and (3) **boundary-spanning** structures and systems. We do not make the claim that this grouping is the conceptual end-all; nonetheless for the purposes of this study it proved to be a useful organizing scheme. Most importantly, it seemed to make sense to informants in our sample of case study institutions.

Mechanisms and Facilitators of Partnerships

Many universities have functions, people, or units that are involved in partnership activities that allegedly have an impact on economic development. Allegedly is the key operative word here; in reality, universities seem to differ markedly in the extent to which a program or activity focused on the external world is adequately staffed, supported, and important. While the following list of programs or activities is probably not exhaustive, it does reflect conventional wisdom about the partnering mechanisms that ought to be in place, as well as providing a useful point of departure for our data collection.

Industry research partnerships. A significant, growing portfolio of social science research documents the impact of university research on industrial innovation and performance. For instance, Mansfield's work[12] estimated that 10% of new industrial processes are attributable to recent academic research, resulting in a social rate of return of 28%. More recent studies confirm the relationship between academic research and industrial performance.[13]

Interestingly, in a later study[14] Mansfield concluded that traditional predictors such as quality of the faculty or size of research and development budget explained only a small amount of the variance in which universities were cited by industry. However, we do know that proximity to a university[15] and direct involvement in partnership-based linkages with industry-university centers[16] can contribute to these benefits.

As we launched this project we expected to find that a variety of factors would affect the amount of research interaction between universities and industry and the benefits that local firms receive. Universities that are aggressively partnering with industry will or should have a robust portfolio of industry-sponsored research, and will have "customer-friendly" structures, policies, and procedures to enable this activity. The latter might include an industry liaison office and flexible contracting procedures. If outreach has a regional economic development intention, the university will make special efforts to involve state-based companies in these research partnerships. We were very interested in how this function worked in our study sample of universities.

Technology transfer. The amount of research performed by U.S. universities, $27.5 billion in FY 1999, provides a tremendous opportunity for technology transfer.[17] There is a direct relationship between the volume of research performed and the flow of invention, although the strength of that relationship varies widely across institutions. Nonetheless, universities have become increasingly active in managing their intellectual property portfolios, particularly since the passage of the Bayh-Dole legislation in 1980.[18] They are also achieving corresponding outcomes in terms of patenting, licensing, and royalties. These activities have tremendous economic value. For instance, one study estimated that $33 billion of U.S. economic activity and 280,000 jobs are attributable to academic licensing of technology.[19] However, the technology-transfer function in a university with sensitivity to regional economic development will also commercialize (when appropriate) faculty inventions via licenses with state-based companies or through local start-ups. The result is parallel involvement in entrepreneurial development and economic development.

Industrial extension and technical assistance. Universities may also be involved with industry by providing problem-solving technical assistance for state-based companies. In most cases, these types of assistance relationships do not involve research or new knowledge, but rather tap into the established expertise of faculty members, graduate students, consultants, and extension staff. There is logical, theoretical, and empirical support for the value of these kinds of partnerships. First, the target for most of these services, small and medium-sized manufacturing operations, are an important but traditionally neglected component of a state's economy. It is also widely recognized that a great deal of industrial innovation and performance growth occurs without an obvious research trigger but instead depends upon optimal or novel use of existing knowledge.[20] Finally, there is a growing body of empirical research that supports the impact that such services can have on economic outcomes.[21]

These services will typically be on a partial cost-recovery basis and may be incorporated into national efforts such as the National Institute of Standards and Technology Manufacturing Extension Program. University faculty members are involved on a project basis, and the programs tend to be incorporated into a college of engineering or business administration. Some programs may address issues of technological infrastructure, such as telecommunications capacities. Several of the institutions in the study sample are land grant universities and thus historically involved in extension activities in agriculture. We decided not to discuss these agriculture-related activities in the case studies *unless* there was some clear involvement in technology-based industry that was consistent with some of the other activity domains. In other words, if the extension mandate was extended to technology-based economic development, the cases tried to reflect this direction.

Entrepreneurial development. Ever since the pioneering and somewhat controversial work of David Birch[22] on the contribution of small, primarily start-up companies to job growth, interest in and attention to promoting entrepreneurship has grown among policy makers.[23] The promise that successful entrepreneurial efforts will grow where they first put down roots has fueled considerable interest in local economic development circles.[24]

We expect that universities that are actively linked to and involved in state and local economic development will operate or partner with local efforts to foster start-up, technology-based companies. In many cases involvement in such activities will be explicitly premised on regional economics and the perceived attractiveness of creating contiguous high-technology industry. The hoped-for benefits include jobs for graduates and perhaps for geographically marooned spouses, the promise of local research partners, and the lifestyle amenities that allegedly go along with being located in a hotbed of technology industry. Activities may include business incubation services and facilities, locally based seed funds, involvement in Small Business Innovation Research (SBIR) grants, entrepreneurial courses and majors, and various entrepreneurial events (e.g., venture forums, conferences).

Industry education/training partnerships. The importance of human capital — talented and highly skilled people — to the knowledge economy is an all but unchallenged premise of the technology-based economic development literature.[25] Predictions of labor shortages for many science and technology fields in the coming years[26] and concerns about "brain drain"[27] have focused new attention on the university's traditional educational mission and how it can help meet state industry's labor needs.[28]

We also assumed that universities actively partnering with firms in science and technology areas would also be partnering in education and training activities. This is likely to encompass a variety of non-degree educational programs that are responsive to the human resource needs of companies, particularly ones that are state-based. These may include graduate certificate programs in technical or management areas, executive development programs, weekend MBA programs, and corporate-focused distance education.

Career services and placement. While nontraditional educational programs will certainly be part of a university's efforts to meet industry's training needs, all universities also have career services functions to enable their graduates to move from the world of classes to the world of work. However, universities with an orientation toward having a state or regional impact may supplement basic services with some novel approaches. There may be special outreach efforts to local companies, as well as feedback to academic units about post-placement needs and opportunities. If a state is mounting special efforts to develop a particular technology industry sector (e.g., biotech), placement services may get involved, for example, by trying to better understand the hiring needs of such employers.

Institutional Enablers – Culture and Rewards

One of our assumptions going into the project was that universities would not be active or effective in various aspects of partnering unless relevant behaviors of faculty, students, and administrators are supported by the values, norms, and reward systems of the institution. For most universities, this will require a deviation from or redefinition of academic tradition.

Anyone who has spent time on a university campus, either as a participant or an observer, will be struck by the almost tribal nature of how certain behaviors or activities are esteemed and others scorned. In order for campus units and individuals to be "engaged," or be effective in "outreach," there needs to be an alignment between relevant norms, values, beliefs, and behaviors. That alignment is what defines an organizational culture. In order to be accepted or encouraged, partnering activities will need to be seen as important, worthy, and central to what the university is all about. In our own personal interactions with universities — as faculty members, staff employees, consultants, and leaders of economic development and policy organizations — we observe huge disparities across institutions along these dimensions. While the authors' antennae may be unduly sensitive, we all have observed the subtle markers of organizational culture in the academic world.

For example, universities that are actively involved in state and local economic development and industry partnering will tend to adopt language in mission, vision, and goal statements that reflects that emphasis. They also tend to incorporate different versions of those statements in reports, publications, press releases, and speeches directed at the external world. In effect, the public language and metaphors that are expressed will have a quite different sound than at other institutions.

Such statements are typically issued at the institutional level, but may be also be found in somewhat different forms at the college or unit level. They also tend to be aggressively disseminated to various leadership and lay audiences. It is a very instructive exercise to snoop around the Internet Web sites of universities — from the perspective of a technology business executive seeking help or a citizen trying to figure out how "their" university makes a difference in their community — and see how apparent that community linkage might be. Similarly, it is useful to take up reading presidents' speeches, and deans' statements of college mission or goals, looking for stirring phrases about making a difference in firms' chances and creating economic opportunity in a region. When the same phrases are repeated over settings and years this says something about the values, beliefs, and goals that make up the institutional culture.

We have observed that universities with active external links are also likely to have an informal and formal system of rewards that encourages faculty to be involved in these activities. These might include positive weighting of such involvement in tenure and promotion decisions, giving attention in campus and community media, providing symbolic acknowledgement via events and awards, and more subtle and informal approval by peers and colleagues. For example, we have run across senior university administrators who have actually started technology companies, which sends a powerful message about cultural approval (or at least tolerance).

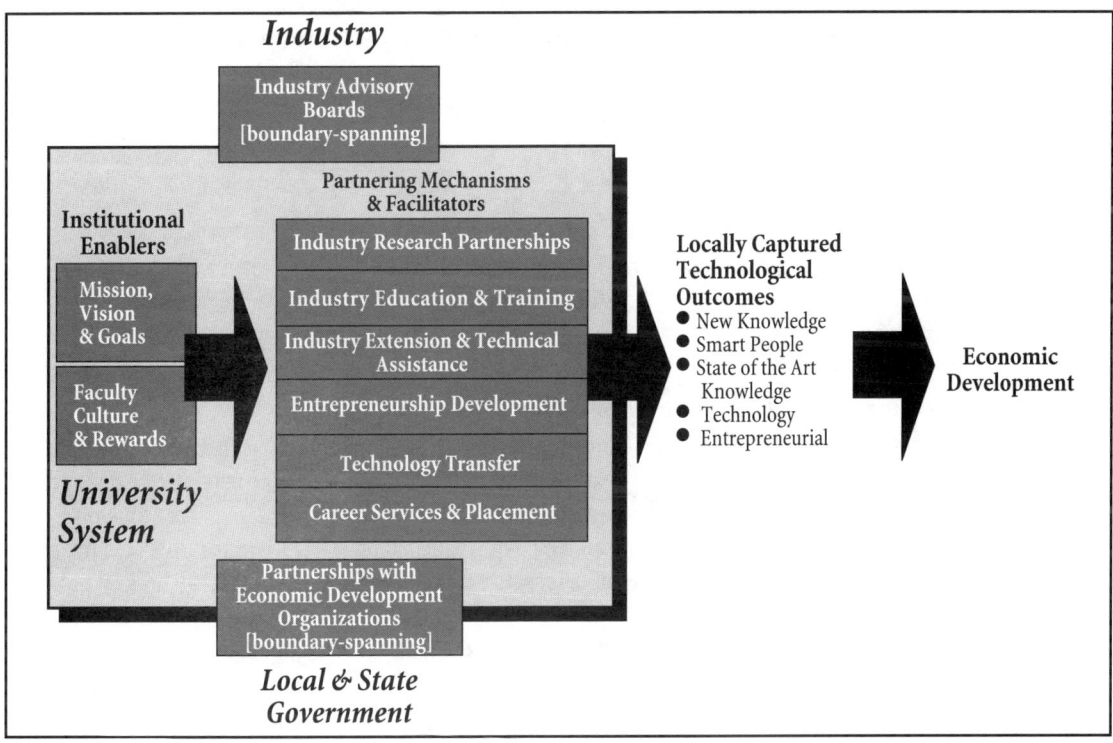

There is an irony about looking at rewards and cultural value statements such as mission pronouncements. That is, while many scholarly observers of academic life consider these factors as critical determinants of institutional and individual behaviors, it is often hard to get faculty members to acknowledge their importance. Everyone looks at themselves as free agents. However, the importance of organizational culture can be realized by noting how few faculty members there are who actually deviate from the traditional role model of scholarship, teaching, and a modest amount of service.

Boundary Spanning Structures and Systems

The basic organizational structures and governance functions tend to look alike at most universities. As the general literature on interorganizational relations suggests,[29] universities taking on a larger role of external partnering likely will have additional structures and systems to manage this interface. We were especially attentive in our case studies to the following:

Formal partnerships with economic development organizations. Universities that are actively linked to state and local economic development will often participate in strategy formulation, governance, and program development activities of state and local economic development organizations. These may include local or state chambers of commerce, state departments of commerce or their equivalent, or local industrial development organizations. Participation occurs at all levels of the institution, from senior leadership to interested faculty and staff. In some cases universities may function as a de facto instrument of state or regional economic development policy. This may extend to university involvement in organized attempts to lure companies from other states or countries.

Industry/university advisory boards and councils. Universities that are significantly linked to the business community will frequently create industry advisory boards and councils. These may exist at the unit and/or institution level and will engage in a variety of activities designed to promote mutual learning between the university and the private sector (e.g., visioning future technology trends, providing feedback on existing academic programs). Some of these take on the flavor of advisory boards on partnering generally, with quite novel reporting relationships.

RESEARCH APPROACH

The *Inovation U.* project is based on a benchmarking approach to data collection with three basic tasks: (1) to develop a performance metric, or proxy thereof, to assess the degree of external partnering of a national population of universities; (2) to identify a few "best in class" institutions; and (3) to describe what those institutions were doing that might differentiate them from their peers.

Benchmarking Performance and Identifying Exemplars

In a project of this sort it is inherently difficult to identify or develop quantitative, objective metrics that might indicate the extent and success of a university's efforts invested in these activities. Instead, the team used a reputation analysis instead. We contacted 55 nationally recognized experts in economic development, regional economics, and the organization of innovation and asked them to be members of a panel of judges. The prospective panel members came from across the country and provided a range of perspectives. They were consultants, researchers on industry-university partnering, university leaders, public policy makers, and individuals from the technology-based private sector. Forty individuals agreed to serve as panel members and all were assured anonymity.

Each panel member was asked to pick from a list of 164 universities[30] those institutions that they felt were "actively and successfully participating in, or linked to, state and local economic development." To conceptually ground the task, each panel member referred to a two-page handout that briefly described 10 "domains" of university activity (e.g., technology transfer, entrepreneurial development, training partnerships with industry) similar to the domains described earlier in this chapter. We asked judges to familiarize themselves with the 10 domain descriptions and then to nominate those universities that they felt were doing an excellent job in these areas. These were "global" nominations as opposed to ratings of each domain for each university on the list. Piloting of the process indicated that few judges had domain-specific knowledge about more than a small group of universities. However, they did feel comfortable making global, reputation-based picks. Eventually 40 completed surveys were returned.

The number of nominations that each of the 164 universities received across the 40 judges was simply aggregated; any single university could theoretically receive up to 40 "votes." These totals were then put in rank order.[31] Sixteen institutions, or about the top 10% of vote getters, became potential "best practitioners." There was a clear break in the vote totals at this level.

Because of limited resources we choose to limit our case studies to 12 institutions. We dropped four universities that made our initial cut for a number of reasons including: a lack of cooperation by institutional representatives, an absence of objective data confirming their involvement with partnering activities, and/or the existence of an extensive literature that already documented that institution's activities.

There was an unknown number of "false negatives," institutions that are clearly involved in external partnering but that the judges didn't pick. The research team knew of a number of smaller or geographically isolated universities that were quite active and successful in these endeavors. The team elected to stay with its research process and the candidate cases that it uncovered, at least for this round of data collection. However, a very useful follow-on study could focus on smaller or rural institutions that are nonetheless involved in partnering.

Case Studies

The next phase of data collection involved case studies of the exemplary institutions. For each of the 12 institutions, the team developed a chapter-length description of policies, practices, and programs related to the 10 activity domains. The gathering and development of case materials generally followed the same path. The process was akin to mutual discovery with our university-based informants, rather than a rigid process of question and answer.

This typically started with a letter contact to the CEO of the university, copied to the chief research officer, the provost or chief academic officer, and the technology transfer manager. The purpose of the initial letter was to describe the goals of the study, explain how their institution had been nominated as an exemplary case, and enlist their support in developing case materials. This was followed by a phone call to the CEO's office, which usually ended up leading to a series of conversations with senior support staff. Eventually, some individual (often the chief research officer) was designated as the principal point of contact for our project.

In subsequent phone and e-mail communication with the point person, a member of the project team again described the nature of the research. During this interaction, he or she also asked the institution to identify "domain champions" (our term) in each of the ten areas of partnership activity. This individual was to be a liaison with the project team for information about that area of activity (e.g., technology transfer). We contacted each domain champion by phone and e-mail, again to describe the purposes of the study. As a starting point, each was encouraged to provide the team with any existing documents, reports, press releases, or studies that would shed light on how a particular partnership activity was conducted at their institution. During this phase, team members also searched institutional Web sites for additional background materials. Each domain champion also received via e-mail a standard set of questions and was encouraged to respond. These covered issues such as the history of a particular activity, its integration with the mainstream teaching and research functions, novel features, and current status. In several of the cases, domain champions sent voluminous hard copy material to the team. Team members frequently followed up with phone interviews, or exchanges of e-mail, to clarify and augment the written or Web-based materials.

One tactic that elicited particularly useful responses was providing informants with examples of a case or cases that had already been completed from another university. Often this stimulated them to share hard-to-obtain documents, historical records, and the like. This occurred in two ways. During the initial development of each case the team provided respondents (except for the very first case) with a small number of sample cases. In addition, when the full array of cases had been developed and compiled into an early draft of this volume, we sent the entire set to original informants, who were given one more chance to correct and provide additional case material. In about half of the cases, we added on-site interviews as well.

On the basis of these data-gathering efforts, the team member assigned to a particular university would typically develop a draft case chapter. In all cases, this early draft included a number of queries and requests for clarification. The drafts (including queries) were bounced back to our university informants at least once, and more often several times. Interspersed with data collection via the Internet were numerous phone conferences and voicemail requests for information. Each of the draft cases took anywhere from three to eight months to complete. It was not a pretty process.

The final drafts became the 12 case study chapters in this book. Each provides some general background and history about the institution and describes novel and noteworthy practices, policies, and programs that characterize its external partnering activities. The material on each university also includes national benchmarking statistics about research scope, extent of industry support of research, and technology transfer performance. A closing chapter provides some concluding comments and suggests next steps for various stakeholder groups.

We have ordered the case chapters in what seemed to us to represent a logical unfolding. First is Georgia Tech, which, by the votes received from our panel of judges, can be considered as the most advanced in the activities studied here. Next, in alphabetical order, we will present the case descriptions of the land grant institutions in the study sample: North Carolina State University, Ohio State University, Pennsylvania State University, Purdue University, Texas A&M University, the University of Wisconsin, and Virginia Polytechnic Institute and State University (Virginia Tech). These are followed by two public universities that are not land grant universities: the University of California at San Diego and the University of Utah. The sample of cases is rounded out by two great private institutions: Carnegie-Mellon University and Stanford University.

WHO SHOULD READ THIS BOOK?

We believe that the examples described and stories told in this volume have great relevance to public policies, programs, and practices. Moreover, we feel that there are a number of stakeholder groups with an interest in the future of U.S. research universities that could benefit from what our research team has learned. They include:

Federal Research Funding Agencies. Despite the growth of industry sponsorship of academic research, the vast majority of support comes from a small number of federal agencies. In particular, these include the National Institutes of Health, the National Science Foundation, the Department of Defense, the Department of Energy, and the Department of Agriculture. In recent years, a number of programs in these agencies have been concerned with or focused on issues of university-industry partnering and the potential for commercial spin-offs from fundamental research. It would be fair to say that interest in state or regional economic development is a minor theme across these same agencies. Nonetheless, we feel that our findings should be of considerable interest to agency officials. Despite recent downturns, the current and future economic fortunes of the country are largely tied to new knowledge and global markets. All of the institutions studied are major and successful players in this arena.

> **Who Should Read This Book?**
> - Federal Research Funding Agencies
> - University Leadership
> - University Governing Boards
> - State and Regional Economic Development Leaders
> - State Legislators
> - Leaders of Technology-Based Industry
> - Private Foundations
> - University Faculty

University leadership. In every case chapter we described instances of university leaders – CEOs, chief research officers, deans – taking strong positions in support of new roles for their university. To a significant degree they are the harbingers of cultural change within the research university. They are ones who must work with their faculty members to define new missions, think through new definitions of scholarship, and look closely at their formal and informal reward structures. We are confident that within the cases described in this volume, university leaders with an itch to change their own institution will find useful examples and the names of peers to call.

State legislators. Not all states are participating at the same level in the knowledge economy, however state legislators are increasingly interested in and informed about the issues addressed in this book. Many want to see their institutions do significantly better in external partnering and involvement in economic development.

University governing boards. In some states or institutions, university boards of trustees or their equivalent increasingly are restive about their institution's involvement in creating state-based economic opportunity. Relatively few members of governing boards have backgrounds as practicing academics, and as a result the mechanisms of institutional change often are not perfectly clear to them. We trust that this volume will provide those individuals with useful practice examples as well as a means of opening a dialogue with their counterparts at the institutions described here.

Leaders of technology-based industry. Business prospects of companies, large and small, are increasingly tied to the research university. These companies are the partners referred to again and again in ensuing chapters. For them, this book should be considered as a companion to the recent study of corporate roles in university partnering by the Business-Higher Education Forum.[32]

State and regional economic development leaders. Every state involved in a technology-based economic development strategy has tried to figure out how to leverage the assets of state-based research universities. Too often, the results are not particularly effective. Many of the institutions described in this volume have developed mutually beneficial working relationships with those agencies in their respective states.

Private foundations. A small number of the major private foundations have a longstanding interest in the American research university. Although their giving agendas are different, all have an interest in maintaining and enhancing the excellence of higher education. We trust that some of the lessons and experiences captured in this book will attract the attention of those interested in gently nudging universities into new roles and responsibilities vis-à-vis the larger society.

Faculty. Last, but obviously not least, are the faculty members of research universities who are obviously the core element in defining institutional excellence. We are firmly convinced that a new breed of faculty member is emerging within the American research university. These are individuals who, while still prizing the excitement of fundamental science and teaching, are also more entrepreneurial in spirit and more willing to take on real world challenges. They are more inclined to be engaged with the industrial world and understand the benefit that those relationships can visit on their scholarship. We hope there will be wide readership of this volume among such individuals and that they in turn will use the information herein as a partial model of what can happen in their own institution.

ENDNOTES

[1] Tornatzky, L.G. (2001). Benchmarking University-Industry Transfer: A Six Year Retrospective. *Journal of Technology Transfer.* 26. 269-277.

[2] Tornatzky, L.G., Waugaman, P.G., and Gray, D.O. (1999). *Industry-University Technology Transfer: Models of Alternative Practice, Policy, and Program.* Research Triangle Park, N.C.: Southern Growth Policies Board.

[3] Kellogg Commission on the Future of the State and Land-Grant Universities. (2000). *Renewing the Covenant: Learning, Discovery, and Engagement in a New Age and Different World.* Washington, D.C.: National Association of State Universities and Land-Grant Colleges.

[4] Loydesdorff, L. and Etzkowitz, H. (1998). The Triple Helix as a model for innovation studies. *Science and Public Policy,* 25.

[5] National Association of State Universities and Land-Grant Colleges (2001). *Shaping the Future – the Economic Impact of Public Universities.* Washington, D.C.: National Association of State Universities and Land-Grant Colleges.

[6] DeVol, R. (1999) *America's High-Tech Economy.* Santa Monica, Calif.: The Milken Institute. (p. 13).

[7] Brooks, H. Research universities and the social contract for science. In Branscomb, L.M. (1993) *Empowering technology.* Cambridge: MIT Press.

[8] Florida, R. (2000). *Competing in the Age of Talent: Quality of Place and the New Economy.* In a report prepared for the R.K. Mellon Foundation, Heinz Endowments, and Sustainable Pittsburgh. Pittsburgh, Pa.: Carnegie-Mellon University.

[9] Berglund, D. and Clarke, M. (1999). Using research and development to grow state economies. Washington, D.C.: *National Governor's Association Best Practices Series.*

[10] Tornatzky, L., Gray, D., Tarant, S. & Howe, J. (1998). *Where have all the students gone? Interstate migration of recent science and engineering graduates.* Research Triangle Park, N.C.: Southern Growth Policies Board.
Tornatzky, L., Gray, D., Tarant, S., & Zimmer, C. (2001). *Who will stay and who will leave? Individual, institutional and state-level predictors of state retention of recent science and engineering graduates.* Research Triangle Park, N.C.: Southern Growth Policies Board.

[11] Gottlieb, P. (2001). *The problem of brain drain in Ohio and Northeastern Ohio: What is it? How severe is it? What should we do about it?* Cleveland, Ohio: Center for Regional Economic Issues, Weatherhead School of Management.

[12] Mansfield, E. (1991). Academic research and industrial innovation. *Research Policy.* 20: 1.

[13] Grossman, J.J., Reid, P.P. & Morgan, R.P. (2001). Contributions of academic research to industrial performance in five industry sectors. *Journal of Technology Transfer,* 26. 143-152.
Toole, A.A. (2001). *The impact of public basic research on industrial innovation: Evidence from the pharmaceutical industry.* Discussion Paper No. 00-07. Palo Alto, Calif.: Stanford Institute for Economic Policy Research.

[14] Mansfield, E. (1995). Academic research underlying industrial innovations: Sources, characteristics and financing. *Review of Economics and Statistics.* 77 (1). (pp. 55-65).

[15] Adams, J. (2000) Comparative localization of academic and industrial spillovers. *Working Paper No. 8292.* Washington, D.C.: National Bureau of Economic Research.

[16] Adams, J. (2001). Industry-university cooperative research centers. *Journal of Technology Transfer.* 26. (pp. 73-86).

[17] National Science Foundation-SRS. (2001). *Academic research and development expenditures, FY 1999.* Washington, D.C.: National Science Foundation. Table B-38.

[18] The Bayh-Dole Act (PL 96-517, the Patent and Trademarks Amendments Act of 1980), named after its senate co-sponsors Burch Bayh and Robert Dole, allowed universities to elect to retain title to inventions arising from research funded by federal agencies and to grant licenses to patents deriving from these inventions. This legislation is a landmark in the development and commercialization of university inventions.

[19] Association of University Technology Managers. (1999). *AUTM Licensing Survey: Fiscal Year 1998.* Norwalk, Conn.: Association of University Technology Managers.

[20] Tushman, M.L. and Rosenkopf, L. Organizational determinants of technological change: Toward a sociology of technological evolution. In Staw, B.M. and Cummings, L.L. (1992). *Research in Organizational Behavior.* New York: JAI Press.

[21] For example, see:
Shapira, P. and Youtie, J. (1997). *Manufacturing modernization: Learning from evaluation practices and results.* Atlanta, Ga.: Georgia Institute of Technology, Georgia Tech Economic Development Institute.
Shapira, P. Manufacturing extension: Performance, challenges and policy issues. In Branscomb, L.M. and Keller, J.H. (Eds.). (1998). *Investing in innovation: Creating a research and innovation policy that works.* Cambridge, Mass.: MIT Press.

[22] Birch, D. (1979). *The job generation process.* (Unpublished manuscript). Cambridge, Mass.: MIT Program on Neighborhood and Regional Change.

[23] National Academy of Engineering. *Risk and innovation. The role and importance of small high-tech companies in the U.S. economy.* Washington, D.C.: National Academy Press, 1997.

[24] Tornatzky, L.G., Batts, Y., McCrea, N.E., Lewis, M., and Quittman, L.M. (1997) *The art and craft of technology business incubation. Best practices, strategies, and tools from more than 50 programs.* Research Triangle Park, N.C.: Southern Growth Policies Board.

[25] For example see:
Berglund, D. and Clarke, M. (1999). *Using research and development to grow state economies.* Washington, D.C.: National Governor's Association Best Practices Series.
Florida, R. The role of the university: Leveraging talent, not technology. *Issues in Science and Technology.* 15. (pp 67-73).

[26] National Science Board (2000). *Science and engineering indicators – 2000.* Washington, D.C.: National Science Foundation.

[27] For example see:
Tornatzky, L., Gray, D., Tarant, S. and Howe, J. (1998). *Where have all the students gone? Interstate migration of recent science and engineering graduates.* Research Triangle Park, N.C.: Southern Growth Policies Board.
Tornatzky, L., Gray, D., Tarant, S., and Zimmer, C. (2001). *Who will stay and who will leave? Individual, institutional and state-level predictors of state retention of recent science and engineering graduates.* Research Triangle Park, N.C.: Southern Growth Policies Board.

[28] For example see:
Carnevale, A.P., Gainer, L.J., Villet, J., and Holland, S.L. (1990). *Training partnerships: Linking employers and providers.* Washington, D.C.: U.S. Department of Labor Employment and Training Administration.

[29] For example see:
Aldrich, H. (1977). Boundary spanning roles and organizational structure. *Academy of Management Review.* (pp. 217-230).
Cummings, T.G. Transorganizational development. In B. M. Staw and L. L. Cummings (Eds.) (1984). *Research in Organizational Behavior.* Greenwich, Conn.: JAI Press.

[30] The list included the top 125 institutions in terms of total research expenditures data as published by NSF, plus other

universities from either Southern Technology Council or EPSCoR states that were typically "flagship" institutions locally, albeit modest in size by national standards.

[31] By a comfortable margin, Georgia Tech received the highest number of nominations.

[32] Business-Higher Education Forum. (2001). *Working together, Creating knowledge.* Washington, D.C.: American Council on Education.

GEORGIA INSTITUTE OF TECHNOLOGY

The Georgia Institute of Technology (Georgia Tech) was founded in 1885 and opened its doors in 1888 as the Georgia School of Technology, with 129 students originally enrolled. The school was the centerpiece of the state's plan for industrial resurgence after the Civil War, and was launched with a $65,000 appropriation from the state legislature. By the 1930s it had begun to grow from its initial trade school orientation, expanding in a number of substantive and programmatic directions. A School of Aeronautics was formed, and the Engineering Experiment Station (now the Georgia Tech Research Institute) opened, providing technical assistance to Georgia industry, a mission that continues to this day in new organizational forms. Renamed the Georgia Institute of Technology in 1948, the school has blossomed into an internationally prominent research and teaching institution. It currently enrolls 14,800 undergraduate and graduate students at the Atlanta campus. The first branch campus is currently being implemented in Savannah, and has already enrolled 130 students in the engineering disciplines. In the FY 1999 National Science Foundation survey of academic research and development,[1] Georgia Tech reported research expenditures of $263.7 million, which ranks 30th among all U.S. universities and 18th among public universities.

Georgia Tech has a number of nationally prominent programs. For example, in national graduate school ratings announced in 2000 by *U.S. News & World Report*, the College of Engineering ranked fourth overall with seven of the 11 programs in the college in the top 10 nationally. The National Academy of Sciences has rated Georgia Tech's graduate program in industrial engineering first in the country; the

Gourman Report has ranked the Industrial Design Program in the College of Architecture as tops in the nation. The school has more than 50 interdisciplinary research centers, many of which are of national standing and scope.

The average SAT scores of Georgia Tech's entering students are among the highest of any public university in the country, and among publicly supported institutions the school is second in the percentage of National Merit Scholars. According to College of Engineering data, between 1991 and 1998, Georgia Tech graduated more engineers than any other university in the country. It also has a commendable record in graduating African-American and women engineers. According to *Black Issues in Higher Education*, Georgia Tech ranks third nationally in the production of bachelor's degree-level African-American engineers, first at the master's level, and third at the doctoral level. Georgia Tech also awards more engineering degrees to women than any other university in the country. Approximately 80% of Georgia Tech undergraduates are enrolled in the Colleges of Engineering, Computing, or Sciences, with more than 60% in engineering alone.

In relation to the objectives of this study, Georgia Tech is perhaps a unique example of external partnering. Virtually every combination of industry relationship or economic development activity can be found at Georgia Tech, and in a very real sense the school is an operating partner with Georgia state government in the implementation and management of a variety of technology-focused initiatives. Perhaps more than any other research university in North America, economic development is an integral, critical component of the mission of the Georgia Institute of Technology, and this has been true from its very inception, along with its commitment to exemplary academics.

MISSION, VISION, AND GOAL STATEMENTS

During the 1880s, Georgia, and the rest of the South for that matter, was struggling to catch up to the rapid pace of industrialization elsewhere in the country. The mission to make Georgia more economically competitive continues to this day. As noted in the Introduction, Georgia Tech garnered more nominations from the panel of experts that was used to identify exemplary institutions for this project. To illustrate the external focus of the institution, this quote from the Vision and Mission section of its Strategic Plan (in which "economic development" is mentioned more than a dozen times) is illustrative:[2]

> *Georgia Tech is a leading center for research and technological development that continually seeks opportunities to advance society and the global economic competitiveness of Georgia and the nation.*

This mission is further articulated in a recent statement from President Wayne Clough:[3]

> *The last century saw Georgia Tech emerge as one of the nation's technological leaders and as a force in the development of the new economy in Georgia. This achievement was attained through a well-honed partnership with state government and the Board of Regents and by hard work and a commitment to excellence. Georgia Tech's momentum was particularly strong in the last decade and was supported by the positive growth of the economy in the State of Georgia and Atlanta.*

This economic development mission for Georgia Tech has its primary organizational home, not surprisingly, in the university's Office of Economic Development and Technology Ventures (EDTV). This group has three major units: the Advanced Technology Development Center (ATDC), Georgia Tech's internationally known business incubator for early stage technology-based companies; the Economic Development Institute (EDI), Georgia Tech's statewide business and economic development service organization; and VentureLab, a new initiative aimed at expanding technology commercialization from Georgia Tech research.

Nearly 40 years in operation,[4] with 200 employees, EDI directly operates several programs functions as a coordinating entity for other activities that involve Georgia Tech and the state of Georgia in the area of economic development. The leadership of Georgia Tech's economic development efforts has been extraordinarily stable, with Wayne Hodges functioning as director since the inception of EDI as a separate operating unit approximately 10 years ago. The senior management team of EDI is deeply experienced, with a number of individuals having both university and community-based economic development backgrounds.

EDI is organized into three broad units and a number of subsidiary programs (which will be discussed below), but its core mission is straightforward:

> *Georgia Tech's Economic Development Institute (EDI) offers an array of services with a common objective: to promote the growth of business and industry in Georgia.*

It should be emphasized that the mission is very much a statewide mandate. While EDI and Georgia Tech are Atlanta based, there is a regional network of offices that spans 18 communities through which services are delivered. In addition to a very accessible Web Site (http://www.edtv.gatech.edu), EDI also publishes a newsletter (*Georgia Tech Impact*), which is distributed to 2,300 individuals on campus and another 4,000 around the state. The newsletter aggressively promotes EDI's mission, services, and products. When the newsletter was created, President Clough urged that it be distributed to all faculty in order to increase campus awareness of the Georgia Tech economic development mission. Another newsletter, *Industrial Advisor*, is focused on manufacturing-related issues and is distributed to 8,000 individuals, typically at the plant-manager level. The newsletters can be viewed in a section of the EDTV Web site (http://www.edtv.gatech.edu/newsinfo.cfm), which has been redesigned to make it even friendlier to manufacturers and economic development leaders around the state.

> **THE GEORGIA TECH CULTURE, FROM PRESIDENT TO ACADEMIC UNIT, IS PERVASIVELY ORIENTED TOWARD OUTREACH AND ENGAGEMENT WITH THE EXTERNAL WORLD.**

However, it would be a mistake to conclude that all Georgia Tech's economic development activities are "contained" within EDI. The Georgia Tech culture, from president to academic unit, is pervasively oriented toward outreach and engagement with the external world. This means that the economic development mission is often realized through a variety of partnerships, which may or may not involve EDI in a formal administrative role.

Championing this mission starts with the president. Wayne Clough has been a frequent, vocal and visible advocate for Georgia Tech making an economic impact on Georgia and the world. He also plays a direct, personal role in large technology-oriented initiatives that illustrate the unique position of Georgia Tech vis-à-vis the state. One of these is the Yamacraw Mission, a $100 million five-year initiative, which is a combined effort by the University System of Georgia, the Georgia Department of Industry, Trade and Tourism, and the Georgia Research Alliance. Dr. Clough serves on the steering committee, and several other Georgia Tech researchers and administrators have been tapped for various planning and leadership roles. Focused on high-bandwidth communications systems, the initiative will build faculty capacity in this area, lure prominent companies to the state, beef up education and training in the field, create a seed fund to support start-ups in the industry, and launch an Electronic Design Center that will commercialize advanced research in the field. Dr. Clough also serves on the boards of the Georgia Research Alliance (see below), one of oldest and largest state technology initiatives in the country, and the Metropolitan Atlanta Chamber of Commerce. With the latter, he has played a key role in the chamber's "Industries of the Mind" campaign, designed to raise awareness and support of knowledge-based industry.

Mission and operational involvement are also found at the unit level. For example, the new Strategic Plan[5] for the College of Engineering calls for the unit to "continue to play and enhance our role in economic development," which is to include support and participation in EDTV activities, playing a lead role in the Yamacraw Mission and the Georgia Research Alliance, and to otherwise "support the location and expansion of technology companies in Atlanta and in the State." In addition to being engaged in economic development, the Strategic Plan also suggests that the college should be a visible champion of its economic development accomplishments: "evaluating, publicizing, and marketing the economic impact of the College of Engineering over the past ten years."

The outreach orientation of Georgia Tech is also enhanced by having as an integral part of its structure a $100-plus million applied research organization, the Georgia Tech Research Institute (GTRI). Most of GTRI's 1,000 employees are located on the Georgia Tech campus and elsewhere in the Atlanta area, although there are facilities in Arlington, Virginia, and Huntsville, Alabama, respectively. The majority of contract work is conducted for federal agencies, particularly in the defense area, although the fraction of industry-sponsored research is increasing (10% of total expenditures in FY 2000). Most of GTRI's research staff is at the master's level, and they hold untenured research faculty appointments. Nonetheless, they maintain a healthy degree of interaction with Georgia Tech faculty members and graduate students, who frequently work on GTRI projects on a part-time basis, which serves to orient the university culture toward applied problems. In addition, GTRI staff frequently teach classes in the academic departments, and a large percentage of the university's co-op students work for GTRI.

A growing fraction of GTRI's work involves Georgia companies and Georgia government entities. For example, Georgia Tech manages a state program called the Traditional Industries Program (TIP), which conducts research and development to improve the competitiveness of three of the state's historically largest sectors: textiles and carpets, pulp and paper; and food processing. Georgia Tech faculty members and staff are performing much of the work, with some participation by GTRI staff. GTRI houses the research arm for the poultry industry, which has been heavily focused on applying computerized sensing and material handling technologies to this industry (e.g., machine vision, robotics, optical biosensors). GTRI also plays an important technical support role for EDI's outreach services to state-based industries, in areas such as environmental health and safety, and materials evaluation and testing.

INDUSTRY RESEARCH PARTNERSHIPS

Georgia Tech has an enviable record of industry research partnerships. National Science Foundation data[6] indicate that Georgia Tech's industry-sponsored research expenditures in FY 1999 were $19.8 million, or 23.8% of total research expenditures. This significantly exceeded the national average of 6.7%, and Georgia Tech ranked second among the top 100 universities. In 1992, industry sponsored research was 13.2% of total research expenditures, indicating a near doubling in less than 10 years. Between 1992 and 1999, while overall research expenditures increased by 46%, industry-sponsored expenditures increased by 164%. Within some units the percentage of industry sponsorship is even higher than the university figures (40% of research funds in the Schools of Electrical and Computer Engineering, and Mechanical Engineering). There are several reasons for the significant scope of industry research funding. One is the value that Georgia Tech places on industry relationships, a theme that is prominent in mission language and strategic plans. For example, the College of Engineering Strategic Plan issued in February 2000 promises that the college will become a model for corporate interaction by:

- *assessing and improving our infrastructure that supports interactions with industry, including contracting flexibility, overhead structure, and intellectual property agreements;*
- *creating strategic alliances with corporate partners that encompass multi-faceted interactions with our faculty and students;*

- *coordinating knowledge of industrial interactions to provide optimum service to companies;*
- *developing mechanisms for bringing together Georgia Tech faculty and local industrial leaders; and*
- *encouraging and streamlining faculty consulting opportunities.*

Second is the generally efficient system of policies and procedures via which research contracts are handled. Early in 1999, Georgia Tech established the Industry Contracting Office, which serves as a strategic delivery system to help the Institute reach its goals. It supports faculty by providing industry, commerce, and the professions with access to Georgia Tech's expertise and resources. The office pays particular attention to providing "one stop shopping," as well as continuity of service between the company and assigned contracting officers. It also works to resolve intellectual property issues quickly, such as nondisclosure and materials transfer agreements.

In September 1999 the Office introduced I-COL, the "Internet Contracting Officers Log," to facilitate project administration and assist faculty. This is a fast and easy way to keep informed about the status of proposals submitted through the Industry Contracting Office. I-COL sends e-mail to advise investigators when an action has been taken regarding a proposal or project. Researchers logging into I-COL will see a list of all their proposals being handled through the Industry Contracting Office and may view the history of any of their own individual proposals.

Third is the accumulated experience and success that Georgia Tech has had in pulling together industry-oriented centers and institutes. There are a number of centers on campus that significantly involve companies as members, financial supporters, or substantive contributors. Among the more significant are the Microelectronics Research Center (MiRC), the Manufacturing Research Center (MaRC), the Georgia Centers for Advanced Telecommunications Technology (GCATT), the Parker H. Petit Institute for Bioengineering and Bioscience (IBB), the Packaging Research Center, and the Institute for Sustainable Technology and Development (ISTD).

Another important feature of center and institute operations, and an important characteristic of the Georgia Tech culture, is the extent to which major research initiatives involve collaboration with other universities in the state. The importance of collaboration is repeated again and again in various mission and strategy documents.

A major contributing factor to Georgia Tech's excellence in industry research partnerships has been the presence of the Georgia Research Alliance (GRA). Founded in 1990, the GRA makes strategic investments in order to build centers of research excellence in Georgia universities, primarily in areas of science that have an obvious linkage to current or future economic growth. These have been concentrated in three strategic areas — advanced communications, biotechnology, and environmental technologies — and have generally supported senior faculty hires and laboratory facilities and equipment. For example, 37 Georgia Research Alliance Eminent Scholar Chairs have been endowed across the six member universities of the Alliance, with a large number of these involving Georgia Tech. Since 1990 the GRA has raised $276 million in state funds, making it by far the most significant component of the state's technology-based economic development strategy.

A unique example of collaboration with established industry can be found in Yamacraw, Georgia's statewide high-technology economic development initiative. Yamacraw is a unique program that aims to make Georgia a world leader in the design of broadband infrastructure systems, devices, and chips. The initiative combines efforts of private enterprise, academia, and state government to leverage Georgia's existing high-technology base and its global leadership in broadband technology research. Georgia Tech is a major part of Yamacraw, with the university president and faculty members from several schools taking part in its activities. In addition, faculty members from several other Georgia universities participate.

The Yamacraw Design Center is the focal point for Yamacraw's broadband communications research efforts, which encompass three target markets: optical networking, high-speed access devices, and content processing. Within these markets, the research thrusts are in the areas of embedded software, broadband access hardware, and system prototyping. Companies that want access to the Yamacraw Design Center's elite faculty researchers and their graduate students can commit $1.25 million over a five-year period or, preferably, commit to hiring 100 high-tech employees in Georgia and pay a membership fee of just $25,000 annually. Design Center members now include Nortel Networks, Broadcom Corp., CIENA, EchoStar Data Networks, National Semiconductor Corp., Star*Core (a joint alliance of Lucent Technologies and Motorola), and Wi-LAN.

Another example of Georgia Tech's commitment to be an active partner in the state's technology base in Atlanta is the new Technology Square development. The project will house the DuPree College of Management, the Global Learning Center, the Economic Development Institute, the Georgia Tech Bookstore, the Center for Quality Growth and Regional Development, a hotel and conference center and other units. The development will be Georgia Tech's first foray across the I-75/85 downtown connect that has formed the eastern border of campus since the 1960s and has heretofore cut Georgia Tech off from the vibrant Midtown business community. The ATDC and Yamacraw Design Center will be in a nearby mixed-use complex known as Midtown Park.

Georgia Tech's extension into Midtown will make its outreach programs even more accessible to Georgia companies and create a new entrance to campus. These units are expected to spark additional technology development in the area, serving as a magnet for innovators and entrepreneurs. The Technology Square/Midtown Park complex will help define Georgia Tech's role in 21st century Georgia.

TECHNOLOGY TRANSFER

Georgia Tech has one of the more active and successful technology transfer programs in the nation, and one that is closely attuned to the economic development mission and entrepreneurial culture of the institution. License income was $2.04 million in FY 1999, a royalty return on investment (royalties divided by total research expenditures) of 0.78%. License income ranks in the 68th percentile, and royalty return on investment ranks in the 53rd percentile of the 142 academic institutions that participated in the *AUTM Licensing Survey: FY 1999*.[7] In new licenses to start-ups in fiscal years 1998 and 1999 combined, Georgia Tech reported a total of 18, placing it in the 89th percentile in the total AUTM licensing survey sample. In the same period, Georgia Tech reported a total of 10 start-ups formed, seven of which were in-state. Georgia Tech ranks in the 94th percentile for total start-ups formed and in the 95th percentile for in-state start-ups formed.

However, the mission thrust, policies, and practices of the office are clearly oriented toward enabling Tech's would-be entrepreneurs, as well as attending to more straightforward licensing deals with established companies. This shift in philosophy has come about in the last decade and is also associated with the entrepreneurial development programs and funding opportunities of the Advanced Technology Development Center (ATDC) incubator. For example, since the establishment of the Technology Licensing Office and the Faculty Research Commercialization Program in 1992, the pace of start-up companies has increased significantly. This is also reflected in increased awareness and support by Georgia Tech leadership. As described by Dr. Charles Liotta, Vice Provost for Research and Dean of Graduate Studies:[8]

> When you license something, you get a certain number of dollars as reward. But when Georgia Tech takes equity in a start-up company, and that company becomes large and profitable down the road, Georgia Tech will profit from it, and so will the economy.

The Georgia Tech Research Corporation (GTRC), which holds title to all intellectual property developed at Georgia Tech, actively encourages faculty participation in start-up companies. Twenty-one start-up companies have been granted licenses for GTRC intellectual property in recent years. In a majority of these cases, GTRC normally takes equity as part consideration for the granting of the license. Many of these start-up companies have become ATDC member companies.

Among the successes is MicroCoating Technologies, which licensed from GTRC a new process for applying thin films. Since 1994, beginning with initial funding from Small Business Innovation Research (SBIR) grants, MicroCoating Technologies has grown in size from two to more than 120 employees. Revenues have, on average, doubled every year since the company was established. The concern was initially backed by a $4 million investment by Atlanta-based Noro-Moseley Partners.

Over the years a number of high-tech companies have been formed out of efforts by GTRI researchers. Examples include Scientific Atlanta, ERDAS, Digital Furnace (now a part of Broadcom), and ChanneLogics. Recognizing the importance of the commercialization process, GTRI has formed the Commercial Product Realization Office to pursue opportunities to work with companies on significant product development opportunities. The focus is on helping companies to successfully move products rapidly to market, including preparation for full production. GTRI's core competencies in electronics, optoelectronics, communications, and information systems are central to many high-tech industries in Georgia.

A recently launched initiative within the Office of Economic Development and Technology Ventures (EDTV) is likely to significantly expand the scope of technology transfer for the university, particularly through the start-up route. VentureLab is to be a "one stop shopping" resource for faculty members interested in commercializing the technology emerging from their labs but who may not have a great deal of knowledge or experience in this area. Four service components will comprise the core of the new program's activities. A technology assessment component will work with faculty early in the process, evaluate the commercial potential of their technology, and determine the most appropriate commercialization path – either licensing to an existing company or forming a start-up. A second component will involve educational outreach to faculty members on principles and practices involved in technology commercialization: protection of intellectual property; the licensing process; and starting, managing, and capitalizing a company. As a third component, VentureLab will have a network of VentureLab Fellows, experienced technology entrepreneurs who can provide advice, mentoring and guidance in launching a technology company. In effect, VentureLab will be building teams that can accelerate the formation and success of the start-up. Finally, the program will make available "gap" funding in the form of PreSeed Awards that can support the creation of a technology prototype or the demonstration of proof-of-concept, making the start-up more attractive to potential investors.

INDUSTRIAL EXTENSION/TECHNICAL ASSISTANCE

EDI's services to business and industry are also the home for a huge industrial extension/technical assistance practice that has been in operation at Georgia Tech for many years. This is operationally and strategically intermingled with the industry training programs mentioned above but also serves companies in a more hands-on manner via assessments and technical assistance projects as well. These activities are organized and delivered via a matrix format in seven substantive domains, although the range of specific staff competencies is much more extensive. The seven focus areas include:

- energy management;
- environmental management;

- information technology;
- lean enterprise;
- process productivity;
- marketing and strategic planning; and
- quality and international standards.

An assessment is typically focused on one or more of the seven areas mentioned above. The assessment may initially involve one or more plant visits by a Georgia Tech EDI staff member (typically less than a day each) and/or having company personnel fill out a standard survey questionnaire. Depending on which of the seven technical areas is involved, and the particular needs of the client company, an assessment involve upwards of several person-days of effort in addition. Within a given technical area, there also may be different types of initial assessments. For example, within quality and international standards, four types of assessment are offered, and similar menus are available in the other areas.

A typical product of the assessment is a short diagnostic report, which informs the company what specific areas of company operation need improvement. This may be accompanied by an on-site or telephone debriefing by the Georgia Tech staff member to discuss next steps. These next steps might include a technical assistance project.

A technical assistance project is typically a longer, more intensive, and costlier engagement with a client company. It involves the development and implementation of an action plan, and the effort may encompass several person-weeks of effort conducted over several months. Paralleling the assessment process, each of the seven technical areas has also marketed a menu of technical assistance project types, although in actual practice these may blur together in a given project. Georgia companies receive five days of consultation free of charge. In addition, a variety of federal agency resources can be applied to assistance project costs. Of the total business and industry services budget approximately 20% derives from client fees.

Service delivery to a company may not necessarily follow the assessment-to-assistance project path just described. In many cases, a corporate client may have a very specific problem and can move immediately to a service engagement — for example, when a company problem can be addressed via a few hours of assistance, a referral or an information search. Seventy professional staff provides the bulk of client services, with 33 located in Atlanta and 37 based in one of the 18 regional offices. In addition, there is extensive case management conducted over the Internet, in order to match specific staff talents to client needs. In many cases, Georgia Tech faculty with specialized expertise will also be brought in on a project. Directors and staff of the 18 regional offices provide the initial point of contact for EDI services, market the program to companies and other clients, and represent the economic development mission of Georgia Tech around the state. Given the economic geography of Georgia, or as one informant described it "Atlanta and everything else," the regional offices are critical to accomplishing the EDI mission and concurrently building and maintaining political support for the programs.

During FY 2001, Business and Industry Services provided help to 1,220 customers through various projects and activities. Follow-up evaluation indicated that 91% of the assisted companies took action on recommendations, 32% reported jobs created or saved, and 44% reported sales increases or cost savings.

Georgia Tech also participates in the national Manufacturing Extension Partnership (MEP), a program of the National Institute of Standards and Technology in the U.S. Department of Commerce. The Georgia Manufacturing Extension Alliance (GMEA) helps the state's manufacturers address their most critical needs in areas such as production techniques, technology applications, and business practices. Help comes primarily from direct assistance by the Georgia in-house MEP staff, but outside expertise is utilized when needed, including from Georgia Tech.

The Georgia Tech Research Institute (GTRI) engages in focused technical assistance and outreach to Georgia companies through several ongoing programs. Ties with EDI's Georgia Manufacturing Extension Alliance (GMEA) have allowed the two organizations to develop an integrated approach. For example, the Waste Reduction and Environmental Compliance Program (Tech WREC), founded in 1983, provides on-site assistance to companies to identify problems and solutions in the areas of hazardous waste deficiencies. Similarly, the Occupational Safety and Health Technical Assistance program, funded since 1978 by the U.S. Department of Labor, conducts company surveys to determine compliance with OSHA standards and regulations. Evaluations typically include assessment of physical, fire, electrical, and machine hazards, as well as exposures to noise, chemicals, and air contaminants. An Asbestos Information Center, initially operated by EPA and now by GTRI, samples the internal environment in schools, office buildings, industrial plants, hospitals, and many other structures suspected of having asbestos-containing materials and recommends asbestos-appropriate actions.

In addition, Georgia Tech hosts the Southeast Trade Adjustment Assistance Center, serving an eight-state region of Alabama, Florida, Georgia, Kentucky, Mississippi, North Carolina, South Carolina, and Tennessee. Supported by the U.S. Department of Commerce, the Center helps companies improve their competitiveness and productivity to address trade inequities. Georgia Tech is also part of three other federal initiatives: (1) the Georgia Tech Procurement Assistance Center, which helps companies sell to federal and state agencies; (2) the NASA Small Business Innovation Research Program; and (3) the NASA Small Business Technology Transfer Program. Last spring, EDI won the Southeast Regional Technology Transfer Center (SERTTC), a NASA technology commercialization initiative serving nine Southeastern states.

ENTREPRENEURIAL DEVELOPMENT

There is a robust climate for entrepreneurial development at Georgia Tech, which spans mission, education, services to faculty, and statewide programmatic leadership. Since 1980 the home of much of this activity has been the Advanced Technology Development Center (ATDC), a technology business incubator that also has statewide program responsibilities. ATDC is now one of the major constituent programs of EDTV and its main, 83,000-square-foot facility is based on the edge of the Georgia Tech campus. Since ATDC opened, it has graduated 81 companies, which have in turn added more than 4,600 jobs to the Georgia economy. Illustrating how Georgia Tech is an asset for the state and intent on promoting partnerships, in 1991 ATDC established a second facility in middle Georgia at Warner Robins, Ga., (largely oriented toward businesses that can serve the Air Logistics Center there), and a third program in 1996 that is co-located with the Georgia Centers for Advanced Telecommunications Technology (GCATT). For all three incubator facilities, total space is 125,000 square feet. During calendar year 2000, ATDC companies attracted $500 million in investment through venture capital, mergers, and acquisition. For calendar year 2001, the total will be over $300 million.

In addition to the usual office and laboratory facilities, ATDC offers an array of assistance services that have been among the "best practices"[9] of the business incubation industry, enabling it to win the National Business Incubation Association (NBIA) "Incubator of the Year" award in 1996. Notable among these is the Faculty Research Commercialization Program (FRCP), which provides faculty researchers with small grants ($30,000 to $100,000) to develop early stage innovations into workable prototypes or to conduct proof-of-concept applied research. While operated by ATDC at Georgia Tech, the FRCP distributes state funds and the competition is open to faculty from all of the Georgia Research Alliance research institutions: Clark-Atlanta University, Emory University, Georgia State University, Georgia Tech, Medical College of Georgia, and the University of Georgia. The focus on commercialization outcomes increases as the program matures. For 1999, FRCP has married each grant recipient with a business advisor, either from the private sector or a university business school. The purpose is to accelerate the pace of business planning. The ATDC services and programs are yielding an increasing flow of rapidly growing start-up companies. In a recent Venture Market South conference sponsored by *Red Herring*, 12 of the 44 firms that were chosen to make presentations were ATDC member companies.

Another example of collaboration with other universities in new company formation is EmTech Bio. This is a research and development center, jointly formed by Georgia Tech and Emory University, that also includes a partnership with the Georgia Research Alliance and ATDC. It will focus efforts on adding value to life science research with a view to commercialization in the areas of genomics/informatics, drug discovery, and bioengineering. EmTech resides in a $2 million facility and is well funded from university sources.

Digital Furnace is a company success story that was bolstered by university partnerships. The company has developed products to improve the efficiency of broadband networks, and was recently sold for $136 million. It has several links to GRA activities. One of the founders, Dr. John Limb, was recruited to Georgia Tech as a GRA Eminent Scholar, and has conducted much of his research in the Georgia Centers for Advanced Telecommunication Technology (GCATT), a GRA-supported facility. Collaborations with Daniel Howard (a GTRI researcher working in GCATT) led to the founding of the company. Its early development was facilitated through the Advanced Technology Development Center (ATDC). The third co-founder, John Lappington, had visited the ATDC incubator located in the GCATT building, and ATDC staff helped get him together with Limb and Howard. To accelerate product development, ATDC leased space for the company in the GCATT incubator, which put them in close proximity to an extensive talent pool of faculty members, researchers, and graduate students. Within 18 months, Digital Furnace grew from 3 to 35 employees, and received capital from Alliance Technology Ventures (which also has GRA roots). Building on the GCATT experience, an incubator will be also be part of Georgia Tech's $58 million Environmental Sciences & Technology building due for completion in the next year.

An additional ATDC program emphasis is somewhat unusual for what is essentially a business incubator. In cooperation with the state of Georgia and local communities, ATDC will host in residence "landing parties" from larger established companies that are considering locating or expanding their operations into Georgia. ATDC provides space and programmatic support, as these companies decide on the feasibility of locating in the state. Thus far, 15 companies participating in the Landing Party program have located in Georgia, yielding more than 1,700 new jobs. For example, Lucent Technologies launched a new product group in the ATDC, which is expected to lead to much larger investments in the state.

Wide-ranging mission and strategic support among the academic units at Georgia Tech buttress these programmatic activities. Witness the language of the most recent version of the College of Engineering Strategic Plan. Therein, as stated in Objective 5, the College is to:

> *Be a model for fostering entrepreneurship, corporate interaction, and economic development.*

Furthermore, among relevant actions for Objective 5, the college will:

> *Provide an environment that stimulates and foster entrepreneurship in our faculty and students by:*
> - *Providing means for educating students and faculty to enable the development of entrepreneurial skills. This will include expanding programs between the College of Management and the engineering schools, such as those developed by BME, ECE, and ME*
> - *Initiating best practice seminars by faculty and others that have successfully initiated new businesses*
> - *Actively supporting and streamlining the process for faculty members and students to pursue entrepreneurial activities (i.e. develop a "path to entrepreneurship"), and to seek SBIRs and STTRs*

- *Providing funds to students and faculty specifically for prototype developments that show promise for business opportunities*
- *Strengthening our co-op program by program by increasing its flexibility and reach (e.g. schedule, international option, public service component) and creating strategic alliances with key business partners*

Georgia Tech's entrepreneurial culture also brings together academic units in interesting partnership activities. To illustrate this crosscutting emphasis, one can point to the recent appointment of David Ku, Ph.D., M.D., to the Lawrence P. Huang Chair of Engineering Entrepreneurship. This endowed professorship is a collaboration between the DuPree College of Management, the College of Engineering, and the School of Electrical and Computing Engineering. Dr. Ku is himself a successful entrepreneur, being the founder of two biomedical ventures, one of which is based on his own research. Other programs involving the DuPree College of Management include undergraduate and graduate certificate programs in engineering entrepreneurship, and a new initiative, being led by Dr. Ku and funded by a $1 million Whitaker Foundation grant, that will focus on the commercialization of biomedical technology. This is part of the increased effort at Georgia Tech to impart entrepreneurial skills and knowledge to engineering and management students as well as faculty.

Also worthy of note is ATDC's new relationship with The Coca-Cola Company through an initiative known as Fizzion. The role of Fizzion is to bring new technology into the world's best-known soft drink company by nurturing start-up firms that have beverage applications and serving as an interface for other sources of new technology. Fizzion start-up companies also are member companies in ATDC and enjoy the benefits of the ATDC program. Fizzion has one company in house, and efforts to connect Coca-Cola to useful Georgia Tech research are expanding.

INDUSTRY EDUCATION AND TRAINING PARTNERSHIPS

Georgia Tech has a long history of providing industry-focused education and training services. Its Continuing Education provides much of the logistic, marketing, and organizational support for these efforts. The basic building block of these activities is the "short course" which generally involves one to five days of contact time and is typically priced from a few hundred dollars up to $2,000. These cover a huge array of topics. For example, the Continuing Education Web site (http://www.conted.gatech.edu/) features more than 50 subjects in which one or more short courses may be offered. These programs reach over 18,000 individuals annually, and attendees range from senior managers to shop floor technical staff. Instructors include many Georgia Tech faculty members as well as individuals brought in from the private sector on a consulting basis.

In addition to open enrollment for individual courses, there are two general ways in which Georgia Tech packages these services. One is the certificate program, in which two to four short courses are bundled and successful completion of the set leads to a professional certificate for the participant, signed by the president of Georgia Tech. There are currently more than two dozen certificate programs; cost for an attendee ranges between $2,000 and $4,000. These programs are nonetheless quite popular with technology-based companies all over the country, which provide financial support for attendance by key staff. In addition to several that are focused on particular technology domains, others oriented toward organizational issues are offered through the College of Management (http://www.dupree.gatech.edu/exed.htm).

Other short courses, seminars, and conferences are packaged to attract Georgia companies, particularly smaller enterprises that might also be served via short-term technical assistance engagements as well. Business and industry Services, within EDI, is the locus for most of this activity. This organization has been operating in one form or another for nearly 40 years, and accounts for 63% of EDI's budgeted activities. They provide an integrated program of services to companies, which combines training, assessments, and technical assistance.

The training component of Business and Industry Services, offered through Continuing Education, focuses primarily on short programs (the one-day workshop is the norm). These are grouped around the seven technical foci of the program and are delivered in settings and locations convenient for Georgia industry participation. In a recent year, Business and Industry Services provided more than 40 training programs, on topics ranging from MRPII/ERP System Test Drives to ISO 9000 lead auditor training. Programs are repeated several times a year, typically in different sites around the state. While most participants get involved through an open enrollment system, other training is provided on a contract basis at plant sites and might be closely aligned with a technical assistance project being implemented in a company. EDI field agents may also make referrals to specific training events. During FY 2001, more 8,000 participants attended 220 training events, workshops, and meetings through the auspices of Business and Industry Services. A special feature during 1999 was a series of 72 Y2K seminars, attended by 995 companies and 2,226 individuals. Approximately 1,500 Y2K diagnostic diskettes were also distributed.

CAREER SERVICES AND PLACEMENT

Georgia Tech provides an extensive set of services and activities to ensure that graduates are appropriately placed in jobs, and as a part of that general function there is also considerable effort devoted to encouraging graduates to join Georgia-based companies. Much of the relevant activity occurs early in the experience of a Tech student, through a rich menu of experiential learning opportunities.

Georgia Tech offers an intensive co-op option, the largest voluntary program in the nation with over 3,400 students currently enrolled. The program has been in operation since 1912. More than 40% of engineering students participate, and about 36% of all undergraduates. It now encompasses virtually all undergraduate degree programs. Under the co-op plan, students will alternate periods of time between on-campus coursework and off-campus placements in companies or other organizations. Nearly 700 domestic employers participate, along with a growing number of international organizations. A centralized campus co-op office (15 FTE staff) arranges for interviews, placements, and referrals and also systematically monitors students' experiences after their return to campus. Co-op is considered an academic program at Tech, and the director reports to the Office of the Provost. In turn, each academic unit that participates has a designated individual (e.g., a vice-chair for undergraduate students) who functions as a liaison with the co-op program. For example, given the volume of students moving back and forth between co-op placement and campus, it is important that certain required courses are taught more frequently than might otherwise be the case. In terms of impact on Georgia, it is noteworthy that about two-thirds of co-op placements involve employers in the state, and about 50% of those result in permanent employment after graduation. The exposure of students to the industrial world also has an impact on the classroom, as the emerging needs of industry become part of the classroom discussion.

For graduates, Georgia Tech has a huge student placement organization, which dedicates significant resources to nurturing and informing Georgia (as well as national) employers. Georgia Tech graduates are aggressively recruited, and the Career Services Office annually organizes over 13,000 interviews with 550 prospective employers. Approximately 75% of graduating students already have a job in hand. The office holds a two-day career fair in the fall, with 350 employers participating (plus a waiting list of 60). Smaller career fairs are also organized for graduates in industrial engineering, computing and business. Career Services also works with the student chapter of the National Society of Black Engineers to host a spring career fair focused on African-American graduates.

Over half of graduating students join Georgia-based companies, and a number of outreach activities are conducted to maintain these relationships. For example, the annual Georgia Employers Career Fair is designed to give graduating Tech students and Georgia-based employers an opportunity to interact. At a recent event, more than 100 Georgia employers attended.

Another effort to assist national as well as Georgia employers in their recruiting efforts occurs through a variety of internship experiences, many of which involve Georgia companies. Presently, more than 2,000 students are registered for the internship program. The program provides a wealth of talent to companies that can also be cultivated for future employment while giving students an opportunity to expand their knowledge base in a real world setting. Many of the internships result in offers of full-time employment after graduation.

FORMAL PARTNERSHIPS WITH ECONOMIC DEVELOPMENT ORGANIZATIONS

Another key part of EDI is the Center for Economic Development Services (CEDS), which has two main client groups: (1) state, regional, and local economic development organizations, public and private; and (2) state, regional, and local units of government. A variety of product and services are provided by a core staff of approximately 20 individuals, mostly based in the regional offices, which is supplemented by 25 part-time associates.

Analytic services constitute the primary product of the Economic Development Research Program (EDRP), which has produced nearly 100 reports over the past 15 years. These include a mix of industry analyses, evaluations, directories, and feasibility studies, which are commissioned by communities, industry associations, the state of Georgia, and various combinations of the above. These typically involve less than three person-months of effort, paid for primarily by EDRP's state funds and by the requesting organization (usually about 20 percent of total cost). During FY 2001 CEDS conducted 87 community economic development projects, and completed 43 fiscal and economic impact analyses. EDRP also publishes a newsletter (*Focus*) three times a year. *Focus* features a lead article covering a current economic development issue, summarizes forthcoming EDRP reports and current projects, updates events of other CEDS programs, and reports on the results of Georgia Tech-related research and services. One of the more novel EDRP products is analytic software (LOCI) that enables a local economic development organization to estimate the costs and benefits of a potential project. LOCI is sold via license fees to either single users or through a site license arrangement, and will be soon featured in a series of short courses that will be offered locally and across the country.[10]

A second functional area of CEDS is the Professional Development Services group, which provides a series of topical seminars, short courses, and conferences to economic development organizations. Recent offerings include the two-day course on economic impact analysis, another on business incubation, and a five-day Basic Economic Development Course. An innovative course experience (which is being repeated) involved a five-day "mobile workshop," which took economic development professionals to communities in adjoining states in which novel policies and practices were being successfully implemented. In FY 2001 more than 720 economic development practitioners attended 13 training events. The logistics for these events are organized and managed by Georgia Tech Continuing Education, although CEDS develops and delivers the substantive content.

A third functional component of CEDS is Community and Technology Services. It delivers technical assistance projects to customers, typically provided by regional office staff but often involving Georgia Tech faculty and/or graduate students. These will generally be planning or implementation assistance efforts, delivered via a consulting relationship. While problem-focused, these engagements attempt to keep the strategic goals of the customer clearly in mind. For example, a growing fraction of this work of late has focused on rural communities' problems with information technology infrastructure, computer access, and training, Web site development, and effective deployment of communication technologies. A pilot effort in this area is expected to be extended to more than 100 rural settings within the next year.

FaciliTech is a fourth relatively new program component of CEDS. It seeks to tie the technical assistance provided through Georgia Tech to the economic development aspirations of Georgia communities. For example, a Georgia-based company may be contemplating a major plant expansion, or a non-Georgia company may be thinking about building a plant in the state. In either case, to sweeten the deal the FaciliTech program can bring to bear the talents of industrial extension staff to formulate a facilities and production technology plan for the prospect company, working in collaboration with the local economic development agency trying to pull off the project. To make this even more attractive, state money is available to expand the scope of free services available for the prospect company, beyond the normal three to five days typical in the Business and Industry Services component. For the recruitment situation, Georgia Tech staff associated with EDI will be in the novel position of providing planning help to an out-of-state company in the process of deciding whether or not to move into Georgia. In some cases, the scope of FaciliTech projects will necessitate pulling in faculty and graduate student help as well.

The newest service offered by this group is the Tourism and Regional Assistance Centers (TRACS). Through feasibility studies and technical assistance, this service helps Georgia communities and economic development organizations evaluate opportunities for developing tourism.

CEDS has played an important role in developing a high-tech economic development strategy. In effect, Georgia Tech has worked formally with local groups to develop strategies that play to their strengths and capacities. Much of this work is related to the Industries of the Mind campaign, which has been championing an enhanced knowledge economy in the state, and the ongoing Georgia Research Alliance strategy.

Industry/University Advisory Boards and Councils

Virtually all of the larger centers and colleges on campus have industrial advisory boards or councils. These include the Packaging Research Center, the Manufacturing Research Center, the Traditional Industries Program, the Center for International Standards and Quality, the College of Computing, the College of Engineering, and the College of Architecture. In addition, the Georgia Tech National Advisory Board functions at the institutional level. The Economic Development Institute also has an advisory board made up of representatives from its major customer sets.

Faculty Culture and Rewards

Under the leadership of the dean of the College of Engineering, a group of Georgia Tech faculty and administrators has examined policies and procedures governing faculty participation in technology transfer activities. New policies have been formulated regarding the process, ownership of intellectual property, licensing, and faculty participation in start-up companies. The goal is to clarify Georgia Tech's policies and procedures as a means of expanding the already very active faculty participation in economic development and technology transfer activities.

Tech faculty may receive a third of royalties from licensing and may hold equity in start-up companies that have licensed Georgia Tech technology. This arrangement has provided sufficient encouragement for a broad range of activities involving both licensing and participation in start-up companies. Such real-world financial incentives are proving to be at least as attractive as awards, recognition programs or anything else the university could do on a symbolic basis.

In the School of Electrical and Computer Engineering, Georgia Tech's largest academic unit, Director Roger Webb supports technology transfer and helps faculty with the sometimes-complex process. "We are pushing this effort hard," Webb says. "There is a general encouragement within the school that is well known, and the posture is that the school will assist in moving the process along. Georgia Tech encourages faculty involvement in economic development and start-up companies under certain conditions."

Approximately 40% of the member companies in the institution's Advanced Technology Development Center involve faculty from Georgia Tech. A good example of the role faculty can play may be found in RF Solutions, the first company funded by the new Yamacraw Seed Capital Fund, part of a major new state economic development initiative. Originally formed by two faculty members from the School of Electrical and Computer Engineering as a consulting enterprise, the company brought on full-time management and other staff to develop its unique technology niche in the growing broadband wireless market. The two original faculty members now serve as technical advisors, but are not involved in the firm's day-to-day operations.

Webb believes faculty should transfer the intellectual property they have developed — either to existing companies or startups — but stay out of the daily company operations. "Faculty aren't good at business things, and they need to have external folks involved to capitalize and run the operation," he says. "And I don't think Georgia Tech wants to be in the business of spinning out faculty as well as technology. I try to discourage faculty from leaving to participate in companies." In all, faculty from the School of Electrical and Computer Engineering are involved in as many as five start-up companies, many of them based on technology licensed through GTRC.

ENDNOTES

[1] National Science Foundation Division of Science Resource Studies. (2001). *Academic research and development expenditures, FY 1999*. Washington, D.C.: National Science Foundation. Table B-33.

[2] Georgia Institute of Technology. (1995). *The Georgia Institute of Technology Strategic Plan*.

[3] Georgia Institute of Technology. (1999). *Annual Report of Institutional Progress to the Chancellor of the University System of Georgia*.

[4] EDI originally operated as part of the Georgia Tech Research Institute, and was spun out as an independent organization approximately 10 years ago.

[5] Georgia Institute of Technology, College of Engineering. (2000). *Strategic Plan*.

[6] National Science Foundation. Division of Science Resource Studies. *Op. cit.* Tables B-33, B-36, B-38.

[7] Association of University Technology Managers. (2000). *AUTM Licensing Survey: FY 1999*. Chicago, Ill.: Association of University Technology Managers.

[8] Robinson, R. (1998). Technology Transfer. *Research Horizons* (Summer/Fall) Atlanta: Georgia Institute of Technology.

[9] Tornatzky, L., Batts, Y., McCrea, N., Lewis, M. & Quittman, L. (1995). *The art and craft of technology business incubation*. Research Triangle Park, N.C.: Southern Growth Policies Board.

[10] Bates, L. (1999). Weighing the pros and cons of attracting new business. *Research Horizons*.(Spring). Atlanta, Ga.: Georgia Institute of Technology.

NORTH CAROLINA STATE UNIVERSITY

Like many of the nation's major land grant universities, North Carolina State University (N.C. State) began as a small, primarily agricultural and technical college. Founded in 1887 as North Carolina College of Agriculture and Mechanic Arts, N.C. State was conceived as a "people's college" and as a vehicle for promoting the economic and cultural transformation of the state during the post-Civil War period. The university experienced gradual growth for much of its early years, and then participated in the post-World War II enrollment surge in the United States and the concomitant growth in federal support for university research. This helped accelerate its transformation from a small, primarily technical college into a comprehensive Research I university. N.C. State continues to emphasize its scientific and technical strengths and its focus on outreach-based economic development.

N.C. State is part of the 16-campus University of North Carolina system. It is the system's largest university, enrolling more than 27,500 students, and the system's flagship science and engineering university. While it does not have a medical school, it contains 10 colleges, offers doctoral degrees in 58 programs and houses four different extension programs

Unlike most land grant universities, N.C. State is located in a relatively urban and industrialized setting. The campus is in the state's capital, Raleigh, and constitutes one point of the Research Triangle Park area along with Duke University (in Durham) and the University of North Carolina at Chapel Hill. The three-county area defined by these universities has a population of about a million, is home to a high concentration of large firms (such as IBM, Nortel, GlaxoSmithKline) and small high-technology companies, and is reputed to have the nation's highest concentration of Ph.D.'s.

In the FY 1999 National Science Foundation survey of academic research and development,[1] N.C. State reported research expenditures of $270.6 million, which placed it 29th among all U.S. universities and 17th among public universities. It ranked fourth among universities without a medical school. The university's engineering program is the 10th largest in the United States; its graduate program was ranked 28th in the country.[2] Engineering programs that were ranked in the top 20 nationally include: nuclear, materials science and engineering, computer engineering, industrial, biological and agricultural, and civil. The chemical engineering department ranked first in the country for research spending. The university boasts 19 faculty who are members of the National Academy of Sciences or the National Academy of Engineering and recently won a Phi Beta Kappa chapter. Students entering its engineering programs in 2000 boasted an average high school GPA of 4.13 and average SAT score of 1250. The university includes over 70 interdisciplinary research centers.

In some respects, N.C. State can be seen as a hybrid of the major types of institutions found in this volume. For example, its service-oriented vision and mission and diverse suite of industry-oriented outreach services clearly mark it as a "knowledge economy land grant" institution, one that has moved from a primary focus on agriculture to one that is oriented to industry. In fact, it was an early pioneer of industrial extension service, one of the technology-focused services that helps define this class. In addition, its location in a relatively urban setting and its proximity to high-technology industry has caused it to respond to the more intense demands for interaction that have helped shape the "engaged" institution.

MISSION, VISION, AND GOAL STATEMENTS

N.C. State has a long and distinguished track record of involvement in and commitment to promoting economic development. For instance, by the late 19th century the university was responsible for operating one of the first Agricultural Experiment Station in the South. By the 1920s N.C. State had established an Engineering Experiment Station and supported a school, the School of Textiles, devoted to the needs of a fledging local industry. Undoubtedly, the university's land grant heritage, with its emphasis on the importance of service and extension, played an important role in these activities.

The values and goals of the land grant tradition continue to support N.C. State's emphasis on economic development and are evident in its current mission statement:

> *Through the active integration of teaching, research, and extension, North Carolina State University creates an innovative learning environment that stresses mastery of fundamentals, intellectual discipline, creativity, problem solving, and responsibility.... North Carolina State University provides leadership for intellectual, cultural, social, economic, and technological development within the state, the nation, and the world.*

And in its goals:

> *... fostering new partnerships, both internally and externally.*

Recent successes, however, including its contribution to the growth of the Research Triangle Park and its innovative Centennial Campus, can be traced to the university's and its leadership's willingness to renew and redefine what it means to be a land grant university in the knowledge economy. For instance, during the mid-1990s N.C. State became one of the first major universities in the country to attempt a top-down, strategic and comprehensive analysis of its economic development options. The externally prepared report that came from this effort, *University Program Partnerships for Economic Development,* indicated that "NC State has the internal capabilities and existing program base that make it logical and realistic to aspire to become the national and international leader in this realm — not just one among able competitors."[3] The report became a major catalyst for expansions, refinements, and reforms in a variety of university outreach structures and programs.

Over the last three years, under the leadership of current Chancellor Marye Anne Fox, N.C. State engaged in a lengthy strategic planning process that tried to address how N.C. State can meet a variety of challenges including a changing national and global economy. The report that came from these efforts, *The New NC State: Becoming the Nation's Leading Land Grant Institution,* was reviewed and endorsed by a multi-sector blue ribbon commission and reinforces and redefines what it means to be a land grant university in the current social and economic environment. Among other things it stressed the importance of "fostering new partnerships internally and externally," endorsed the university's ambitious business partnering model based on the Centennial Campus (see below), recommended the creation of a university-level outreach/extension vice-chancellor position, and highlighted the importance of moving from a one-way extension model to a more interactive model of engagement. The plan also endorses four new multidisciplinary academic initiatives: genomic sciences, environmental sciences, materials sciences, and computer networking. Each of these academic initiatives is intended to strengthen research as well as create opportunities for economic development, and all were strongly endorsed by the business community.

There is ample evidence that the broader university community has embraced the university's focus on extension/engagement and technology. First, most of the college mission statements echo the importance of outreach/engagement. For instance, the College of Engineering mission statement articulates a goal to "enhance economic development and improve the quality of life of our citizens." Even programs such as psychology, which have traditionally been detached from industrial and economic development ties, show signs of this influence. Four of the department's five programs, industrial/organizational, ergonomics, school, and "psychology in the public interest," have clear ties to external constituencies. Finally, the university has four distinct extension services focused not only on agriculture, but also on manufacturing, textile technology, and the humanities.

INDUSTRY RESEARCH PARTNERSHIPS.

Industrial research is a significant and important component of N.C. State's research portfolio. NSF data[4] indicate that the university's industry-sponsored research expenditures in FY 1999 were $31.5 million, or 11.6% of total research expenditures. This was above the national average of 7.4%, and ranked N.C. State 14th among top-100 U.S. universities on this measure. N.C. State ranks fifth among land grant universities in industry research support and second among land grant universities without a medical school. In 1992, industry support accounted for 14.2% of total research expenditures. This modest decline appears to be due to a very dramatic increase in overall research support that was proportionately less industrial in nature. During this time period, total research expenditures increased by 89% while industry-sponsored expenditures increased by 55%.

A number of factors appear to have contributed to N.C. State's success in this area. From a historical standpoint, the university's industry-friendly land grant philosophy is certainly a key ingredient. From its inception, N.C. State has viewed working with and for industry and the external community as central rather than peripheral to its institutional mission. However, at least four other factors have also been significant contributors to its enviable track record of research partnering: its proximity to and involvement with one of the world's largest research parks, Research Triangle Park; its early investment in and commitment to cooperative research centers; the development of its own visionary university-based "technopolis," the Centennial Campus; and the creation of the Kenan Institute, a "captive foundation" committed to financially supporting and promoting science and technology-based partnerships.

The creation and growth of Research Triangle Park (RTP) has played a major role in the growth of N.C. State's research connections to industry. RTP is a 7,000-acre public/private planned research park created in the 1950s through the combined efforts of private and government officials.[5] In 1960 RTP was home to three research and development companies with about 500 employees. Today it is the largest research park in the United States and hosts 106 research and development organizations and 45,000 employees. Over the years a truly symbiotic relationship has developed between N.C. State and RTP. Firms have cited the proximity and responsiveness of N.C. State's large, high-quality engineering and science programs as one of the major motives for moving into the park. At the same time, N.C. State has been able to attract nationally prominent faculty and increase the quality of its student population because of the opportunity to interact with RTP's industrial community.

N.C. State also has been very proactive and effective since the early 1980s in building research centers involving industry as substantive and financial partners. The university started one of the first National Science Foundation (NSF) Industry/University Cooperative Research Centers (IUCRC), the Center for Advanced Communications and Signal Processing, and built on that experience in two ways. First, it continued to compete successfully for a variety of NSF and other federally sponsored centers.[6] It has been home to five NSF IUCRCs, a NSF State/IUCRC, a NSF Engineering Research Center and, more recently, the Center for Environmentally Responsible Solvents and Processes (CERSP), a NSF Science and Technology Center involving several universities.[7] At the same time, N.C. State learned to develop a variety of partnership-friendly structures and policies to enable such relationships. For instance, it created a role and eventually an office that specialized in industrial research agreements, and it provides a significantly reduced overhead charge for industrial memberships in centers. More recently, it has implemented a system whereby colleges can directly implement industrial research contracts of $25,000 or less, and do so at a reduced overhead rate, as long as the firm signs a standard agreement.

Today, N.C. State hosts approximately 40 industrially focused centers that are home to more than 300 firms. It derives approximately one-third of its industrial research support through these centers. Given the university's accomplishment in managing industry partnerships, it is not too surprising that the newest addition to this suite of centers is the Center for Innovation Management Studies (CIMS). CIMS, originally based at Lehigh University, supports research on research and development management and the innovation process. N.C. State also helps manage Oak Ridge National Laboratory in Tennessee (with six other universities and Battelle Memorial Institute). This arrangement will allow joint university/lab faculty positions, joint proposals and research contracts, and joint seminars. Finally, the College of Engineering manages the Mineral Resource Laboratory, an educational and research facility in Asheville, North Carolina, dedicated to enhancing minerals-related work in industry.

N.C. State also has succeeded in developing its own visionary concept of a research park, the Centennial Campus. Begun in 1985 with a deeding to the university of surplus state land close to the main N.C. State campus, Centennial Campus has become a unique 1,334-acre planned academic-industry community or "technopolis."[8] When completed the Centennial Campus will include a cluster of academic and industrial research facilities, a hotel and conference center, residential options, a golf course, and a middle school. The Campus is conceived as much more than a real estate development; it is entirely consistent with the university's larger goals and mission. Industrial partners (ranging in size from start-ups to large corporations) and other partners are expected to make a long-term commitment to one of the university's academic programs. Further, most research facilities are multi-tenant buildings that co-locate academic and industrial researchers. Over the past several years, development of the Campus has begun to accelerate. Currently, Centennial Campus is home to more than 70 companies, government agencies and a business incubator. The concept behind the Campus stresses close, interactive and long lasting ties with industrial partners. In many respects, Centennial Campus has become the crown jewel of a broad and long-standing tradition of research partnering with industry.

Finally, the university's industry partnering efforts have benefited from the creation of the Kenan Institute for Engineering, Technology & Science. The Institute was established in 1992 with a $20 million endowment from the Kenan Charitable Trust. Although it is part of the N.C. State community, it has the flexibility to invest its endowment in quite creative ways, both inside and outside the university. As such, it has served as a catalyst for the creation of a number of industrially oriented partnerships involving N.C. State as well as other institutions in the Research Triangle. These include: the Kenan Center for the Utilization of Carbon Dioxide in Manufacturing; the Technology, Education and Commercialization Program; and a number of smaller initiatives. The institute's expansive mission has positioned it in a role that is quite complementary with the partnering aspirations of the university:

> ... to develop partnerships in basic research, education, commercialization and public outreach with individuals and organizations dedicated to the advancement of science, engineering and technology as a force in improving the economic and social well-being of the nation and the world.

As a connected but independent foundation, the Institute's use of discretionary funds has helped it stimulate ambitious partnerships with a variety of public and not-for-profit organizations outside the university as well. These focus on, among other things, K-12 enhancements, improvements in science and technology public policy, and economic development. In relationship to this project, the Kenan Institute's impact appears in a number of the other domains including: entrepreneurship, formal partnerships with economic development organizations, industrial extension, and technology transfer.

TECHNOLOGY TRANSFER

The Office of Technology Transfer (OTT) — part of a recently restructured research, contracts and grants function — handles technology transfer activities at N.C. State. It employs seven professionals and four support staff and reports to the vice chancellor for research and graduate studies. Like most technology transfer offices, OTT works closely with faculty to address disclosure, patenting, and copyright issues, and in negotiating licensing and royalty arrangements.

License income was $7.8 million in FY 1999, and royalty return on investment (royalties divided by research expenditures, or ROI) was 2.9%. License income ranked in the 89th percentile, and royalty ROI ranked in the 88th percentile, of the 142 academic institutions that participated in the *AUTM Licensing Survey: FY 1999*.[9]

N.C. State reported a total of 43 new licenses to start-ups in fiscal years 1998 and 1999 combined, placing it in the 94th percentile in the AUTM licensing survey sample. N.C. State reported 13 new start-ups formed, 12 of which were in-state. N.C. State ranks in the 96th percentile for total start-ups formed and in the 96th percentile for in-state start-ups formed. In terms of the potential regional impacts of technology transfer this record is quite commendable.

Over the years, N.C. State has taken a number of steps to increase the odds that commercialization will happen locally. For instance, OTT has been very open to commercializing intellectual property by taking an equity position in a local start-up as opposed to focusing on up-front royalty payments. With the same goal in mind, the OTT has the flexibility to negotiate lower royalty rates for firms that agree to commercialize the technology locally. A penalty clause kicks in if the licensee moves out of state, and thus protects the university's financial interests.

In another novel approach, the university has had some success in attracting "intellectual property donations." These involve arrangements whereby firms donate intellectual property to universities and receive tax breaks in return. N.C. State is then free to further develop and market the technology. Several of these deals are already producing significant royalty streams. In an attempt to orchestrate these kinds of arrangements, N.C. State and the University of North Carolina at Chapel Hill have formed the Patenting and Technology Transfer Initiative. PATTI is affiliated with the Center for Environmentally Responsible Solvents and Processes and focuses on carbon dioxide-related technology. It utilizes the engineering, chemistry, law, business, and information science expertise at both UNC-CH and N.C. State to identify desirable patents, to develop donation proposals and secure donations, and to formulate commercialization plans for donated technology. Because both universities have considerable expertise in CO2-technology, donated patents may be bundled with homegrown patents for licensing. One corporate participant commented, "[PATTI is] the first proactive effort by a university to seek intellectual property related to a core research strength. This model will catalyze other universities to foster stronger ties between programs in business, science, engineering and information sciences."[10]

For many years the university has helped faculty entrepreneurs attract private venture capital, but recently it has gone one step further. In 1998, N.C. State created Centennial Venture Partners (CVP) in collaboration with the North Carolina Technology Development Authority (NCTDA), an incubator promotion organization. The fund was capitalized with $10 million in investments from the endowment funds of N.C. State's various college foundations. Follow-on (matching) funding attracted from other investment sources equals approximately 12 times CVP's investment. The fund is managed outside the university and targets technology owned by the university, its alumni, and by industry tenants of the Centennial Campus (who, by definition, have an ongoing relationship with at least one N.C. State research program). In its first two years of operation, CVP invested in 15 companies and was responsible for the creation of more than 240 local high-tech jobs. These efforts have been supplemented by additional N.C. State-NCTDA partnerships including establishing the Entrepreneurial Development Center @ NCSU (a business incubator) on Centennial Campus. As in other domains covered in this report, the Centennial Campus is an asset in achieving the university's partnering and economic development goals.

INDUSTRIAL EXTENSION/TECHNICAL ASSISTANCE

While all land grant universities have had a commitment to agribusiness and forest products extension activities, N.C. State was one of the pioneering institutions to extend that approach to other sectors. Its Industrial Extension Service, established in 1955, was one of the first university-based extension programs in the nation to offer technical and industrial management services to industry. N.C. State has continued its commitment to extension and outreach to this day and is home to three formal extension programs, each of which is targeting a different industrial sector: the Cooperative Extension Service (agriculture), the Industrial Extension Service (IES), and the Textiles Extension Service.[11]

Of these, the most significant vehicle for industry targeted extension is the IES. While IES is housed in and reports within the College of Engineering, it has strong organizational ties to state government. For instance, its literature describes IES as "university affiliated" and as representing the "university and government communities." As a consequence, IES has a statewide mission to promote economic development and fulfills its mission by partnering with a broad spectrum of state agencies and departments, including the community college system. Although a handful of IES services are provided by staff who have joint appointments with academic departments at N.C. State, full-time staff provides the vast majority of IES services and training based around the state.

The largest component of the IES is its federally leveraged Manufacturing Extension Partnership program that has a total budget of $6 million a year. Other programmatic components include Industrial Liaison, Forum for Competitive Advantage, the Solar Center, and the Industrial Energy Program. The primary areas of emphasis in service provision and training are lean manufacturing and quality improvement. Targeted industries include metalworking, furniture, polymers, and construction. Most IES clients are small manufacturing enterprises with 500 employees or less. IES also places a strong emphasis on environmental and safety issues. It coordinates "The Greening of NC" Network, a full-service, environmentally focused network of federal and state agencies. A recently completed strategic plan will concentrate future efforts on greater functional integration across these areas.

During the 1999-2000 program year IES provided almost 6,000 free services, 225 fee-based services, disseminated over 35,000 publications, and conducted 250 research and service projects. Although IES receives much of its support from state government, leveraging is a big part of its funding strategy; it receives funding from 76 different sources (e.g., separate grants and contracts). IES service recipients reported $129 million in economic benefit and received three state-level and two national awards for new products during the 1999-2000 program year.[12]

The Textile Extension and Applied Research Service (TEARS) provides education, training, and technical assistance services to the state's largest manufacturing industry. It is housed in the College of Textiles, the largest textiles college in the western world. While most of TEARS services are delivered within North Carolina, its mission has always targeted the textiles industry in general, and services have been provided throughout the southeast and nationally. For example, as the textiles industry has become more global in its operations, TEARS has responded by offering some of its training in Mexico and by translating its training materials into Spanish. During the 1999-2000 school year, its applied research program conducted more than 110 testing and product development projects and received fees approaching $800,000. Program staff members are often on the road conducting in-plant programs. As traditional manufacturing continues to move off shore, the college and TEARS have increased their training, research, and service focus on high-technology, high value-added applications. The College's Nonwovens Cooperative Research Center is a good example of this trend.

The major strengths of N.C. State's extension activities are undoubtedly the size, breadth, and diversity of services it provides. However, a recent self-study suggested that the integration and coordination of extension services was not optimal and that the university needed a "full-time leader for campus-wide and state-wide engagement."[13] As a consequence, the university created its first university-wide executive extension position — the vice chancellor for university extension and engagement. This position was filled during spring 2001, and the incumbent has assumed responsibility for all formal and informal extension activities on campus and will attempt to promote greater integration and coordination of these efforts. Another noteworthy change in extension at N.C. State is the already mentioned emphasis on a more interactive or "engagement-based" approach to extension and outreach. Programs appear to be embracing this shift in both word (e.g., using the vocabulary of "engagement" in their mission statements) and deed (e.g., surveying end-user needs and developing more customized programs). For example, when one peruses the university's home page on the Internet an "extension and engagement" tab (http://www.ncsu.edu/extension.html) will steer the user to other pages in which these activities are presented by college, organizational unit, interest, and location.

ENTREPRENEURIAL DEVELOPMENT

Like most universities with strong scientific and technical programs, N.C. State can point to a significant number of "entrepreneurial success" stories that have sprung from the efforts of individual faculty and graduates, including SAS Institute (the world's largest privately held software company) and Cree Research (a manufacturer of light-emitting diodes). However, over the past decade N.C. State has tried to go beyond the serendipity of individual success by strengthening and institutionalizing factors and conditions that encourage entrepreneurial activity among its students and faculty and within the local community. There is growing evidence that these efforts are beginning to bear fruit. According to university records, over the past two years 20 companies have emerged from university laboratories and created hundreds of jobs.[14]

A great deal of the credit for campus-based entrepreneurial development can be given to a small number of faculty members. For instance, the Technology Education Commercialization (TEC) Program was developed by a handful of faculty in the College of Engineering and the School of Management (and supported by a grant from the National Science Foundation and the Kenan Institute for Engineering, Science and Technology). TEC is a multi-semester course that provides undergraduate and graduate students with hands-on experience with new product development and commercialization. Initially, TEC teams focused their attention on "mining" university labs and research projects for promising inventions. More recently, it has broadened its horizons and has begun to provide commercialization assistance (with help from IES) to entrepreneurs and start-up companies in the local area. As of 2001, the program had aided the commercialization efforts of more than a dozen companies. Those companies have attracted more than $100 million in venture capital and created more than 250 jobs for North Carolina.

The Engineering Entrepreneurship Program, a program for undergraduates that extends over several semesters, was developed by a faculty member in electrical and computer engineering to encourage and support student entrepreneurship. Student participants get course credit while attending seminars on entrepreneurship and participating in teams that are organized like start-up companies. The University Entrepreneurs Network, a group that sponsors seminars, special projects, and social gatherings in support of technological entrepreneurship, complements these efforts. Finally, the College of Management sponsors a graduate concentration in e-commerce and hosts the award winning "E-Commerce Learning Center @ NCState", a web-enabled educational tool that includes 1,000 hyperlinks to educational material on e-commerce (http://ecommerce.ncsu.edu).

The university's Centennial Campus also provides a very fertile environment for activities of campus-based and outside entrepreneurs. The combination of state-of-the-art facilities and labs, the ability to partner with university programs, and access to the university's talented pool of faculty and students has attracted a significant number of start-up companies. Some of these are located in the Entrepreneurial Development Center @ NC State, a technology incubator facility. Established by the North Carolina Technological Development Authority (NCTDA), the facility has space for 36 companies, offers the usual array of direct and brokered support services, and also has the unique location of the Centennial Campus as well as potential access to the early-stage capitalization described above.

INDUSTRY EDUCATION AND TRAINING PARTNERSHIPS

N.C. State offers a diverse collection of industry-focused education and training through a variety of institutional offices and academic units. Most of these are offered through the Division of Continuing Studies, the Industrial Extension Service (IES), or one of the smaller outreach and extension programs. The bulk of these are offered on a fee-for-service basis. During the 2000-2001 academic year, considering all providers roughly 350,000 participants enrolled in noncredit learning activity at N.C. State.

The Division of Continuing Studies has been in operation for 75 years, offering a diverse selection of technical, management, and other courses. Nontraditional courses are offered through several units: the Division of Continuing and Professional Studies, a unit that offers customized and regular non-degree courses and seminars in topics such as accounting, engineering, and management; the Computer Training Center; the Institute for Environmental Technology Education; and the Distance Education Division, a unit that offers courses in topics as diverse as management skills, principles of electricity, and air conditioning. In 1999-2000 the Division of Continuing Studies offered 516 distance education credit-courses to 5,606 registrants and nondegree courses/seminars to 153,400 nondegree participants. Unlike at many other universities, which often enlist community members to teach, full-time staff teach most of the continuing education courses.

The Industrial Extension Service (described in more detail in another section) courses are targeted at a broad spectrum of technical and managerial topics with heavy emphasis on environmental, manufacturing, quality, and civil engineering/construction. During 1999-2000, IES conducted industrial education programs for more than 11,000 industry managers and engineers from more than 2,000 firms; 108 events (e.g., training sessions) were held at company facilities. While most of the courses are offered in Raleigh, many are offered at various locations around the state (in partnership with the state's community college system) and nationally. The Textiles Extension Service also offers training programs and courses on textile issues (36 programs, 471 participants) either in plants or at more centralized locations. Short courses, addressing relatively high-level issues, serve another 800 participants a year. Over the past few years a great deal of effort has been invested in converting various courses into distance education formats. In recognition of the growing importance of distance learning, N.C. State appointed an associate vice chancellor for distance education and learning technology in 2001.

> **FINALLY, THE UNIVERSITY'S COMMITMENT TO A MORE INTERACTIVE CONCEPT OF "ENGAGEMENT" (AS OPPOSED TO EXTENSION) APPEARS TO BE HAVING AN IMPACT.**

There appears to be several keys to N.C. State's strong record in this area. Certainly, the importance attached to these kinds of activities in university and college mission statements has been critical. (The College of Management mission statement calls for it to offer "high quality executive education and outreach programs"). The foresight to invest in continuing education facilities is another factor. The construction more than 25 years ago of the McKimmon Center, a dedicated continuing education conference facility that has two dozen meeting rooms and can host meetings of up to 1,200, allowed the university to develop a large and diverse collection of instructional offerings. Although this facility is no longer spanking new, it has been updated with satellite reception equipment, computer terminals and other specialized instructional technologies. Plans for a new executive conference center on the Centennial Campus should complement these capabilities. Finally, the university's commitment to a more interactive concept of "engagement" (as opposed to extension) appears to be having an impact. While always customer conscious, N.C. State's IES has begun a structured program of market research to ensure that the courses and services it offers meet the current and emerging needs of its target audience.

CAREER SERVICES AND PLACEMENT

Like most major universities, N.C. State's Career Center is national in scope. The fact that N.C. State has ranked first or second in the number of students hired by IBM over the past three years gives some indication of how highly regarded their graduates are by large, national employers. However, the university also attempts to aid small local employers.

The university's cooperative education programs and placement service provide a variety of services that assist local and state-based employers. The Cooperative Education Program at N.C. State is one of eight programs in the country to receive accreditation from the Accreditation Council for Cooperative Education. During the 1999-2000 academic year, it placed more than 800 students in co-op job opportunities. Over 70% of these placements were in the Research Triangle Park area and 90% within North Carolina. The Career Center sponsors a variety of job fairs at which N.C. firms are heavily represented, with a recent event on Centennial Campus attracting over 2,000 students. These efforts are complemented by college-level efforts such as the College of Engineering's "Annual Engineering Career Fair." In addition, staff from the Career Center run workshops throughout the state for employers on "how to attract the best students." A placement service Web site allows firms to access a database of students registered with the placement service. Finally, staff from the Career Center routinely meet with representatives from local industrial development groups and chambers of commerce to provide advice on how to tap into the university's pool of talented graduates. University records indicate that approximately 58% of undergraduates take jobs in the state.

Formal Partnerships with Economic Development Organizations

The university's most significant linkage to economic development organizations is structured, once again, through the Industrial Extension Service, including its formal linkages with the state's community college system. IES staff are represented on a large number of economic development-related agencies including: State Economic Development Board, a variety of North Carolina Department of Commerce task forces that address industry needs, North Carolina Citizens for Business and Industry (the state's chamber of commerce). IES is represented on the state's Economic Development Committee and regularly conducts joint projects with the National Academy of Manufacturers, as well as participates in more locally oriented manufacturing councils, committees of 100, chambers of commerce and economic development groups across the state. For example, IES is an active participant in two councils of government and has developed grant proposals with the North Carolina Rural Center, the Center for Entrepreneurial Development, and the Technology Development Board.

Once again, Centennial Campus and the organizations it hosts and attracts have become effective vehicles for linking N.C. State with economic development interests. As described earlier, N.C. State has partnered with the North Carolina Technological Development Authority to develop an incubator for start-up companies on Centennial Campus. In addition, N.C. State hosts the North Carolina Progress Board, a state-funded initiative to benchmark and support progress in a number of social and economic domains. The Centennial Campus leadership has also developed a Centennial Campus/Southeast Raleigh Partnership that is designed to encourage employment and job creation for an economically depressed part of the city. The Kenan Institute has partnered with both local (Wake County Public School System) and regional (Southern Growth Policies Board) organizations. As an example of the kind of opportunities Centennial Campus is likely to create in the future, the U.S. Department of Agriculture opened an eastern regional hub for the Animal, Plant, Health and Inspection Service on the Centennial Campus in May 2000. The facility allows scientists to collaborate with policymakers to protect American plant resources and agriculture trade.

Industry/University Advisory Boards and Councils.

N.C. State makes extensive use of industry advisory boards and councils. For instance, all of the university's business- and technologically oriented colleges have advisory boards with significant industrial representation that are actively involved in strategic planning and in the evaluation of instructional and other programs. The IES and its MEP program have very active advisory boards with heavy industrial representation. In addition, N.C. State's extensive investment in consortia-based industry-university research centers ensures that there is substantial industrial guidance provided to these research efforts. Finally, industry has been well represented on the committees that have guided the various strategic planning activities covered in this report.

Faculty Culture and Rewards

There is evidence that both faculty culture and, to some extent, the university's reward structure supports N.C. State's commitment to technology-based economic development. For instance, a special committee of the faculty senate listed "technological and managerial innovation" and "engagement with the people and organizational constituencies outside the university" as two realms for faculty responsibility. In addition, the university has developed a variety of mechanisms to acknowledge faculty contributions in these areas. The university has sponsored an Inventor's Awards Luncheon for more than 10 years, provides Outstanding Extension Awards, and recently created an Academy of Outstanding Faculty Engaged in Extension. On a more concrete level the university is in the process of increasing the share of royalties given to inventors. Historically, inventors received 25% of gross royalties in technology transfer deals, which has been increased to 30% in 2001, and will be boosted again to 40% in 2003.

In addition, the university's recently revised promotion and tenure guidelines, or "realms of faculty responsibility," now contains language that is quite supportive of the kinds of activities and priorities highlighted throughout this chapter. For instance, one item addresses the importance of "extension and engagement with constituencies outside the university," another stresses "managerial and technological innovation." In addition, the teaching item highlights the importance of "interdisciplinary and multidisciplinary learning," while the research item makes a point to acknowledge applied research that produces "practices and technologies useful to society." Taken together, North Carolina State University's mission, culture, and reward system send a powerful message to faculty about the importance the university community attaches to activities that contribute to technology-based economic development.

Endnotes

1 National Science Foundation Division of Science Resource Studies. (2001). *Academic research and development expenditures, FY 1999.* Washington, D.C.: National Science Foundation. Table B-33.
2 *U.S. News & World Report.* Ranking of university graduate programs (http://www.usnews.com)
3 Klein, E. (1997). *University program partnerships for economic development.* Raleigh, N.C.: North Carolina State University.
4 National Science Foundation. Division of Science Resource Studies. Op. cit. Tables B-33, B-36, B-38.
5 For more details see Link, A.N. *A generosity of spirit: The early history of the Research Triangle Park.* Research Triangle Park, N.C.: Research Triangle Foundation of North Carolina.
6 These centers include: the Center for Advanced Computing and Communications (joint with Duke University), the Center for Advanced Processing and Packaging Studies (joint with University of California-Davis and Ohio State University), the Center for Integrated Pest Management, the Nonwovens Cooperative Research Center, the Silicon Wafer Engineering and Defect Science Center, and the Lymphocyte Technology Center.
7 CERSP is a multi-university center that includes the University of North Carolina at Chapel Hill, North Carolina A&T, and the University of Texas at Austin.
8 The total acreage of the Centennial Campus includes approximately 200 acres surrounding the Veterinary school, which will be developed as the Centennial Biomedical Campus.
9 Association of University Technology Managers. (2000). *AUTM Licensing Survey: FY 1999.* Chicago, Ill.: Association of University Technology Managers.
Association of University Technology Managers. (1999). *AUTM Licensing Survey: Fiscal Year 1998.* Norwalk, Conn.: Association of University Technology Managers.
10 See CERSP Web site: http://www.nsfstc.unc.edu/resources/partnerships/PAATI
12 N.C. State also hosts a Humanities Extension/Publication program.
12 N.C. State Industrial Extension Service. (2000) Annual report. Raleigh: North Carolina State University.
13 North Carolina State University. (2001).*The new NC State: Becoming the nation's leading land grant institution.* Raleigh, N.C.: North Carolina State University.
14 N.C. State Office of Technology Transfer. (2000). *Annual Report.* Raleigh, N.C.: North Carolina State University.

OHIO STATE UNIVERSITY

Founded in 1870, The Ohio State University (Ohio State) is one of the largest and most well known of public land grant universities. It has 36,000 undergraduate students and 12,000 graduate students enrolled at the main campus in Columbus, and another 7,000 enrolled at five branch campuses around the state. It offers a comprehensive menu of degree programs and research foci, through 25 colleges, 56 interdisciplinary research groups, and professional schools of law, medicine, veterinary medicine, business, and pharmacy. Being the only land grant school in the state, it also offers extension programs in all 88 Ohio counties. Most importantly for this project, Ohio State has gone through something of a renaissance over the past few years. This has involved an exciting rethinking of mission, goals, and investment — particularly as they pertain to contributing to the knowledge economy of the state. While these changes are still being implemented, and the economic downturn has slowed growth, nonetheless the long-term benefits thereof are slowly being realized. Ohio State is a national benchmark about how creative leadership and planning can turn a large institution toward a new path.

In the FY 1999 National Science Foundation (NSF) survey of academic research and development,[1] Ohio State reported research expenditures of $322.8 million, which ranks 19th among all U.S. universities and 12th among public universities. As part of its "2010 objective" (to have 10 programs in the top 10, and 20 in the top 20, by the year 2010) the university believes that is has attained – or is about to reach – national stature in several areas of research and scholarship. This long-term objective is led by a small number of targeted investments in programs that have the potential to reach this goal. In the science and technology area a sample of these selective investments include: bioengineering — particularly minimally invasive surgery; cardiovascular bioengineering and medical imaging; material sciences — particularly sensors, electrical materials, and computational design of new materials; and information technology — particularly computer visualization, motion capture, and wireless technology. Other programs on campus outside of the science and technology area also are also achieving national stature. For example, *U.S. News & World Report* ranks Ohio State's full-time MBA program in the top 25.

In terms of the objectives of this project — to portray institutions that are actively linked to and involved in state and local economic development — Ohio State represents an interesting case. It is clearly an institution that is in transition from a large, relatively uninvolved (in technology-led economic development that is) land grant school to one that aspires to be Ohio's leading asset in growing a knowledge-based economy. While not there yet, the Ohio State story is very instructive for other institutions with similar aspirations.

MISSION, VISION, AND GOAL STATEMENTS

As far as playing a role in technology-based economic development in Ohio, the university has clearly put its stake in the ground. For example, the academic plan[2] released in October 2000 described six strategies and 14 supporting action initiatives. Of most relevance to this chapter, strategy number six is to "help build Ohio's future." That translates into action initiative number 14:

> *Become the catalyst for the development of Ohio's technology-based economy. Increase collaborations with the private sector to enhance research, successfully transfer University technology, and provide experiential learning and career opportunities for students. Implementation: Make SciTech a national leader in technology transfer and University-related enterprise development. Position TechPartners as a nationally recognized vehicle to increase the University's competitiveness; attract top faculty, students and research funding; and create a tangible positive impact on Ohio's economy.*

That mission thrust is repeated at various levels, and the most vocal and visible champion is President William "Brit" Kirwan. Many of the initiatives and new energy on campus are a direct result of his leadership. The following is an illustrative excerpt from one of his speeches:

> *In the Information Age Economy, where success is rooted in the strategic application of technology and knowledge management, the lines between business and academia are being blurred by partnerships that deliver value to a company's bottom line, just as they advance a university's academic and research missions. Ohio State's Office for Technology Partnerships leads us to best practice technology partnerships and supports the University's mission toward top 10 public research institution status.*

These new institutional goals are increasingly expressed at the unit level as well. For example, a recently developed set of promotion and tenure guidelines with the College of Food, Agricultural and Environmental Sciences expresses a more expansive vision and mission of what the College is all about. They have broadened the concept of scholarship to include the transformation and application of knowledge, and have legitimized the use of patents as an indicator of research excellence.

Much of this relatively recent emphasis on technology-based economic development has its conceptual origins in an earlier, broader planning and mission articulation effort in the area of outreach and engagement. Building off Ohio State's historic role as a land grant institution, that effort produced a number of position papers that focused academic units more on external partnerships across a variety of social issues

INDUSTRY RESEARCH PARTNERSHIPS

NSF data[3] indicate that Ohio State's industry-sponsored research expenditures in 1999 were $52 million, or 16.1% of total research expenditures. This placed the university sixth among the top 100 U.S. universities in the fraction of its research expenditures supported by industry. To illustrate the impressive growth trajectory, industry sponsorship of research in 1992 accounted for 6.9% of expenditures. During this 1992-1999 period, while overall research expenditures increased by a respectable 59%, industry sponsored expenditures increased by an extraordinary 271%.

Ohio State prides itself on being both an originator and an emulator of "best practices" in university-industry partnering. This includes user-friendly policies and procedures at both central administrative and unit levels, inviting Web sites that describe the capacities of the institution, and a culture that is very supportive of these arrangements. These practices are particularly prominent in units that historically have had large portfolios of industry-sponsored work (the Colleges of Engineering, and Food, Agricultural, and Environmental Sciences). For example, the university has launched an annual Technology Partnership Awards program, to recognize exemplary university-industry collaborations. Ohio State has also established a primary point of initial contact for industry, through its Office of Technology Partnerships, and has developed clear guidelines for industrial contracts (e.g., *Procedures for High Risk Industrial Contracts*) that minimize red tape and delays for companies. These changes have created a receptive environment for industry-sponsored programs, small and large. Among the latter are several major centers with a strong industrial orientation in the College of Engineering.

As one example, the Center for Advanced Polymer and Composite Engineering (CAPCE) is building a base of research, engineering education, and technology transfer in advanced polymer and composite manufacturing technology. The research concentrates on manufacturing polymeric materials via melt, powder, and reactive liquid processing and forming from sheet and bulk materials. Interactions among materials part design, processing conditions, and product properties are key concerns. The program is structured according to three thrust areas: thermoplastic processing, thermoset polymers and composite manufacturing, and integral attachment (snap-fit) design (http://www.capce.ohio-state.edu/About_CAPCE.html). More than 20 companies participate in CAPCE, which is part of the National Science Foundation's portfolio of centers.

The Ohio Supercomputer Center's (OSC) Technology Policy Group is addressing Ohio's technological infrastructure readiness through a partnership with PriceWaterhouseCoopers called E-Com Ohio. E-Com Ohio is the first state-based effort to take on the challenge of developing and using a methodology and analytic tools to assess a state's readiness for global e-commerce. Illustrating the flexible partnership structure that Ohio State has developed, the center is housed at the university's affiliated research park called Scitech but is administratively managed by the university. The funding comes from the state Board of Regents, Ohio State, as well as other member universities, but OSC has a separate governing board.

OARnet is a division of OSC and is a major regional Internet service provider, serving nearly 100 universities and colleges in Ohio as well as government agencies and corporate enterprises. The engineering expertise of the organization lends itself to developing and testing next generation Internet technology. In 1999 OARnet was selected by the University Corporation for Advanced Internet Development (UCAID) to lead the Ohio consortium examining applications and infrastructure for Internet 2. In addition, OARnet has received funding from the State's Technology Action Fund to test applications emerging on the Internet 2 network.

OSCAR is an example of a large interdisciplinary research project being conducted in partnership with industry. OSCAR is working with the State of Ohio Coal Development Office, and industry representatives, to test a technique for removing harmful products produced in the combustion of high-sulfur coal, and to find a commercial use for the ash byproduct of the combustion process. Participating units on campus include the Department of Chemical Engineering, Department of Civil and Environmental Engineering and Geodetic Science, the McCracken Power Plant (Ohio State's physical facilities) and the Ohio Coal Development Office. If the scale up demonstration of this project is successful, it could prove beneficial to the Ohio coal industry as well as energy producers generally (http://www.eng.ohio-state.edu/nie/nie722/722_research.html#OSCAR).

Perhaps the most important ingredient of success in the area of industry research partnerships (as well as in technology transfer and entrepreneurial development) is the innovative approach to creating a system of industry engagement, which in turn derives from an extensive and thoughtful planning and strategizing process. In 1998 President Kirwan created the University Technology Partnerships Task Force, charging them with answering the challenge: "What can Ohio State do to become a leader in this area?" That led to a 20-page report issued in March 1999 titled *Turning Great Research Into Innovative Products*, which described Ohio State's recent performance in this area, provided illustrative best practices that might be adapted, and made several strategy and action recommendations.

In addition, the report contributed to the creation of the Office for Technology Partnerships. The office was intended to pull together under one organizational umbrella and location the university's licensing function, its collaborative research activities with industry, its forays into entrepreneurial development of university technology, and a more recent, somewhat diverse, mandate to encourage statewide and community-based initiatives in technology-based economic development. A September 2000 report titled *Connecting Knowledge with a Global Marketplace* describes in much more detail the accomplishments and vision of the office. One of the major accomplishments has been to get all of the component functions into contiguous office space on the second floor of the Ohio State Research Foundation building. On many campuses, functions such as these that are nominally complementary have a hard time coordinating because of physical separation.

TECHNOLOGY TRANSFER

The Office for Technology Licenses is one of the on-campus offices that are part of the Office for Technology Partnerships. As such, it now reports to the assistant vice president for technology partnerships. The office is now housed with several other organizations that encompass Ohio State's integrated, "one-stop-shopping" approach.

Based on data from the Association of University Technology Managers (AUTM), Ohio State license income was $1.6 million in FY 1999, for a royalty return on investment (royalties divided by total research expenditures) of 0.5%. License income ranks in the 64th percentile, and royalty ROI ranks in the 43rd percentile of the 142 academic institutions that participated in the *AUTM Licensing Survey: FY 1999*.[4]

Looking at the number of new licenses to start-ups in fiscal years 1998 and 1999 combined, Ohio State reported a total of 11, placing it in the 52nd percentile in the total AUTM licensing survey population for this measure. Looking at new start-ups formed, Ohio State reported none during this period, perhaps reflecting some of the past ambiguity in policies regarding equity participation (see Entrepreneurial Development, below).

Up until a few years ago, the staffing of the Office for Technology Licenses was minimal, although there are now five full-time people. The office is most heavily involved with those colleges that have been historically active in technology, primarily engineering and agriculture. Staff from the office may sit on planning committees in these colleges and may participate in faculty searches, particularly with candidates who have a strong interest in patenting or entrepreneurial activities. Additionally, the office has a wide range of other campus contacts. For example, it has also worked closely with professors in the College of Arts who have been active in the development of new approaches to computer-based animation.

Ohio State's licensing office has at least two advantages over other universities. First, the director has been at the university since the early 1990s and continuity has been greater than most universities. Second, the director has solid relationships with key deans and center directors. This helps to quickly resolve issues and make sure that information about intellectual property (IP) relevant to the college is available and understandable. One example of this are the various updates on IP and licensing policies that are inserted into deans' newsletters and other materials that are routinely distributed to faculty members. Relatively frequent presentations on IP developments have been given to the Deans' Council meetings and to associate deans for research at their meetings.

The office has tried informational outreach seminars for faculty but the attendance has been low. In lieu of those events, the approach is to work with deans to bring the licensing director and staff into college staff meetings, departmental meetings, and industry advisory meetings. Faculty members have learned about protecting intellectual property and how to work with the technology transfer office. Invention disclosure rates have been increasing at a 20% to 25% annual rate since the office has been more active in outreach and increased the scope of its services.

In future years, the involvement of the technology transfer function in deals that are more entrepreneurial in nature is likely to increase significantly. As described below (see Entrepreneurial Development), there are a number of external partnerships now underway that are focused explicitly on this type of activity.

INDUSTRIAL EXTENSION/TECHNICAL ASSISTANCE

The College of Agricultural, Food, and Environmental Sciences is the organizational locus of an extension apparatus that serves every county in the state. Although traditionally focused on the agricultural sector and allied industries, it increasingly has concentrated on higher value-added industries and problems of economic development at the community level (http://www.comdev.ohio-state.edu/cdsp.html).

Within this broad mission and mandate Ohio State University Extension offers a variety of training, outreach, and leadership development activities. Some of these are primarily focused on skills and knowledge, while others try to facilitate the processes of community change and leadership development. Some of the topics addressed in these activities include the following: economic development; business retention and expansion; business attraction; access to capital; industrial sites and buildings; development policies; small business development; downtown development; home-based business; entrepreneurship; workforce development; labor management; wages and benefit assessment; family incomes; marketing; tourism; and international issues (http://www.comdev.ohio-state.edu/; http://www.comdev.ohio-state.edu/cdprog.html#c). Obviously, many of these issues go far beyond the traditional emphases of agricultural extension and are quite consistent with the shifts in the university's mission and goals described elsewhere in this chapter.

ENTREPRENEURIAL DEVELOPMENT

While yet to realize national standing in terms of performance metrics, Ohio State has made extraordinary strides in strengthening entrepreneurial development activity. One thrust has been in the improvement of internal policies, procedures, guidelines, and culture pertaining to faculty entrepreneurs. Prior to the recent changes, faculty members at Ohio State who were interested in building a start-up company around their inventive activity faced a difficult road, a situation not dissimilar from other research universities. A second thrust in gearing up entrepreneurial activity has been the forging of robust partnerships with organizations that are external to the university, but that are deeply involved in entrepreneurial development. Primarily through this creative use of partnerships, Ohio State has created a full-service entrepreneurial development infrastructure.

Regarding policies and procedures, Ohio State has enacted or set in motion several internal reforms. An existing law in Ohio, in effect, precluded university employees from having an ownership interest (equity position) in a start-up company based on university-developed technology. Changing this situation demanded legislative relief, however the first step involved a statewide campaign of education and advocacy led by the Office of Technology Partnerships and the University Governmental Relations Office. It focused primarily on Ohio General Assembly. The work of a statewide collaboration of business, legal and educational communities led to the passage of S.B. 286 in 2000 by the legislature. The law enabled Ohio public universities to be more flexible about faculty and state equity holding and mandated that they develop guidelines for implementation. At Ohio State this has translated into a campus-wide discussion and the drafting of a set of guidelines. The final version thereof was reviewed in a series of public meetings on campus and was adopted by the Board of Trustees in early 2001. Since then five companies have been formed involving faculty.

In addition to the guidelines, in 2000 the Faculty Committee on Patents and Copyrights completed a revised Intellectual Property Policy. While not focusing exclusively on the start-up situation, it nonetheless clarifies expectations and roles regarding intellectual property protection.

Externally, Ohio State has excelled in forging partnerships with community organizations actively involved in entrepreneurial development — sometimes with Ohio State technology and sometimes not. In fact, these developments have resulted in a new "branding" of the Office of Technology Partnerships into TechPartners. While officially an Ohio State-based organization, four of the seven partners are outside the university.

One of the four external partners is Scitech, a research park that is located adjacent to the university but operates through a separate nonprofit corporation. The mission of Scitech is to promote on-campus research alliances between businesses and the university and to provide facilities to house companies that collaborate with Ohio State researchers, including university spin-off enterprises. One way to ensure alignment of Scitech with the university is through the Board of Trustees for the corporation. The university president chairs Scitech's Board, and members include the Ohio State vice president for research, deans from the College of Engineering and the College of Food, Agricultural, and Environmental Sciences, a university trustee, and community and business leaders. Scitech targets as potential tenants those companies that hire students, engage in cooperative research relationships with Ohio State, and license technology from Ohio State. Through a long-term master development agreement with Ohio State, Scitech renovated 48,000 square feet of existing space and added 50,000 square feet of new space in 2001. Currently, 25 companies reside in Scitech Park, including 12 that reside in the business incubator.

Scitech has also incubated another member of the TechPartners group, the recently established Technology Commercialization Corporation (TCC). TCC occupies a niche between commercially creative Ohio State researchers and the intellectual property they create and the local entrepreneurial community, particularly early stage institutional venture capital funds. The function of the TCC is to groom raw technology into well-packaged, business opportunities suitable for first round (seed stage) venture capital investments. TCC works closely with early investors, and will have a special relationship with the $40 million seed venture fund that the Technology Leadership Council has formed in Columbus. In recognition of the seed fund's lead investor, it has been named the Battelle Technology Fund.

For any particular core technology, TCC accomplishes commercialization by securing intellectual property rights, conducting developmental research to specify the market opportunity, conducting a focused development program to reduce the technology to operational practice, building a new corporate entity, and preparing the company for the first formal round of financing. Success at the technology commercialization phase prepares the early-stage company to initiate a product or service that fulfills a significant market need and helps it create a team that can execute the market strategy. This accomplished, TCC helps the start-up company connect with other aspects of the regional technology enterprise infrastructure, such as admission into the local technology business incubator, the Business Technology Center (BTC). BTC also serves as a tenant feeder to Scitech's higher quality multi-tenant facilities. In its first year the TCC made five investments, two being licensees of university technology and three that were tenants of the BTC incubator (see below).

The Ohio State University Foundation and the University Development Office (the unit responsible for organizing and securing gifts and donations to Ohio State) have been assisting in fund-raising activities for the TCC. They work with Scitech, which has secured nearly $4 million from government, university friends, and corporate sources. The board of trustees of the Ohio State University Foundation has formulated an advisory committee from among its members to guide its fund-raising efforts for technology commercialization. In parallel, a group called the Technology Commercialization Advisory Board has emerged, which consists of venture capitalists, technology entrepreneurs, active and retired business executives, and Ohio State officials.

Most recently, the TCC secured funds to establish a small pre-seed fund of approximately $700,000, half from the State's Technology Action Fund, $250,000 from a venture capital group, and $50,000 each from the College of Engineering and Scitech. This pre-seed fund will be invested to evaluate new invention disclosures, existing intellectual property assets, and nascent technological developments from the College of Engineering. The focus will be on technological innovations that show promise for launching high-growth start-up businesses that would eventually enter the information technology, telecommunications, and wireless markets. Technologies that are identified as having the greatest potential for commercial success will receive additional investment to advance the technology toward commercialization. Validation and collaboration with industry participants and early investors will be a high priority in order to quickly determine these markets' appetite for supporting a potential new venture. Other pre-seed funds are being planned for technology areas such as agriculture and the biosciences and medicine.

To further support entrepreneurial ventures, the university has advanced its relationships with the venture capital industry through a so-called "affinity" VC investment strategy. An affinity fund is an independent, professionally managed venture capital fund which, while investing broadly, also makes best efforts (and provides convincing evidence thereof) to identify and invest in start-up companies commercializing inventions originating at the university or otherwise located in central Ohio. In return, upon recommendations from The Office of the Treasurer to the Board of Trustees Investments Committee, the university will make investments in the range of $500,000 to $2 million in each such fund. All of this is done with advice and counsel from relevant legal, financial, and technology groups at Ohio State.

Ohio State leadership has played an important role in the development of the Columbus Technology Leadership Council, another entrepreneur support entity. The council is a membership organization, involving principals of Columbus-based technology companies, that conducts a variety of educational, networking, and business mentoring activities. The Leadership Council established as an objective the creation of the Battelle Technology Fund, which reached a first close of $20 million with an eventual target of double that amount. The seed venture fund will be available to Ohio State-linked start-ups, as well as other community-based companies. The council is also one of the members of TechPartners.

The fourth non-university member of TechPartners is the Business Technology Center (BTC), which is a Columbus-based technology business incubator. The BTC has recently expanded its facilities from 25,000 square feet to 65,000 square feet. Included in the expansion are wet lab facilities for biotech start-ups, which meshes well with strengths at Ohio State. In addition, BTC will continue its emphasis on information technology companies with the advent of a "platform lab," a facility geared to software development. Start-ups with Ohio State origins are expected to be a primary source of tenants, and half of the 14 current tenants are companies that are built on university-originated technology. The expansion will more than double this number of tenants.

The entrepreneurial resurgence at Ohio State will also benefit from new financial resources from the state of Ohio. A Technology Action Fund (TAF) established in 1999, supports early commercial development of technology, including proof-of-concept projects and prototyping. This money is awarded via a statewide competitive proposal process. Also under discussion by the legislature is a plan (called The Ohio Plan or TOP) to create new university-based research centers in three areas: nanotechnology and advanced materials, information technology, and biotechnology. These competitively funded centers will be expected to produce state-of-the-art research that has commercial potential for the Ohio's new and existing technology companies. The state has also created a competitive biotechnology research and technology transfer fund based on the tobacco settlement, which is slated to spend upwards of $36 million within the next two years. Even though the economic slowdown and K-12 funding needs have curtailed growth of these initiatives, they are expected to regain momentum downstream.

In addition to the changes described above, which primarily affect would-be faculty entrepreneurs, there has been parallel activity in educational programs for students. In partnership with Arthur Andersen and other sponsors, the Fisher College of Business (FCOB) launched a business plan competition this year. Student teams participated in workshops led by program sponsors who provided guidance in business conception, planning and development, as well as execution and funding. The latest College of Business initiative is a new Entrepreneurship Center. In future years, the Office of Technology Partnerships will seek to expose university-developed technologies to student teams as commercialization opportunities and use their skills in developing business plans.

Furthermore, students are being exposed to local entrepreneurs with success stories in a number of small-group, mentoring environments. The Executive Luncheon Series Program brings leaders of local, fast-growing technology companies to campus, where they can engage entrepreneurial faculty and students. Experiences such as these are critical to building an entrepreneurial environment at Ohio State and in the community.

INDUSTRY EDUCATION AND TRAINING PARTNERSHIPS

In order to be responsive to regional and state-based employers, several units on campus have either revised existing education programs or launched new initiatives. Some of these lead to a degree or formal credential, while others are less formally structured.

For example, in response to companies' requests for a greater emphasis on teaming, the Fisher College of Business revised its full-time MBA program, placing a greater emphasis on group projects and consensus building. The 21-month curriculum develops critical thinking skills, global perspectives, and real-world leadership experience. The college has also expanded its Evening MBA program to meet the growing needs of employers, with an increased emphasis on group problem solving as well. In addition, the college offers an Executive MBA (EMBA) program for a more elite group of attendees drawn from individuals who already hold managerial positions. The EMBA classes meet only three days a month, but the Internet and a dedicated Web site enable group interaction and faculty guidance. All of these revised degree programs are conceived within a context of creating 21st century managers who must thrive in a world that is increasingly global and connected.

In addition to formal degree-granting programs, the Fisher College of Business offers a nondegree Management Certificate Program. This covers the usual business topics such as human resource management, workplace diversity, employment law, accounting, finance, marketing, logistics, information technology, negotiation, and corporate strategic planning.

Finally, College of Business faculty also deliver a number of custom-tailored programs for individual corporations, professional and trade association, and other organizations. These programs are generally preceded by on-site research and needs analyses that include interviews with company leadership. The intent is to craft the educational program to the culture and needs of the corporate client. Again, there is a strong interest in serving regional employers as well as entities based outside of Ohio. One example is the Ford Lean Manufacturing Program. This course series was developed to provide MBA interns with concepts and knowledge pertaining to the lean-manufacturing methods originally developed in Japan. The program is intended to prepare students to be more effective sooner at jobs with Ford Motor Company and its suppliers.

Not surprisingly, the College of Engineering also has been involved in a variety of educational programs to meet the needs of industry. For example, it is developing a program in collaboration with IBM to train students in a modeling technique for circuit testing, called verification. Lucent has funded a series of advanced software engineering courses as well.

The Ford Living-Learning Program is a particularly interesting industry-university educational partnership that involves linkages between the Colleges of Engineering and Business, and Ford Motor Company. An industry-focused residential environment has been created on campus that affords students an opportunity (http://www.osuhousing.com/LLC/llc-ford.html) to get deeply involved in the challenges of working in that industry. In addition to providing a residence, the program involves students in research opportunities focused on the automotive industry, internship and service learning experiences, plant trips, and an extended summer orientation with the company. Engineering students (primarily from mechanical engineering) and business students participate in the program.

CAREER SERVICES AND PLACEMENT

Ohio State's career services are quite responsive to the needs of industry employers, particularly those that are based in Ohio. The activities of the college of Engineering are illustrative (at Ohio State, much of this activity tends to be decentralized to the college level). It hosted more than 700 recruiting visits by companies in the 1998-99 school year, with 51% of participants being Ohio companies. The college also sponsors three career fairs annually, with upwards of 200 companies participating in each. It collaborates with the Columbus Technology Leadership Council and the Columbus Chamber of Commerce on recruiting strategies. Engineering co-op and internship programs involve 70% of students prior to graduation, and the college runs training workshops for employers that participate in the program. The college's strategy is rounded out by an Internet-based job listing service and an annual publication of a recruiter's guide, with procedures, campus contacts, and statistical information. As a result of these various procedures, the college reported that 60% of employed graduates accepted jobs in Ohio in the 1998-1999 academic year.

FORMAL PARTNERSHIPS WITH ECONOMIC DEVELOPMENT ORGANIZATIONS

Over the past few years Ohio State increasingly has become connected to local economic development organizations. Through extensive networking and coordination the university is well represented in virtually all major economic development discussions that occur in the region and at a statewide level.

The historical relationship of agriculture extension offices with every county in the state, for instance, has expanded over the past decade to include economic development functions. Today, extension offices are deeply involved in aspects of economic development ranging from economic analysis and development officer training to proposal development and networking in order to access university resources.

Two groups in central Ohio play a lead role in economic development. The first is the Greater Columbus Chamber of Commerce. The university is actively involved from the board level down to various committees. The president of the chamber is a leader in many important community development discussions, including the biannual compact concerning the distribution of state funds for community facilities and projects, many of which involve Ohio State. For example, in FY '98 Scitech received $4 million from the community portion of the state's capital budget, $2 million of which was directed to the expansion of the local technology business incubator, the Business Technology Center. As described above, both of these organizations are actively partnered with Ohio State. The chamber also convenes a monthly meeting of all local chief economic development officers, and the university participates in the meeting.

A second key group advancing local economic development is the Columbus Technology Leadership Council. This organization was formed in 1998 based on the lead recommendation from a task force that the mayor's office convened. Ohio State played a key role in bringing technology leaders together and helped to staff the organization until a president was hired in 1999. Ohio State's president, Brit Kirwan, was invited to be the first chairman of its board, which was largely composed of technology business executives. He now serves as the founding chairman and member of the executive committee. The council has become the voice for technology-based enterprise in the community, and some of its early initiatives are bearing fruit, such as the venture capital fund described above.

In addition to these groups, other alignment activities occur. At the city level, the mayor's cabinet meets with university officials periodically, and economic development is one agenda topic. A local venture capital group convenes regular meetings to ensure that technology intermediary groups remained aligned with one another's activities. Last, TechPartners by its nature aligns the activities of the university and the local intermediaries most closely affiliated with the university.

INDUSTRY/UNIVERSITY ADVISORY BOARDS AND COUNCILS

At Ohio State there is a strong tradition of advisory boards, both formal and informal. Virtually every college has a dean's advisory council composed largely of alumni from business and civic organizations related to the interests of the particular college. These groups do more than participate in an advisory capacity. They are actively involved in fund raising, serving as access channels to industry contacts, and being advocates for prospective student recruits and placements.

Formal advisory boards exist in many other ways. Notable is the Alumni Association, a separate but affiliated entity of the university. The membership is approximately 120,000; Ohio State claims that 1 of every 100 university graduates in the United States is an Ohio State alumnus.

This broad level of commitment was evident in the fall 2000 completion of the university's "Affirm Thy Friendship" campaign. The campaign goal of $1 billion was exceeded by $230 million, and of the total $411 million came from corporations. The university's Office of Development employs about 60 development officers who have constituent (college, academic unit, and geographical and specific gift foci) responsibilities. The relevance for this chapter is that each one of these people represents a contact point for corporate relations. Additionally, University Development has a central unit that targets corporate and foundation prospects and fosters partnership activities.

Another example of an advisory group is the coalition of venture capitalists, business developers, legal counsel, state government officials, and representatives from Ohio's universities that was assembled to address the statutory inadequacies associated with faculty participation in start-up companies commercializing university technology. This coalition forged a consensus among disparate groups that led to the unanimous General Assembly passage of a bill alleviating the problem. That same group remained active in reviewing versions of start-up participation guidelines that emerged from Ohio State. Other examples of these kinds of advisory and consensus building activities are evident in the statement by a university technology program manager that "in the technology arena, Ohio State has learned not to inhale its own smoke."

As is the case with most universities, various additional task forces are created to examine new areas and advance university initiatives. Two are relevant for the discussion on technology partnerships and demonstrate the evolution of the advisory function.

Soon after his arrival on campus, President Kirwan appointed a University Technology Partnerships Task Force. The task force was composed of leaders from the university's faculty and administrative ranks, government, and the business community, and led by a steering committee composed of senior university executives and the chairman of the Ohio State Board of Trustees.

The task force examined six groupings of technology partnerships: industrial liaison, industrial research contracting, technology licensing, access to specialized equipment and facilities, technology commercialization, and early stage venture funding. The task force engaged the services of an external research and consulting organization to conduct a benchmarking study of Ohio State's peer institutions and to identify best practice partnerships in those universities. The study[5] also assessed Ohio State's comparable policies, practices, and plans in these six areas, recommending actions that would allow Ohio State to become a best practice university in this arena. Action recommendations were developed for each of six technology partnership areas, which in turn were reformulated by the task force into the five core strategies around which the university has built its technology partnerships activities.

As part of the task force's third strategy (to fortify the community's technology enterprise infrastructure), the Office for Technology Partnerships worked with two ad hoc committees. First, a subcommittee of the Ohio State Foundation Board was created to advise the university on improving technology commercialization and executing a venture capital fund. This group met over a two-year period and a nucleus of people have followed the activities and contributed in many ways. A parallel ad-hoc committee — composed of business development, venture capital, and university officials — was formed around the same topic. From the university the group included the president, treasurer, and dean of the Fisher College of Business, and was chaired by the assistant vice president for technology partnerships. Among the activities of this group was setting criteria and reviewing venture capital proposals for university investment, and reviewing the business plan for the Technology Commercialization Corporation (TCC). Once TCC became operational, this group evolved (with some changes) into an advisory board for the TCC.

FACULTY CULTURE AND REWARDS

The 1998 Task Force on University Technology Partnerships came to the conclusion that incentives and rewards for involvement in economic development are one important driver of change, and this item was one of the five core strategies to execute as part of their plan. It is clear that in the past few years both conducting industrially supported research and participating in entrepreneurial technology commercialization increasingly have become accepted as integral to the broader academic experience. Today at Ohio State, attracting top faculty and students is based on the notion that academic research and technology partnerships are not an either/or proposition.

Four activities clearly indicate the shifting culture. First, in the wake of the General Assembly passage of S.B. 286, the university has set forth clear, empowering guidelines for employee participation in entrepreneurial companies. These guidelines have passed through the university governance process and are now operational. They provide great policy support for entrepreneurial endeavors. Related to this are the revisions of intellectual property policy that the Faculty Committee on Patents and Copyrights recently completed; these included a greater recognition of the legitimacy of entrepreneurial endeavors.

The second harbinger of culture change occurred when the university's Office of Academic Affairs accepted new promotion and tenure guidelines developed by the College of Food, Agriculture and Environmental Sciences. These policies reflect a new flexibility for inclusion of entrepreneurial and economic development activities in promotion and tenure decisions.

Third, annual technology partnership awards give formal recognition to "best technology partnerships practices" of faculty and companies that work with faculty. The annual speaker is the governor. Other similar recognition and awards events occur in colleges and at a university level. While modest in scope they are symbolically important.

Fourth, as noted above, the president of the university continues to actively proclaim and champion the role of industry partnerships in his speeches, writing, and public pronouncements. His role in shifting the culture of Ohio State cannot be overstated.

ENDNOTES

[1] National Science Foundation Division of Science Resource Studies. (2001). *Academic research and development expenditures, FY 1999.* Washington, D.C.: National Science Foundation. Table B-33.

[2] The Ohio State University. (2000). *The Ohio State University academic plan.*

[3] National Science Foundation. Division of Science Resource Studies. *Op. cit.* Tables B-33, B-36, B-38.

[4] Association of University Technology Managers. (2000). *AUTM Licensing Survey: FY 1999.* Chicago, Ill.: Association of University Technology Managers.
Association of University Technology Managers. (1999). *AUTM Licensing Survey: Fiscal Year 1998.* Norwalk, Conn.: Association of University Technology Managers.

[5] Battelle Memorial Institute Technology Partnership Practice. (1998). *Technology partnerships: Benchmarking The Ohio State University and its peer Institutions. An action plan for positioning The Ohio State University for leadership.* Cleveland, Ohio: Battelle Memorial Institute.

PENNSYLVANIA STATE UNIVERSITY

In terms of size and scope of operations, The Pennsylvania State University (Penn State) is clearly one of the premier land grant, research-intensive universities in the country, and also boasts one of the largest unified outreach networks in American higher education. Founded in 1855 as a small agricultural college, it became the state's sole land grant institution in 1863 following the passage of the Morrill Act in 1862. The university began to experience significant growth early in the 20th century. By the 1930s, it was well along in establishing a statewide presence through undergraduate education, its agricultural extension activities, and its educational and assistance outreach in other areas. Since then, Penn State has expanded to become a world-class university with a three-part mission: education, research, and service. However, that mission is construed to place a heavy emphasis on outreach and external partnering.

The main campus is located at University Park, Pennsylvania, where approximately 40,000 students are enrolled. Over the years and in partnership with the commonwealth of Pennsylvania, Penn State has developed an extensive system of branch campuses and affiliated institutions. These are now located in 24 locations, covering every region of the state, and enroll an additional 40,000 students. There are more than 427,000 alumni of Penn State, making it one of the more visible and esteemed institutions in the country, and its presence in the state is pervasive. According to a recent State of the University speech[1] by President Graham Spanier, "one out of every two households in Pennsylvania has a person participating in a Penn State program," including cooperative extension, resident, continuing and distance education, service, and research.

In the FY 1999 survey of academic research and development expenditures by the National Science Foundation[2] Penn State reported research expenditures of $379.4 million. This ranked 14th among all U.S. universities and ninth among public universities. Penn State has consistently ranked among the top 10 universities in the number of faculty who win prestigious Fulbright Scholarships for study abroad. Numerous Penn State faculty hold membership in the National Academies of Sciences, Engineering, or Medicine. Penn State is considered world class in acoustics research (an outgrowth of work with the Navy) and in the study of advanced materials, specifically electronic-semiconductor materials, diamond and diamond-like materials, polymers, ceramics, powdered metallurgy, and biomaterials. In the emerging discipline that intersects the life sciences and information technology Penn State is developing competencies in bioinfomatics. The Department of Geography has been ranked number one in the United States by the National Research Council (NRC). The university has historic strength in plant and animal biotechnology research. It also has outstanding programs in the colleges of Engineering, Agricultural Sciences, Earth and Mineral Sciences, Health and Human Development, and the Eberly College of Science. The recently established Life Sciences Consortium pulls together expertise from a wide array of units and disciplines across the campus. There is also a Materials Research Institute, a Children, Youth, and Families Consortium, and an Environmental Consortium, all of which report directly to the vice president for research and are campus-wide in scope. In fact, nearly one-third of Penn State's research is interdisciplinary in nature, and is organized through either Intercollege Research Programs (IRP) or the Applied Research Laboratory. This encouragement of interdisciplinary research also is reflected in the role that the university plays in economic development and community outreach.

Penn State is an example of an institution that is the dominant publicly supported university in its home state, along with being a land grant school, and which has very self-consciously taken on the mission of fostering economic and social development as an integral theme in everything it does. Moreover, its reach in performing this mission cuts across disciplines, activities, and sub-regions of the state. It is clearly an "engaged university" as discussed in the introductory chapter.

Mission, Vision, and Goal Statements

Penn State leadership has quite clearly articulated the role that the university should play in societal betterment. Interestingly, this role is portrayed as being complementary to more traditional responsibilities in education and scholarship. In a recent campus publication, appropriately titled *Integrated Impact*,[3] Penn State's president is quoted as follows:

> *I believe that we can and should be identified as the leading model of how a university simultaneously provides excellence in undergraduate education; graduate education; research, scholarship, and creative activity; technology transfer and promotion of economic development; continuing and distance education; cooperative extension; public and professional service; the promotion of health and human development; and the cultural advancement of our society.*

These general themes are echoed and restated by various units on campus, particularly those that have a more visible role in relating to Pennsylvania economic development. For example, the Industrial Research Office states the university mission as:

> *To improve the lives of people in Pennsylvania, the nation, and the world through integrated programs in teaching, research, and public service.*

Similarly, in a sidebar introduction to a brochure[4] on the Penn State Innovation Park, President Spanier (who chairs its governing board) again reiterates the theme, as follows:

> The Penn State Research Park encourages a close working relationship between the University and the business community. We are pleased to expand and enhance our role in economic development through the Research Park and to include industry representatives in our extended University family.

He has also lent the legitimating mantle of his office to the increased efforts of the university to commercialize faculty-developed technology and to partner with industry:[5]

> We're doing more of it today – we have our antenna up when there's a faculty member's research that may have potential in the commercial sector. In the past, many faculty may never have seen their research outside of the lab.

These illustrations do not exhaust the use of mission and goal statements to articulate the outreach role in the Penn State context. Two themes, in particular, are worth noting about these statements and other mission language. One is the concept of *integration* between the external outreach activities and on-campus education, research, and scholarship. In effect, making a difference in the "real world" is portrayed as integral to the Penn State experience. Second is the extent to which practical impact is not seen as the exclusive domain of engineering and the sciences. Rather, outreach in areas such as education and health improvement is similarly valued. For example, another university publication[6] from Penn State Research and Technology Transfer provides 39 pages, organized region-by-region, of nearly 100 Penn State research projects that have made a difference in areas as diverse as environmental remediation, substance abuse, rural health care, and Alzheimer's disease. On a Web page[7] reachable through the main university site are described 19 ways ("a sample") that Penn State makes life better for residents of the state, which again spans the gamut from conducting research, to training doctors for Pennsylvania, to reaching out to inner-city youth.

INDUSTRY RESEARCH PARTNERSHIPS

NSF data[8] indicate that Penn State's industry-sponsored research expenditures in FY 1999 were $65.7 million, or 17.3% of total research expenditures. In 1992, they were 15.3% of total research expenditures, indicating a commendable increase in an already excellent level of performance. Between 1992 and 1999, overall research expenditures increased by 36% while industry-sponsored expenditures increased by 54%. The percent of FY 1999 industry-sponsored expenditures was above the national average of 7.4% and ranked fifth among the top 100 U.S. universities. Nationally, among top-50 research universities, Penn State has been ranked in the top three, with Duke University and the Massachusetts Institute of Technology, for industry-sponsored research and development expenditures. In contrast to many universities, about half of industry-sponsored research at Penn State involves Pennsylvania companies. In FY1999, 367 Pennsylvania companies supported 648 projects at Penn State. Not surprisingly, there is a well-developed structure for managing industry research and an attempt to be "customer-friendly" in terms of policies and procedures concerning industry research partnerships.

The Industrial Research Office (www.research.psu.edu/iro) functions as the primary point of entry for Penn State research partnerships with industry. The IRO is located within the Office of the Vice President for Research, reporting through the assistant vice president for research and technology transfer. It is currently staffed by a senior director, a contract specialist, two professional staff who function as liaisons to industrial clients, and two administrative support staff. The mission of the IRO is straightforward:

To establish long-term, mutually beneficial relationships between Penn State, industry, and government in order to stimulate cooperative research activities.

The list of partnership-stimulating activities is extensive. The office undertakes several facilitating activities, including organizing visits by faculty and students to companies, hosting company visits to the campus, linking faculty to companies around major programs or smaller projects, and maintaining databases of faculty capacities. For example, Penn State works with the Community of Science (COS) to maintain an online database of faculty areas of expertise. This is available gratis to faculty at Penn State and at other institutions that participate in COS, and for companies that subscribe to the COS service.

The IRO, as a function of its service to industry (and faculty), will do COS searches. It publishes (hard copy and online) a Penn State Research and Technology Directory, which lists over 200 research centers and laboratories, including a contact person, phone and fax numbers, and an Internet address. In addition, a company can download from the IRO Web site a "Request for Information" form, specify its needs and interests, and fax it to the office.

The office also develops directories of Penn State capacities in specialized domains of research. A recent effort was an 82 page Environmental Research Directory that describes faculty members' interests and expertise, as well as the foci and capacities of centers, institutes, and laboratories. Complete contact information is also provided, and the document has been widely disseminated to potential sponsors in government agencies and industry. The IRO also publishes a CD-ROM with all of the above information plus intellectual property available for licensing. In addition, the IRO enables industry to access research facilities like the Nanofabrication users facility, and the national Electron Beam Physical Vapor Deposition (EBPVD) coating center.

The IRO is generally viewed as the "marketing and sales" function for science and technology within the university. In this context the IRO makes industry aware of intellectual property available for license, research talent, and facilities. The IRO also packages the resulting partnership. It does the early stage negotiations and nondisclosure agreements and assists in proposal preparation. This effort greatly enhances the win rate with industry and adds considerable value to the industry/university partnership. The IRO functions as the liaison with the commonwealth of Pennsylvania in securing leverage funding for technology development through the array of economic development incentive programs.

The IRO has crafted several "special" partnerships with firms using master agreements that broadly define the relationship and provide for an enhanced oversight relationship. This effort is not unlike "affiliates" programs at other institutions. However, the liaison service that Penn State provides to industry is free. When mutual interest has been determined, and a connection established between a company and a Penn State researcher, the IRO also plays a role in facilitating contracting procedures.

There are more than 180 centers and consortia that are to some degree industry-sponsored at Penn State. The centers focus on all aspects of Penn State research competencies. IRO plays an active role in the formation of the centers by assisting in the crafting of the industrial agreements and operating documents. The IRO also assists in the identification of state and federal funding resources and in proposal preparation. Perhaps the most important role for the IRO in center formation, however, is in the identification and nurturing of potential industrial sponsors.

Penn State has been active and successful in using master agreements, particularly with those companies that have long-term multiproject relationships with the university. The Industry Master Agreement is a protocol that the IRO developed several years ago to enhance research and tech-transfer partnerships with industry. The agreements provide for a menu of options for sponsored work and captures issues generic to the partnership up front. For example, one such agreement calls for establishing an oversight team of corporate and university officials charged with monitoring the partnership, a process for solicitation and evaluation of proposals, a comprehensive approach to new project development, and IRO-dedicated management of the overall relationship. This particular relationship resulted in $1.5 million in sponsored research this year.

Another asset that fosters industry research sponsorship is Penn State Innovation Park. In its current configuration, the park offers 118 acres of space to companies large and small. The first buildings were opened in 1994, and the first privately developed multi-tenant building was completed in 1998. A second multi-tenant building is under construction. In addition to space for companies, the park also has the Penn Stater Conference Center Hotel, with accommodations for meetings of up to 1,500 participants. The park has fiber-optic connectivity throughout and ready access to regional transportation links. Preference for tenancy is given to companies with a strong interest or track record in collaborating with Penn State in research, education, or training. There are currently 38 tenants in the park, including those in the business incubator. These tenants employ more than 750 individuals. Of note, Penn State's entire Technology Transfer Organization (Ben Franklin Technology Center, Industrial Research Office, Intellectual Property Office, PENNTAP, the Research Commercialization Office, and the Small Business Development Center) is also located in the park. This centralized access is attractive to tenant companies, as well as to the industry community in general.

In fact, all of Penn State's main campus activities in research administration, research and technology development, industrial liaison, business incubation, business development, technical assistance and commercialization activities are under one roof under one command in the Innovation Park. This represents a powerful tool in technology-based economic development. This cluster also allows internal and external constituents (customers) a one-stop access to Penn State resources and research opportunities.

TECHNOLOGY TRANSFER

License income was $2.83 million in FY 1999, for a royalty return on investment (royalties as a percent of total research expenditures) of 0.76%. License income ranks in the 72nd percentile, and royalty ROI ranks in the 51st percentile of the 142 academic institutions that participated in the *AUTM Licensing Survey: 1999*.[9] Penn State reported 30 new licenses to start-up companies in fiscal years 1998 and 1999 combined, placing it in the 86th percentile in the total AUTM licensing survey for this measure. Penn State reported eight new start-ups formed in the same period, seven of which were in state. Penn State ranks in the 84th percentile for total start-ups formed and in the 85th percentile for in-state start-ups formed. These results reflect the activities of the technology transfer office, the research strengths of the institution, and the increasingly robust infrastructure in support of commercialization through start-ups.

Since start-up companies are particularly important for anchoring economic development benefits within the state, it would be useful to point out some of the relevant recent changes in university policies and practices of the Intellectual Property Office. For example, the establishment of the Research Commercialization Office was clearly an attempt to accentuate the start-up mission with a new set of operating philosophies and policies.

EIEICO Inc. is an example of how the approach can work effectively. The company was established based on licenses to a "technology platform" of three patented Penn State inventions with product applications in the meat and dairy industries. Title to the inventions is held by Penn State Research Foundation (PSRF), and PSRF will retain an equity interest in EIEICO, the start-up licensee. Faculty members and students involved in original development of the inventions will receive a portion of any economic gain. The company's investors and management will hold the remaining ownership interest. EIEICO will operate as a parent company and establish subsidiary companies for the portfolio of licensed inventions. Dr. Eva J. Pell, vice president for research and dean of the graduate school, says, "This new model for technology transfer, in which related inventions are bundled into the same start-up company, offers those who invest in EIEICO a higher probability of seeing a winner. It also aligns the interests of the inventors and the university with those of the financial and management shareholders."

The university will benefit from this arrangement by fulfilling its outreach mission and providing products and economic benefit for the public good. In addition, the university has the potential of realizing additional financial gain from the downstream sale of its equity interest.

INDUSTRIAL EXTENSION/TECHNICAL ASSISTANCE

Penn State is home to one of the "granddaddies" of the university-affiliated industrial outreach programs. Established in 1965, the Pennsylvania Technical Assistance Program (PENNTAP) has provided technical assistance services to more than 20,000 clients throughout the state. The services are provided free, and the clients are small manufacturers (48%) and other businesses. The assistance generally involves a mix of short-term technical counseling, technical information and information search services, and referrals to other sources of expertise. PENNTAP has won several awards for excellence from both national and state organizations.

In 1999, PENNTAP provided 900 cases of technical assistance to 620 clients in all 67 counties of the state. Those clients reported $9.9 billion in economic impact, and 310 jobs created or retained. The annual budget for the program is $1.5 million, of which about half comes from Penn State, and the balance from state and federal agency support. As an unusual expression of mission alignment, Penn State's monetary support comes out of its own budget, not as a pass-through of a state grant or contract. As in most states, there is a Manufacturing Extension Program (MEP) in Pennsylvania, which is also supported by federal and state sources (plus client fees). PENNTAP is not formally part of MEP but does have subcontractor partnership agreements with most of the MEP centers.

The PENNTAP staff consists of 10 technical specialists, a technical librarian, administrative support staff, and a few part-time student assistants. All of the technical specialists who work directly with companies have particular areas of expertise as well as industry experience, and all are employees of Penn State. The PENNTAP director reports to the assistant vice president for research and director of technology transfer. This gives the program a campus-wide mandate to seek appropriate expertise, which it would not have if located within a single academic unit.

The technical areas in which PENNTAP provides assistance run the gamut of needs that are typically experienced in manufacturing (e.g., materials handling, metal forming and fabrication, industrial engineering) but also extend to areas such as forest products, environmental issues, occupational safety and health, product development, and statistical analysis. Only three of the 10 technical specialists work out of the University Park campus; the balance of staff members are based at other Penn State campuses or in offices at MEP partner organizations. Nonetheless, the PENNTAP technical staff coordinate their own efforts and with efforts of other service providers through e-mail, by regular personal contact, and by participating in regional service provider network meetings. Illustrative of the scope of internal coordination, in 1999 nearly 30% of PENNTAP's 900 cases involved PENNTAP technical specialists getting help from other PENNTAP specialists to formulate a response to the client. Also, 40 cases were referred from one PENNTAP technical specialist to another because of more appropriate expertise or geographic proximity. In terms of external coordination, in 1999 33% of PENNTAP's cases were the result of referrals to PENNTAP from other organizations. Similarly, about one-third of PENNTAP cases involved referring clients to other organizations or resources for additional or extended assistance beyond the assistance provided by the PENNTAP technical specialist.

While clients are not charged for assistance services, any engagement is limited to 20 hours of contact time (excluding travel). On rare occasions fees will be charged for additional specialized services. In some cases, a company's problem will be sufficiently complex that a referral will be made to a faculty member, another program, a federal lab, or a trade association. These additional resources may involve a fee, which is negotiated between the company and the service provider. Out of 900 assistance engagements in 1999, 140 involved referrals to Penn State faculty, staff, or students outside the program. In most cases, Penn State faculty will provide assistance at no cost or arrange for the involvement of a graduate student at a very nominal cost. Occasionally, an assistance engagement will lead to a contract research project. In these cases, the IRO may play a role in identifying appropriate faculty and/or facilitating the contract arrangements. In addition to the hands-on technical assistance, PENNTAP also provides customized technical information searches. These are also free, and a client company may send to the program a technical information search request, specifying the kinds of information desired, key words, and potential publications to search. There is typically some back-and-forth interaction to verify the nature of the search before the program will deliver a product, usually within a week or two.

In most academic departments in which faculty or students frequently get involved in PENNTAP, these assignments are considered worthwhile and consistent with the research, education, and service goals of the unit. Faculty members report that they use their interactions with PENNTAP clients as examples in their classroom instruction. In addition, the program itself has hosted a reception for faculty members and staff, to acknowledge 300 individuals who had provided assistance to clients. Each person received a personalized certificate, and the president of the university and a senior official from state government both gave laudatory speeches.

One important strength of the program has been its fairly disciplined approach to gathering evaluation data from clients. This involves systematic follow-up and the development of statistical profiles of outcomes. The performance measurement and evaluation system has received a best-practice designation from the U.S. Economic Development Administration.

Several things are noteworthy about Penn State's industrial extension activities. One, it almost surely will have long-term fiscal and political support. PENNTAP seems to be a permanent part of the Penn State organizational landscape, which has interesting implications for maintaining a culture for involvement in economic development. Second, it has a relatively prominent organizational home. That is, rather than being hidden in a department or college, where it might be vulnerable to the budgetary exigencies and disciplinary constraints at that level, it has a much wider mandate. Third, it is operationally integrated with other technology-oriented outreach functions, as has been elaborated elsewhere in this chapter. Fourth, PENNTAP has been able, in most cases, to offer these services gratis to state-based companies. Few assistance programs elsewhere in the country can make the same claim.

ENTREPRENEURIAL DEVELOPMENT

Despite the fact that Penn State is physically isolated from national centers of commerce (or maybe because of that circumstance), it has made significant progress in developing a physical and programmatic infrastructure for entrepreneurial development. Much of this activity is centered at Innovation Park but it also involves the active collaboration with and support from several organizational entities on campus and in the community. This cooperation is basically institutionalized because virtually all of those entities report to the same assistant vice president.

In 1998, the university formed a new Research Commercialization Office designed to focus Penn State's efforts in fostering start-up companies based on research-generated technology. The office works on identifying, assisting, and accelerating commercial opportunities resulting from knowledge created by faculty, staff, and students. A key component of the assistance is the encouragement of seed investment in Penn State commercialization projects from angel investors or venture capital firms.

The Research Commercialization Office works closely with two local technology business incubators. Facility management is provided by an economic development organization in the community, and both incubators involve companies with strong connections to Penn State. The Zetachron Center for Science and Technology Business Development is a 10,700-square-foot wet lab facility and currently houses seven companies. Companies include: Centre Ingredient Technologies, a producer of natural flavors and fragrances; Mitotyping Technologies, a mitochondrial DNA lab servicing the criminal justice market; Salimetrics, a producer of non-isotropic immunoassays for research and development testing labs; and EIEICO, a company commercializing three technologies in the agricultural market. The second incubator, located in the Penn State Research Park, houses 12 tenant companies representing a wide range of industries. Companies include: The Forecast Institute, specializing in weather prediction software; Lomic Incorporated, a producer of gas metering software products; Licom Inc., a developer of fiber-optic technology products; and eight different Internet-related service providers. Of the 19 tenant companies, approximately half have resulted from a knowledge base emanating from Penn State or a licensed technology from Penn State's Intellectual Property Office. The majority of the companies actively employs or utilizes undergraduate and graduate student interns in their staffing strategy. Several incubator graduate companies have hired their former interns or Penn State graduates.

A third asset for entrepreneurial development is the regional office of the Ben Franklin Partnership (BFP), which is also located in the Penn State Research Park. This is a statewide $25 million program at four centers, one of which is based at Penn State. For existing companies, the program can provide funding (on a competitive basis) for projects that typically focus on process or product improvement. For the university, the program can partially support an industry-oriented center or institute. For start-up companies, the program can support the development of a promising technology into a working prototype. Only a small fraction of projects directly involve the commercialization of Penn State technology, but nonetheless university faculty and students are involved in several aspects of BFP program activities, ranging from working on projects to reviewing proposals for potential funding. Again, because of the co-location of this program with the other technology transfer offices, there are numerous opportunities for leveraging among the programs. Locating the program in the Penn State Research Park also sends a clear message to the region and the state that this is an important part of the university's mission.

Although less focused on high-tech companies, Penn State's Small Business Development Center (SBDC) serves a variety of companies in a contiguous multi-county area. The center is staffed with three permanent employees, three student employees, and an outside consultant. It is funded by a mix of monies from the state's Department of Community and Economic Development and from Penn State. Organizationally, the SBDC reports to PENNTAP (see above) and in turn to the vice president for research. The center provides a wide variety of business assistance services and training often with help from university faculty or staff. Most of the services are delivered free of charge or for a modest fee. The latter are coordinated through Penn State's Office of Outreach and Cooperative Extension.

INDUSTRY EDUCATION AND TRAINING PARTNERSHIPS

Penn State provides a wide variety of industry-focused education and training offerings, either through its branch campus system, via distance learning, or in the form of new industry-oriented degree programs. Among the latter is the formation of a new School of Information Sciences and Technology. The school was launched in response to urgent workforce shortages in the information industries, both in Pennsylvania and nationally. Industry executives, who emphasized the need for management and communication skills as well as technical expertise, guided development of the program. Almost 600 students are enrolled in the school, about 200 at University Park and the rest at branch campus locations. The IST school has significant industrial support and has a guaranteed placement of all of its first class in a highly competitive IT industry. A four-year baccalaureate degree is available at the University Park campus and other selected locations. Other campuses also offer the two-year associate degree. Master's and Ph.D. programs will be available in the near future, as will IST certificate programs. IST students who cannot study in residence also have access to courses and certificate programs via Penn State's World Campus, a Web-based interface for providing anytime/anywhere learning.

The branch campus system at Penn State provides affordability to students who must stay in their community for personal and financial reasons and allows for programmatic flexibility at the local level in response to workforce demands in industry. For example the Penn State Erie Campus (Behrend College) offers degrees in plastics and advanced materials technology in response to the significant industry cluster in the region; the Dubois campus of Penn State offers programs in powdered metal technology; the Mont Alto campus offers forest products; and the Capital Campus in Harrisburg offers degree programs in environmental science and technology.

Penn State has created a first-of-a kind in the state (and one of a very few in the United States) Semiconductor Training Program in the Innovation Park facility. This two-year associate degree program prepares technicians to work in clean-room environments within the semiconductor industry. The first three semesters are offered at many of the community colleges and branch campuses across the state with the final semester in the clean room at the University Park campus. Technicians are trained on state-of-the-art equipment (e.g., an operational six-inch wafer line and a class 10 clean room). This $20 million facility is part of the nano-fabrication users facility, a National Science Foundation funded industry/university research consortium with a focus on next generation "system on a chip" prototype products and processes. A second unique program resides within the Sintered Materials Center whose technology and research focus relates to the powdered metals industry. This industry is uniquely clustered in Pennsylvania where it manufactures more than 39% of the world's powdered metal parts. The center is another example of industry/university/state government partnership with over 80 industry partners, and $1 million in state funding support. The center boasts a field training and technology assistance site located at the Penn State Campus in Dubois. The Dubois center is located in the heart of the powdered metals industry cluster where approximately 4,000 workers are employed in more than 40 firms.

CAREER SERVICES AND PLACEMENT

The Eberly College of Science, the Smeal College of Business, the College of Engineering, and the School of Information Sciences and Technology have cooperative education and internship programs for undergraduates. In the College of Engineering, 48% of the nearly 1,000 students who participate in the cooperative education program work for companies in Pennsylvania. The College of Engineering staff works with the high-tech councils in eastern and western Pennsylvania to establish co-ops, internships, and jobs for Penn State students. Staff members also work with the Chamber of Business and Industry of Centre County (CBICC) and the Private Industry Council of Centre County (PICCC) to develop local opportunities for University Park students.

While the career fairs at the University Park campus usually host national companies, Commonwealth Campuses tend to invite regionally based companies. In the fall of 2002, the Office of Career Services will host a special career fair called "@pgh.cafe" (http://www.tc-p.com/atpgh.cfm), sponsored by Pittsburgh Technology Council and Pittsburgh companies.

Penn State also intersects with industry on issues of human resources via statewide programmatic initiatives. The state of Pennsylvania has programs in place that encourage workforce development in key industrial sectors that have a high potential for growth. These programs are tied to the technology development initiatives described above. The industry clusters that predominate in this investment strategy include plastics, tool and die, powdered metals, advanced materials (semiconductors and ceramics), biotechnology and the life sciences, environmental science and technology, and information technology.

Many of the programs at Penn State reflect both technology opportunity and human resource needs. Examples include the Semiconductor Manufacturing Training Program, the Information Science and Technology Program, the Sintered Materials/Powdered Materials Program, the Plastics Technology Development/Deployment Centers Program, and the e-Business Resource Program.

FORMAL PARTNERSHIPS WITH ECONOMIC DEVELOPMENT ORGANIZATIONS

Contrasted with many other institutions, Penn State's formal partnerships with state and local economic development organizations are probably more operational and real than symbolic. It has a long fiscal and operational partnership with the Commonwealth of Pennsylvania regarding existing programs and has been at the policy table for many years as the state has developed new programs to address economic development in the knowledge economy. Its role and visibility among the state's political and economic development leadership is of long standing, and has generally transcending party and ideology.

Penn State officials hold memberships in and participate on various committees of the Pennsylvania Chamber of Business and Industry and the Pennsylvania Economic Development Association, for example. The university is also heavily engaged with the Pennsylvania Department of Community and Economic Development in both program implementation and policy development. As previously mentioned, the university administers one of the state's four Ben Franklin Technology Centers, which supports industrial technology development, as well as PENNTAP (Pennsylvania Technical Assistance Program). The university also participates in a variety of economic policy planning activities, such as Pennsylvania's Technology 21 planning process completed last year, and is a member of the Pennsylvania Technology Investment Authority.

In addition to this interface with statewide economic development organizations, Penn State officials also work with a wide variety of local and regional economic development organizations across the state. Pennsylvania has more than 1,500 local and regional community and economic development organizations. These include county and municipal economic development offices, county industrial development corporations and authorities, small business development centers, regional planning and development commissions, housing and redevelopment authorities, community action agencies, private industry councils, Ben Franklin Technology Centers, industrial resource centers, and many others. With nearly 100 Penn State campuses and extension offices, the university has a presence in every one of Pennsylvania's 67 counties. Through these locations, Penn State officials help provide leadership on a daily basis to these and other types of economic development organizations. Correspondingly, many of these organizations are represented on Penn State campus and Cooperative Extension advisory boards throughout the state.

INDUSTRY/UNIVERSITY ADVISORY BOARDS AND COUNCILS

There are more than 180 industry-driven research and technology development centers and laboratories whose research and strategic agenda is in part or predominately developed by industry boards and center members, as well as academic units with strong ties to industry. For example all departments within the College of Engineering have strong industry and professional advisory councils (IPACs) that help the department develop programs, curriculum, and research that are relevant to market demand. The IPACs consist of industry leaders in the field, key professional societies representing the discipline, and key alumni.

Penn State has helped to organize and manage a wide variety of industry advisory boards, councils, and consortia. For example, one of the newest is the Transportation Research and Education Consortium established this year in partnership with the Pennsylvania Department of Transportation and Pennsylvania industry to address public and private research and education needs in the transportation sector. Others examples of industry-driven centers include the Center for Innovative Sintered Products with more than 70 industry members; the Pennsylvania Nanofabrication Manufacturing Technology Partnership, governed by an advisory board comprised of leading semiconductor manufacturing firms; the Penn State Erie Plastics Technology Center, with more than 70 industry members; the 35-member Pennsylvania Housing Research Center which promotes better and more affordable housing for Pennsylvanians through technology; and the 30-member Penn State Center for Excellence in Metal Casting, developed in partnership with the Pennsylvania Foundrymen's Association.

Still others include the Penn State Berks Food Manufacturers Training Consortium which addresses workforce training needs of more than 20 major Pennsylvania food processing companies in and around Berks County, Pennsylvania, and the Penn State York Industrial Training Consortium, which provides workforce training programs for six of the largest industrial employers in York County, Pennsylvania. Finally, Penn State has been instrumental in helping to develop consortia independent of the university in new industry sectors. An example here is the 100-member Pennsylvania Biotechnology Association, which was started within Penn State but now serves the statewide interests of this industry. Through these types of advisory boards, councils, and consortia, Penn State is able to extend its research and education capabilities to thousands of Pennsylvania companies beyond the 368 firms that directly sponsored research at the university last year.

FACULTY CULTURE AND REWARDS

In addition to the many examples of mission language and public advocacy in support of an aggressive outreach posture for Penn State, there are many informal examples of units and colleges supporting faculty involvement in economic development activities and programs. There also are instances of formal acknowledgement programs and a more positive consideration of these activities in tenure and promotion considerations. For example, the office of the vice president for research and the Penn State Research Foundation held a Penn State Inventors Reception in recognition of the 46 patents issued to more than 100 faculty, staff, and students during 1999.

Perhaps the best expression of cultural support for many of the activities described in this chapter is found in the outreach and cooperative extension function of the institution. Headed by a vice president, it publishes a quarterly magazine, *Outreach*, that documents the community improvement work of Penn State faculty and staff around the state. In 1990 the unit published a plan[10] for strengthening the outreach function, which received wide visibility both on campus and around the state.

In addition, there have been extensive recent discussions on campus trying to reshape the definition of scholarship, as well as to address the issue of faculty rewards for outreach. A group entitled the University Scholarship and Criteria for Outreach and Performance Evaluation (UniSCOPE) learning community has released a report[11] that calls for considering the three mission areas of the University – teaching, research, and service – as alternative forms of scholarship, each with its dimensions of excellence and modes of recognition. Technical assistance and consultation are considered as viable types of activity, patents and licenses are considered appropriate vehicles for delivering research scholarship, and corporations are a legitimate "target student" audience. In parallel, a Faculty Senate Committee on Outreach Activities has convened and recommended policies that will define outreach, recommend evaluation methods and criteria, and suggest approaches to recognition and rewards. Obviously these two groups have complementary and perhaps overlapping tasks; one likely result should be a clarification of Penn State's culture and rewards regarding outreach, including the industry partnerships that have been described in this chapter.

ENDNOTES

[1] Spanier, Graham. (1998). *State-of-the-University address.*

[2] National Science Foundation Division of Science Resource Studies. (2001). *Academic research and development expenditures, FY 1999.* Washington, D.C.: National Science Foundation. Table B-33.

[3] Penn State Research and Technology Transfer, Partnerships for Economic Development. *Integrated Impact.* University Park, Pa.: Penn State University.

[4] *A Vision. Penn State Research Park. Growing tomorrow's technology today.* University Park, Pa.: Penn State University.

[5] Cited in *Penn State Research Park newsletter.* Second Quarter, 1999.

[6] Penn State Research and Technology Transfer, Partnerships for Human Development. (1999) *For the Health of Pennsylvania.* University Park, Pa.: Penn State University.

[7] http://www.psu.edu/ur/about/nineteen/19ways.html

[8] National Science Foundation Division of Science Resource Studies. (2001). *Academic research and development expenditures, FY 1999.* Washington, D.C.: National Science Foundation. Tables B-33, B-36, B-38.

[9] Association of University Technology Managers. (2000). *AUTM Licensing Survey: FY 1999.* Chicago, Ill.: Association of University Technology Managers.
Association of University Technology Managers. (1999). *AUTM Licensing Survey: Fiscal Year 1998.* Norwalk, Conn.: Association of University Technology Managers.

[10] Office of the Vice President, Outreach and Cooperative Education. (1999). *The plan for strengthening outreach and cooperative education.* The Pennsylvania State University, June, 1999.

[11] The UniSCOPE Learning Community. (2000). *UniSCOPE 2000: A multidimensional model of scholarship for the 21st century. A UniSCOPE learning community challenge to the Penn State community of scholars.* Unpublished paper.

PURDUE UNIVERSITY

Purdue University is one of the larger land grant, research-intensive universities in the country. Opened in 1874, the university now has more than 60,000 students on the main campus at West Lafayette, Indiana, and satellite campuses elsewhere in Indiana. In the National Science Foundation FY 1999 survey of academic research and development,[1] Purdue reported research expenditures of $226.4 million, which ranks 38th among all U.S. universities and 25th among public universities. Although the university does not have a medical center at the West Lafayette campus, it has world-class status in many of the other disciplines that are present. For example, Purdue claims to have granted more Ph.D., master's, and bachelor's degrees in engineering than another university in the country. Its School of Agriculture has consistently been considered among the top five, and the university has major strength in biotechnology, management, education, pharmacy, and veterinary medicine. There are 34 centers and institutes, many of which have national prominence and long-term federal support. According to *Computer World*,[2] Purdue leads the nation in the production of information technology undergraduate degrees. Purdue also is the largest producer of technology bachelor's degrees of any public institution and ranks in the top three in the production of engineering bachelor-degree holders.

Purdue is a prime example of a university that has publicly and prominently embraced the role of being an economic development asset in its state and the larger global economy. It is also an example of an internally coordinated, carefully managed approach to this challenge.

Mission, Vision, and Goal Statements

Although many of the activities within Purdue's "portfolio" of economic development-related programs are of relatively long standing, within the last few years there has been an increasing emphasis on coordination within an institution-wide mission, vision, and structure.

For example, the Purdue Web site makes it easy to find the institution's current stance on engaging the external world. In the Partners section (http://www.purdue.edu/Purdue/Partners/), it states:

> Purdue University is a powerful resource for the economic development of Indiana. Under the leadership of President Martin C. Jischke and Dean of the School of Technology Don K. Gentry, the University is working closely with government offices, business and agricultural leaders, and educators to ensure that the state realizes the maximum possible advantages from Purdue's many resources.

Behind that Web site statement lies an interesting recent history of organizational rethinking and reorganizing. In 1998 then-President Steven C. Beering endorsed a concept paper[3] that proposed the establishment of a campus-wide Office of Economic Development. While pointing out the many existing activities in units and schools across the campus, the paper argued for the benefits that might be achieved by greater "coordination, communication, visibility, synergism, and public understanding." The paper went on to propose the establishment of an Economic Development Cabinet (whose membership would include leaders from the university, state government, and the private sector), as well as an Economic Development Consortium or Council, internal to the university, to foster cooperation, coordination, and program development. In addition, the paper proposed 23 specific action strategies under the categories of leadership, planning, communication and marketing, and programmatic initiatives. Shortly thereafter, Dr. Don K. Gentry, dean of the School of Technology, was appointed to serve as the first assistant to the president for economic development and charged to begin fostering many of the detailed recommendations of the concept paper.

An Economic Development Council was formed, with Gentry as chair first, followed by President Jischke. It serves primarily a conceptual and coordination function. Its members include four deans, four vice presidents, and two assistants to the president. It meets monthly to develop policy recommendations, to provide planning direction, determine strategy for implementation, and provide integration and coordination between the various operating groups. The council has construed economic development to include human capital development, innovation and research, commercialization of products, technology transfer, job creation, and access to financing. The geographic mandate is to "create a statewide partnership between Purdue, the state, and local communities." However, the authority, budget, and responsibility for pursuing these goals at an operational level lies with various service units of or associated with the university as described in this chapter. The council has also expanded its committees to include local leadership in the planning process. Recently Don Gentry has assumed a full-time responsibility as the vice provost for engagement.

During the 2000-2001 academic year the university developed and published a five-year strategic plan,[4] which featured engagement as one of three major goals to be addressed in order to achieve national preeminence. Engagement would involve, among other things:

- A position of national leadership in knowledge and technology transfer
- A vital role for the university in strengthening Indiana's economy and improving the qualifications of the state's workforce

Among the key strategies for engagement are to:

- Develop an organizational structure for promulgating university efforts to engage key local, state, national, and international constituencies to increase community and economic development and quality of life endeavors
- Increase partnerships to enhance commercialization of research, entrepreneurial initiatives, support for startup companies, and assistance to the state and to business, industry, and agriculture
- Educate, retain, regain, and retrain the workforce in targeted fields with skills necessary to build a strong state economy and expand continuing education and lifelong learning opportunities.

As this chapter demonstrates, Purdue has made significant progress over the past 10 years to fulfill that vision of preeminence.

INDUSTRY RESEARCH PARTNERSHIPS

NSF data[5] indicate that Purdue's industry-sponsored research in FY 1999 totaled $28.9 million or 12.7% of total research expenditures. This exceeds the national average of 7.4%, and puts Purdue ninth among the top 100 U.S. universities. Between 1992 and 1999 overall research expenditures increased by 61% while industry-sponsored expenditures increased by 128%.

Purdue has an extremely active and robust program of industry-university research partnerships, which is organized through the Office of Research and Technology Programs (OIRTP), reestablished in 1994 and currently headed by an assistant vice president for research.[6] Previously, Purdue had a smaller and less active function but came to the conclusion that the university needed to facilitate industry-sponsored research and to coordinate with federal programs that required industry-academic collaboration. The three-person office considers its role as a "window to Purdue for industry and a window to industry for Purdue faculty."

Organizationally, OIRTP is part of the university administrative structure, and the OIRTP director reports to the vice president for research and dean of the graduate school. OIRTP functions in many ways like an industrial relations office for the 34 centers and institutes on campus, all of which involve industry, and many of which make special efforts to get participation from smaller companies. OIRTP will help with the centers' development and industry outreach efforts, and assist in bringing together faculty from different units and disciplines.

OIRTP conducts outreach to the industry community and helps industry locate university resources in response to its needs. It publishes a professional-appearing, slick paper newsletter twice a year, which goes to 2,000 industry research people nationwide. A typical issue highlights university research programs of potential interest to industry (e.g., departments, centers), as well as describing specific "partnership opportunities," such as sponsoring students or projects. In cooperation with the Office of Technology Commercialization, the newsletter spotlights a small number of technologies available for licensure. OIRTP also contributes articles on industry partnerships to the university's monthly publication *Research Review* targeted to all faculty on campus and to companies located in the Purdue Research Park. A recent article highlighted two start-up companies involving professors from the Chemistry Department,[7] and articles on funding opportunities through the National Science Foundation and private foundations. In many institutions, these opportunities would not be juxtaposed nor seen as equivalent in their legitimacy.

OIRTP also makes available to industry the services of Connect Indiana. This includes a Web site that announces various seminars, workshops, and events. It features a reasonably friendly search mechanism allowing companies to enter needs and interests and discover expertise and facility resources that might be a good match. For example, the search engine will typically identify several faculty members with expertise in relevant areas, and the prospective industry partner can then peruse a condensed version of their vitae, with research interests, publications, experience, and contact information. The software to run and update the site was written at Purdue specifically for Connect Indiana. The expertise information is from Community of Science (COS), a private company that provides this service to universities, and it is updated on a regular basis. The facility information is gathered from various sources at the university and is also updated continually.

Aside from the Web site, Connect Indiana is a single point of contact for Indiana companies seeking help from Purdue. Companies can engage the service on a one-time basis or become a no-cost member of Connect Indiana. Organizations that use the site are asked to register as members primarily so Purdue can send them regular e-mail about programs and events that might be of interest. The registration data (which is kept confidential) is also used to notify users of significant changes in the site. Private sector and government organizations inside and outside the state of Indiana access the site on a regular basis.

Once mutual interests about a potential partnership are identified, OIRTP provides staff resources to help organize the relationships. This mostly involves coordinating and facilitating the services of offices and functions on campus. For example, staff have worked with the contract office to develop and implement simpler, menu-driven sponsored project agreements. Purdue has standard agreements and several standard clauses that can be inserted or changed in contracts without further approval. With more expansive or complex agreements, such as strategic partnerships that might involve a "cluster" of projects conducted over a period of time, OIRTP negotiates the principles and the contract office prepares the agreement. Purdue has been encouraging the use of master agreements with companies, under which faculty members can make specific project proposals without having to worry about delays from contract negotiations. There are currently about six strategic technology partnerships in place with companies such as Caterpillar and Rolls-Royce/Allison. Recently, the attractive features of strategic partnering with Purdue helped to persuade Siemens to significantly expand a plant site that they had purchased in the Lafayette area and were about to close. The university worked closely with local economic development leadership to bring this about.

On an ongoing, campus-wide basis OIRTP also chairs the Industrial Research Activities Committee (IRA), which provides a vehicle for coordinating the university's approach to industry-sponsored research, apprises faculty of industry partnership opportunities, and addresses emergent policy issues. OIRTP leadership and/or staff also serve on the Purdue Research Park Advisory Board, Indianapolis and Central Indiana's Technology Partnership Steering Committee, the Lafayette High Technology Task Force, and the Lafayette Venture Club Board.

TECHNOLOGY TRANSFER

Purdue's Office of Technology Commercialization (OTC) has the responsibility for managing the institution's technology transfer activities. The OTC is housed within the Purdue Research Foundation and reports to the vice president for research. Its activities include educating faculty about technology transfer concepts and policies, protecting university intellectual property; marketing and licensing technologies to both established and start-up companies, conducting a monthly Entrepreneurs' Forum to help create an entrepreneurial culture on campus, and operating both a "gap-funding" program as well as an internal seed capital fund to invest in its start-up companies.

Purdue's patenting and licensing function has been reasonably productive when compared to national norms, particularly in terms of entrepreneurial paths to commercialization. License income was $2.15 million in FY 1999, a royalty return on investment of 0.97% (royalties as a fraction of total research expenditures). License income ranks in the 69th percentile and royalty ROI ranks in the 60th percentile of the 142 academic institutions that participated in the *AUTM Licensing Survey : FY 1999*.[8] Purdue reported a total of 30 new licenses to start-up companies in fiscal years 1998 and 1999 combined, placing it in the 83rd percentile. In the same period, Purdue reported a total of eight new start-ups formed, four of which were located in state. Purdue ranks in the 84th percentile for total start-ups formed and in the 72nd percentile for in-state start-ups formed.

Technology transfer activities at Purdue are noteworthy on several counts. For one, the university has been quite novel in terms of the integration of technology commercialization activities across various units and functions. Many of the programs described elsewhere in this chapter (Purdue Research Park, the system of incubators, Gateway, OIRTP) have some hand in the commercialization of faculty technology, and they seem to be able to work cooperatively. For example OIRTP chairs a Technology Commercialization Working Group (TCWG) that involves line people from several groups on campus involved in economic development, particularly in the commercialization of faculty inventions. It ensures cooperation and a smooth flow of the commercialization process.

> **THE UNIVERSITY HAS BEEN QUITE NOVEL IN TERMS OF THE INTEGRATION OF TECHNOLOGY COMMERCIALIZATION ACTIVITIES ACROSS VARIOUS UNITS AND FUNCTIONS.**

In the early '90s, Purdue developed a set of policies and approaches that enable the establishment of faculty start-ups. An endorsing letter from the president to faculty, dated December 18, 1995, attached a document that a Purdue Research Park committee drew up,[9] providing a very laudatory view of faculty start-ups. It acknowledges service expectations for faculty and outlines in quite accessible language the rules and procedures regarding conflict of interest, leaves of absence, departmental permissions, and oversight. The document also describes resources (such as those discussed above) that the faculty member can use in developing his or her business. This is not a lawyer's document, trying to protect at all costs the flanks of the university. Since 1995, changes in university policy also have allowed Purdue to take equity as a part of its license agreements. Purdue currently holds equity in 10 spin-off companies. Moreover the pace of start-up companies licensing Purdue technology has significantly accelerated, from two between 1992 and 1994 to 17 between 1999 and 2001. The number continues to rise.

Through the Purdue Research Foundation, the university has become a partner with several venture capital funds to generate support for the new and expanding businesses located at the Purdue Research Park. It has invested $1 million in each of two funds as a way to foster long-term relationships with venture funding. There are no requirements that the start-up companies in the portfolio must come from Lafayette, but that has occurred nonetheless.

Purdue has also created the Trask Pre-Seed Capital Investment Program, which provides small initial investments for faculty start-up companies. The program is limited to a one-time investment of up to $250,000 and is intended to help develop the technology and the company so it can be more competitive in acquiring private seed and venture funding. The capital program made four investments in start-up companies in the first year of operation. This program supplements the Trask Technology Innovation Awards, which provides small, competitive grants to faculty seeking to increase the value of intellectual property that has already been disclosed to the Office of Technology Commercialization. These awards can range up to $100,000 for a period of one year. Proposals to both programs are reviewed in terms of commercial and technical potential. For the Pre-Seed Capital Investment Program, the applicant must have a business plan and a license agreement in place with the university.

INDUSTRIAL EXTENSION/TECHNICAL ASSISTANCE

Purdue has a small but energetic program of industrial extension and assistance that has been in existence since the mid-1980s. In consists of the Technical Assistance Program (TAP) and a parallel Technical Information System (TIS). TAP provides problem-solving consulting services to Indiana companies, with typical engagements involving no more than a few days level of effort (five days of Purdue's time are provided free of charge under state of Indiana funding). A typical project would address a manufacturing firm's problems of plant layout, process improvement, product design, environmental compliance, or quality and cost management. A faculty member will usually lead an assistance project, often working with a graduate student. Projects beyond five days are conducted on a contract-for-service basis. Since inception of the program in 1986, TAP has conducted more than 4,000 technical assistance projects that have, based on evaluations, resulted in total cost savings for clients of $16.6 million and increased sales for clients of $146.3 million.[10] In addition to the direct assistance projects, TAP places about 90 undergraduate students in summer internships with Indiana companies. TAP has nine faculty members with appointments that range from 10% to 30% of their time, 20 graduate students with a 50% time commitment, and 4.5 full-time equivalent administrative and clerical support staff. Other faculty members are involved on an as-needed basis. Faculty participation is generally restricted to tenured faculty, given that TAP participation still is neutral at best in terms of tenure and promotion are concerned. However, most faculty members who have a partial appointment with TAP tend to stay with the program for several years and report considerable professional satisfaction from the work.

The Technical Information Service (TIS) is a program that complements TAP. Operated by the Purdue University Libraries with support from the state and user fees, the program functions as a custom information search and document delivery service for companies and other organizations. In 2000, TIS conducted 343 search projects and shipped more than 11,000 documents. TIS also assists clients in the identification of Web sites that are particularly appropriate for their information needs.

Taken together, TAP and TIS serve more than 600 Indiana companies annually. They have an annual budget in excess of $1.55 million, of which $1.2 million comes from the state of Indiana, and the balance from client fees. During its history over 2,000 of the state's 10,000 manufacturing companies have been provided assistance, and there have been many repeat customers.

TAP works closely with other Purdue economic development-related activities (most described in this chapter), and with state-level programs such as the Indianapolis-based Indiana Business Modernization and Technology Corporation (BMT), the state affiliate of the federally funded Manufacturing Extension Program. TAP supports BMT outreach services to small manufacturing companies, and participates in the statewide Machine Tool Alliance, which involves 100 companies in a program of training, networking, and information sharing. On campus, TAP works with the Indiana Clean Manufacturing Institute (pollution prevention), the Centers for Excellence (a School of Technology program that provides consultation assistance and training to companies), and the Business and Industry Development Center.

Purdue has requested additional funding from the legislature to expand TAP from the current three sites to 12 locations. This would enable TAP to deliver consulting and assistance services from Purdue's regional campuses and affiliated universities. Currently, many areas of the state underutilize TAP because of the existing delivery structure.

ENTREPRENEURIAL DEVELOPMENT

By design, the bulk of the programmatic focus on entrepreneurial development is located in the Purdue Research Park. The park was established in 1961 on a 650-acre site two miles from Purdue's main campus. It currently houses 75 businesses employing more than 2,000 people. The park is "smart" in that it continually updates the telecommunications capacities for residents, including a direct fiber-optic link to the university. It is home for established businesses that want an enhanced research partnership with Purdue. The park also provides facilities and services oriented toward start-up companies, some of which are based on university-developed technology.

The park has been quite aggressive in providing business incubation space and services. The Business and Technology Center is a 28,000-square-foot incubator that includes laboratory facilities, business services, and consulting services provided by both the local Small Business Development Center (SBDC) and Purdue's Business and Industry Development Center (BIDC). The 13,000 square foot Hentschel Center, is yet another incubation facility for mid-tech ventures.

These incubators have recently been buttressed by two additional facilities in the park. The Purdue Technology Center was finished in 1999, and added an additional 60,000 square feet of space for start-up companies. This facility incorporates several "smart" conference rooms, including state-of-the-art videoconferencing and multimedia facilities. These are available to tenants of all of the incubation facilities in the park. Another facility, the 48,000-square-foot Innovation Center, was also completed in 1999. It is intended to serve as a "post-graduation" venue for companies that have grown beyond the size constraints of the other incubators. With the various incubator and post-incubation facilities that are currently operational, Purdue has one of the largest university-affiliated physical infrastructures for entrepreneurial development in the country.

Augmenting the excellent facilities for incubating companies is the Purdue Gateways Program, which focuses on the particular needs of Purdue researchers involved in commercializing their promising inventions via a start-up. It provides (or brokers) services such as business evaluation, planning, product development, access to early-stage capital, and formation of the management team. Each early-stage firm is pared with an experienced mentor whose background is matched with the company he or she takes on. Gateways sees itself operating similarly to product development systems in place at companies such as 3M and Hewlett-Packard. Gateways also is available to any start-up business that agrees to have some interaction with Purdue, such as licensing Purdue-developed technologies or collaborating with Purdue researchers. Many of those ventures also request space in the Purdue Technology Center complex. Gateways currently has two full-time staff and an annual budget slightly less than $300,000 per year. Staff resources are also buttressed with undergraduate and graduate research assistants from various units on campus, particularly the Krannert School of Management.

Recently, Purdue has proposed the development of a statewide network of high-tech incubators. This is in response to a study committee report of the Indiana General Assembly, which called for the state to create and provide initial funding for five regional centers. These would be modeled after the programs based in the Purdue Research Park and would involve Purdue staff in feasibility analysis, operational planning, consulting, and staff training at the regional centers. As of 2001 the state was favorably inclined, but had not yet funded the network because of revenue shortfalls.

Research Park support of entrepreneurs actually began before the incubation programs with the Business and Industrial Development Center (BIDC). BIDC was established at Purdue in 1983 to foster entrepreneurial business development activities in the state, to assist the state in industrial recruitment, to help citizens and businesses access Purdue's resources, to operate economic development pilot programs, and to provide a small-business oriented general business counseling service. BIDC has a statewide mission but is nonetheless a university department that is included in the base budget of the institution. BIDC interacts daily with other university-based economic development initiatives and also works closely with regional economic development organizations throughout the state. The Purdue Technical Assistance Program (TAP) grew out of a BIDC pilot. Currently BIDC is developing a computer-education program is being developed for clients of the state's welfare-to-work program. If successful it will be spun out to be operated by another university unit.

Industry Education and Training Partnerships

Purdue has a variety of education and training programs primarily oriented toward nonresident students working in industry. These range from graduate programs tailored to the needs of executives and managers to shorter courses for technical staff in industry. The programs take place at both the main campus at West Lafayette, and throughout the state. For example, the Krannert School of Management offers several executive level educational programs of particular relevance to Indiana companies. Faculty from the school routinely participate in the programs, and 20 individuals in the Krannert Executive Education office staff the programs. The annual operating budget exceeds $3 million.

The Executive Master's Degree (EMS) draws participants from around the country who attend courses in a dedicated executive education building at the Krannert School. The program is organized around six two-week resident sessions spread over a two years. The format is intended to permit participants to remain in their current job situation but periodically journey to Purdue for an intensive educational experience. The on-campus experience is supplemented with interaction among students and with faculty via the Internet. This approach has been popular with both students and sponsoring companies.

The Weekend EMS program holds classes each Saturday during the school semester. It is for Indiana residents exclusively. In fact, it was launched in response to requests from the surrounding community to offer such a program. It is quite similar to other weekend programs offered around the country.

The Engineering/Management Program is a one-week, nondegree program held annually via a cooperative arrangement between the Krannert School and the School of Engineering. The participants tend to be engineers and technical specialists who want management training. About a third of the students come from Indiana, with the balance from all over the country.

A more recent addition (begun in 1999) is an Executive MBA in food and agribusiness management. This program involves four two-week residential sessions spread over two years, three of them at the Purdue main campus and a fourth at the campus of a partner institution, the Wageningen University in the Netherlands. Internet interaction is also emphasized in this program.

The School of Technology offers a master's of science in technology, delivered in a distance-learning mode with students attending three weekend seminars per semester and interacting with the faculty over the Internet for the rest of the required work. This popular program is designed to serve individuals working in industry. The first group of students from five states graduated in May of 2000.

A much larger system of educational delivery, targeted toward pre-baccalaureate students in engineering technology fields, is offered by the Purdue School of Technology through its Statewide Delivery System. These are degree programs, mostly associate's in applied sciences plus some bachelor's programs, that are offered in 12 locations throughout the state. In 1998 a total of 1,879 students were enrolled, and 172 degrees were conferred (144 associate's and 28 bachelor's). All degree-seeking students are admitted to Purdue University, regardless of which physical campus they attend, and Purdue provides all of the faculty, laboratory equipment, and administrative support. Virtually all students are residents of Indiana, and because the vast majority are employed, classes are typically taught in the evening.

All curriculums in the School of Technology are designed to serve the current and future technological needs of business and industry. Additionally, every degree offering at the sites in the Statewide Delivery System is grounded in a local needs analysis. This includes a labor-market study by Purdue's Office of Manpower Studies and a planning process that involves local industry and government leaders. As a result, the mix of degree programs is quite different across locations reflecting the composition of the local industry. However, nearly all of the degree programs have their counterpart at the main campus, and all credits are transferable to other Purdue locations. The two- and four-year curriculums are consistent to allow for ease of transfer between the 12 locations of the school. More than 300 business and industrial representatives serve on program advisory committees to assist faculty in keeping the curriculum current. More than 900 bachelor's degrees in eight fields of technology were produced in 1999 with a job placement rate of 99%.

Finally, each of the campuses of the Statewide Delivery System is involved in variety of special programs tailored to the specific needs of local industry and business. These may include one-time nondegree courses at an employer location, for-credit short courses, various certificate programs, and a variety of informational outreach activities to the community. For example, Purdue recently developed and delivered a series of courses to Raytheon, with the objective of converting a group of engineers with varied backgrounds into software engineers.

CAREER SERVICES AND PLACEMENT

Purdue has an active and aggressive placement service that is directed toward national as well as state-based employers. Regarding the latter, the university holds an annual High Tech Job Fair for Indiana companies, which provides state high-tech companies the opportunity to compete for Purdue graduates. The event has room for 100 companies and has been held twice thus far. Each year, companies are trying to fill more than 500 full-time positions in areas such as software, information technology, e-commerce, pharmaceuticals, insurance, aerospace, engineering, and advanced manufacturing. Follow-up evaluations indicate that companies see the event as a tremendous boost to their recruiting efforts.

In addition, there are numerous internship opportunities with national and state-based companies. For example, TAP annually places 90 students in summer internships with Indiana companies. TAP helps employers identify the majors and skills needed and provides resumes of interested and qualified students. Many employers are able to find students who are from their local area. TAP faculty members support the students with advice and feedback, often visiting them on-site during the summer. Not surprisingly, many of the internships result in offers of full-time employment after graduation.

FORMAL PARTNERSHIPS WITH ECONOMIC DEVELOPMENT ORGANIZATIONS

Purdue is involved in a range of local, regional, and state economic development organizations, and the nature of that participation varies widely. For example:

- State Department of Commerce. Through various units and individuals, Purdue provides technical assistance, research, and marketing support.
- State Economic Development Council. Purdue is represented on the governing board, and various planning and action committees.

- Central Indiana Economic Development Corporation. The university is represented on the board and is a corporate partner.
- Indianapolis Economic Development Corporation. Purdue is on the board and is a corporate partner.
- Greater Lafayette Progress Council. Purdue is represented on the board.
- State Chamber of Commerce. Board membership.
- National Council on Competitiveness. Board membership.
- Business Modernization and Technology Corporation. Corporate membership and service delivery partnership with TAP.
- Indiana Small Business Development Centers. Membership and joint work with TAP.
- Indiana Department of Industrial Management. Outreach to companies through TAP.
- Indiana Information Technology Association. Member and active participant.
- Access Technology Access Indiana. Purdue is currently a lead organization on the board of this statewide technology transfer organization.
- Lafayette High Technology Task Force. Purdue is represented on the steering committee.
- Central Indiana Partnership. Purdue helped to found the effort, and continues to participate.
- Indianapolis Economic Development Corporation. Purdue helped found the effort and continues to participate.

Purdue is obviously playing leadership roles in many of these organizations and has been otherwise supportive of each group's efforts. As the state's land grant university it acknowledges its role and responsibility to foster economic growth through outreach and service. This charge is not only instrumental to the mission of the university but top-level administrators encourage and participate in the efforts. It is summarized in the president's theme for the entire outreach and economic development effort of the university: " Purdue university, the engine to power Indiana's economic growth."

INDUSTRY/UNIVERSITY ADVISORY BOARDS AND COUNCILS

Perhaps most indicative of Purdue's high-level commitment to an economic development role, the president has formed a Council of Advisors drawn from business, industry, and government leaders to advise his administration on issues of economic development.

Other external advisory councils operate at the unit and college level throughout the institution. Some of the service programs (e.g., TAP) clearly focusing on an industrial clientele have advisory councils as well.

As a land grant university, involvement and partnerships with business and industry are a part of the ongoing efforts of the university. All schools and many programs have business and industrial advisory committees to assist in determining program directions for the future, to assist in partnerships for laboratory development, and to provide placement support for the graduates.

FACULTY CULTURE AND REWARDS

While there are no formal references in the language of tenure and promotion procedures or processes that reinforce the economic development activities of faculty, there are a variety of ways in which the university has publicly, informally, and symbolically endorsed the faculty's role therein. For example, in the faculty start-up document described in the previous section, the opening paragraph states the following:

Purdue's research mission involves components of both basic and applied research. A cardinal feature of applied research is the utilization of the results to solve a real-world problem of societal interest. It follows naturally that technology transfer activities are a companion to the applied research mission. The technology that is exported from the University has direct and indirect economic impact on the community, State and Nation. Therefore, the research activities of the faculty have an important impact beyond the usual academic results.

Purdue also finds ways to acknowledge the success of faculty, staff, and students involved in external partnerships. For example, an annual Burton Morgan Entrepreneurship Competition is conducted for students, and winners receive significant publicity and administrative support from the Gateways program. It annually awards $50,000 in prize money and the winner gets a free office in the incubator.

The most recent strategic plan has also been quite explicit on how performance toward the engagement goal will be measured, which is likely to have significant implications in the future for faculty rewards and culture, either informally or formally. The administration will be tracking such things as:

- Faculty involvement in engagement activities
- Number of license agreements and patents for technology transfer
- Number of start-up companies
- Number of regional technology centers
- Number of partnerships
- Graduates' career placement and retention in Indiana and in the state's key economic clusters

Obviously Purdue is committed to building a new kind of land grant institution to serve its state and region through technology-based economic development, partnerships, and engagement. It is clearly a model for its peers.

ENDNOTES

[1] National Science Foundation Division of Science Resource Studies. (2001). *Academic research and development expenditures, FY 1999*. Washington, D.C.: National Science Foundation. Table B-33.

[2] The Student Population Boom. *Computerworld*. October 19, 1998.

[3] Purdue University. (1998). *Indiana's Land Grant University Serving Indiana, the Nation, the World through Excellence in Education, Research and Service*. Unpublished paper.

[4] Purdue University (2001). *Purdue University. The Next Level: Preeminence. Strategic Plan for 2001-2006*. (http://www.purdue.edu/oop/strategic_plan/)

[5] National Science Foundation. Division of Science Resource Studies. *Op. cit.* Tables B-33, B-36, B-38.

[6] Currently, Dr. John A. Schneider (jas@purdue.edu)

[7] Schneider, J. (1999). Two West Lafayette Companies Win Tibbitts Awards. Purdue Faculty-Owned Bioanalytical Systems Inc. and Spectracode Inc. *Research Review*. West Lafayette, Ind.: Purdue Research Foundation. (December 1999, January 2000, p. 1).

[8] Association of University Technology Managers. (2000). *AUTM Licensing Survey: FY 1999*. Chicago, Ill.: Association of University Technology Managers.
Association of University Technology Managers. (1999). *AUTM Licensing Survey: Fiscal Year 1998*. Norwalk, Conn.: Association of University Technology Managers.

[9] Purdue University. (1995). *Purdue University. Faculty-Owned and Operated Businesses: Policy, Guidelines, and Procedures.*

[10] Purdue University Technical Assistance Program. (1998). *Purdue Powers Manufacturing. Annual Report – Year Ending June 30, 1998.* West Lafayette, Ind.: Purdue University.

TEXAS A&M UNIVERSITY

Texas A&M University (TAMU) was established in 1876 as the first public university in Texas, and the state's land grant university. TAMU has grown into a large comprehensive public university. The university enrolls 44,026 students and has 2,400 faculty members. It is the only U.S. university to be ranked among the top 10 nationally in total enrollment, budget, endowment, and number of National Merit Scholars enrolled.[1] TAMU reported research expenditures of $402.2 million in fiscal year 1999, which ranks 11th among all U.S. universities and eighth among public universities in total research expenditures in the FY 1999 survey of academic research and development expenditures of the National Science Foundation.[2] TAMU is the flagship of a multi-institution system, which includes the state's other land grant institution (Prairie View A&M University), eight other regional universities, a health science center, and eight statewide research and public service agencies. The latter relate closely to the university's research and extension missions and include the Texas Engineering Experiment Station, the Texas Agricultural Experiment Station, the Texas Transportation Institute, and the Texas Wildlife Damage Management Institute.

The university's main campus is at College Station, 90 miles northwest of Houston, 170 miles northeast of San Antonio, and 165 miles southeast of Dallas. Although the College Station/Bryan area has more than 130,000 permanent residents, the university is not located in one of the state's major population areas, a pattern of other land grant institutions. This "isolation" from major business and population areas has created both an obstacle and the necessity for creative thinking and action. TAMU is unique in that it has been designated as a sea grant and a space grant university; one of only a few institutions that are designated land, sea, and space grant institutions. In addition to research and education, this unique status also broadens its outreach mission and capabilities.

In addition to the federal land grant provided under the Morrill Act, the state of Texas also provided a land grant to TAMU and the University of Texas. This state land grant has provided income that has been reinvested well (the granted lands are oil lands), allowing the state to spend the proceeds on projects to grow and expand the two universities. This fund is now known as the Permanent University Fund. The fund is controlled by the state legislature but monies from the fund cannot be appropriated except to the TAMU System and the University of Texas System. Traditionally, the Permanent University Fund has been used to finance building projects and other physical infrastructure needs. A recent constitutional amendment regarding the fund has broadened the definition of infrastructure to allow investment in new faculty positions, computing and communications infrastructure, and strengthening graduate programs.

Over the past 40 years, TAMU has evolved from being a primarily undergraduate, all-male, military college focusing on agricultural and engineering education to being a comprehensive research university with both a large and diverse undergraduate student body and a robust graduate and research enterprise. This evolution was guided in a purposeful manner by a series of leaders supported by state and national constituencies. In the evolution, the faculty has been strengthened, as has the emphasis on research.

MISSION, VISION, AND GOAL STATEMENTS

As a land grant institution, TAMU has always accepted a strong service mission. The service mission readily spilled over from the agriculture units (the College of Agriculture and Life Sciences, the Texas Agricultural Experiment Station, Texas Cooperative Extension, the Texas Forest Service, and the Wildlife Damage Management Service) to engineering and other units of both TAMU and the overall system. Faculty members and administrators understand that the university needs to take this responsibility seriously.

TAMU has expressed this changing focus in *Vision 2020*,[3] a document that states what kind of institution TAMU wants to become by the year 2020, and what needs to happen if this vision is to become a reality. The 12 change steps it contains are expressed as "imperatives." With each imperative come specific goals. *Vision 2020* is a vision stated in specific terms and a broad-brush long-range plan based on that vision.

The *Vision 2020* report resulted from a process begun in 1997, when the president appointed a steering committee of campus leaders and external stakeholders with the mission of developing a vision of becoming a leading public university by 2020. The steering committee appointed task forces that worked on specific issues. A major effort identified a national "consensus top 10" universities and benchmarked TAMU against institutions in this group. By the completion of the visioning process, more than 250 people from the campus and various stakeholder communities had participated in the process of defining goals, setting priorities, and identifying what was needed to achieve the goals.

The vision for TAMU is to become "one of the ten best public universities in the United States." The report identifies the current "ten best,[4] using a number of measures of universities' achievements and benchmarks TAMU's current standing among the selected 10 best.

The statement of the *Vision 2020* mission and core values prominently includes service and such statements as contribution to society and engagement with colleagues in industry. The first imperative on faculty excellence includes a statement describing the academic environment as one which "values and rewards innovations and great ideas …" The ninth imperative on building community and metropolitan connections points out, among other things, that faculty researchers "need private sector sponsorships and commercialization support." The 12th imperative on meeting a commitment to Texas refers back to the university's original purpose "to prepare educated problem-solvers to lead the State's development" and goes on to affirm this mission: "TAMU, if it aspires to national prominence must first stay committed to Texas."

TAMU officials point out that this ambitious vision and plan was possible as a result of TAMU's 40-year evolution from being an undergraduate, male, military institution to being a research university. During this time, it opened the student body to women, added new graduate programs, strengthened existing ones, and upgraded the faculty. Since the early 1980s, state financing has been directed at improving the research capabilities of the university, as well as coping with an increasing undergraduate enrollment. By the late 1990s, it appeared clear to the leadership and the outside stakeholders who participated in the *Vision 2020* process that the vision of becoming a "top ten" institution was now realistic.

Carrying this vision out will be expensive, and leaders concede that the state of Texas will have to make more investments, as will private givers and research sponsors. One TAMU official described the *Vision 2020* report as a "gathering of collective will" to make improvement and move forward. There is considerable optimism that the buy-in among faculty, administrators, and external stakeholders is sufficient to move toward the vision.

To move forward, a follow-up organization complete with selected benchmarking metrics has been put in place. The steering group includes external stakeholders from both public and private sectors. The implementation steering committee will be staffed from the president's office. A subcommittee comprised of campus and stakeholder representatives will review and advocate each imperative.

INDUSTRY RESEARCH PARTNERSHIPS

Business-sponsored research at TAMU has been a significant element of its sponsored research portfolio. The National Science Foundation data[5] show that TAMU's industry-sponsored research expenditures in 1999 were $34.8 million, 8.6% of total research expenditures. In 1992, they were 9.4% of total research expenditures. During this time period, overall expenditures increased by 31% while industry-sponsored expenditures increased by 21%, which resulted in a decrease in the share of industry-sponsored research. In FY 1999, industry-sponsored expenditures were 8.6%, just above the overall national ratio of 7.4%, and ranked 26th among the 100 largest U.S. research universities using this measure.

The mainstay of TAMU industry-sponsored research in the past has been the petroleum industry. This tracks closely with the Texas industrial economy and the traditional source of in-state jobs for TAMU graduates. In more recent years, TAMU has been working to bring in other industrial groups more representative of the broadening Texas economy. This includes the telecommunications industry and the computing equipment industry. TAMU also has worked to develop industry research consortia that will "lock in" support for extended periods.

TAMU is also participating in multi-university efforts to strengthen research ties with industry. For one, it is participating in a consortium of Texas universities and companies with a presence in Texas in the field of telecommunications technology.[6] It also is working with other Texas universities to develop a coordinated statewide program in biotechnology linked to state wide economic development goals and objectives.

TAMU leadership has linked its research development objectives with other university outreach efforts to business.

For example, long-term research relationships often are bolstered if a company foresees access to trained graduates. Thus, companies' recruiting objectives are considered and TAMU science and engineering graduates have grown in demand (see Career Services below). Access to continuing education resources for staff development also influences research relationships, building a strong tie to regional businesses desiring workforce development resources. TAMU leadership understands that together these activities become more valuable to companies than they are separated and uncoordinated. The Dwight Look School of Engineering, which has the largest undergraduate student body in the country, and is ranked 11th by *U.S. News & World Report*, is a real attraction to business and has led to close linkages and the establishment of new corporate design centers in the Bryan/College Station area.

The Compaq Design Center illustrates the success of this linking approach. In 1997, on the basis of existing research relationships, Compaq Computer Corporation located a small software design center at College Station to take advantage of readily available part-time student employees. The opportunity to provide real-world work situations for students was important to the university, and access to well-trained software developers — even on a part-time basis — was important to Compaq. Since its establishment, the center has hired more than 200 students, and has offered more than 85% of them full-time jobs with the company upon graduation. The center now has 10 full-time employees, and is more productive than similar activities at other Compaq locations. In addition to the Design Center, collaborative research projects with TAMU faculty continue. Compaq will be moving the Design Center to the TAMU Research Park in the near future.

> **THE COLLEGE OF ENGINEERING TAKES A SYSTEMATIC APPROACH TO BUILDING AND MAINTAINING RESEARCH RELATIONSHIPS.**

Other companies have followed Compaq's lead. Nortel and Texas Instruments have signed umbrella research agreements with the Engineering Program (The Look College of Engineering, Texas Engineering Experiment Station (TEES), Texas Transportation Institute (TTI), and Texas Engineering Extension Service (TEEX)), FMC's petroleum equipment business, and Toshiba's power equipment business have set up similar operations to that of Compaq, or are in the process of doing so. A number of other companies are considering placing design centers in the Bryan/College Station area to take advantage of the university's large talent pool.

The College of Engineering takes a systematic approach to building and maintaining research relationships. A three-member ad hoc faculty committee is organized to maintain relationships with a company's executives when a relationship begins. Umbrella research agreements are put into place to facilitate setting up several research projects with a company. A network of advisory panels at the department and college level encourage involvement (see Advisory Committees below). These tactics are intended to build relationships that last and develop beyond the individual project level.

TAMU has leveraged its ability to quickly set up interdisciplinary and interdepartmental efforts to meet industry's needs. The university matured as a research institution at a time when interactivity and collaboration were necessitated by limited resources, and the culture has stuck. A collaborative, service-oriented culture has proven effective in attracting industry research collaboration.

Finally, strategic leadership decisions have strengthened the overall research enterprise. The Vision 2020 planning effort affirmed the overall importance of research to the future growth of the institution. The president has demonstrated support by strengthening the stature of the chief research officer and by allocating resources for functions such as intellectual property protection (see Technology Transfer, below) and initiation of interdisciplinary programs and projects. *Vision 2020* also recommends establishing a Center for Business and Industry responsible for "marketing the intellectual capabilities of the University to the private sector, nurturing new spin-off and incubator companies resulting from local University/private sector collaboration, and promoting the growth of the University's Research Park."[7]

Technology Transfer

The TAMU System Technology Licensing Office (TLO) provides a system-wide function. It reports to the system's vice chancellor for business services. In the management of innovations emerging from TAMU, the TLO reports to the university's chief research officer. The technology transfer function began in individual components of the system such as Texas Engineering Experiment Station (TEES) and Texas Transportation Institute. By 1988, TEES committed to the creation of a licensing office. These early efforts were not coordinated or accountable to a single university or system official, although a system-wide patent policy had been put in place in 1985 in reaction to the Bayh-Dole Act of 1980.

TAMU officials stated that until recently, TAMU faculty members did not enjoy a "culture of developing intellectual property." Others pointed out that early inventions were almost universally licensed to existing companies that were collaborating in the research. Inventions went to research sponsors, and faculty members did not think about the start-up route to commercialization. Indeed, the 1980s were a time the university was rapidly expanding its externally sponsored research activity, and little energy or resources were available to encourage faculty participation in intellectual property development or formal technology transfer.

In 1992, the chancellor of the system created a central technology transfer and licensing office and centralized the authority to manage and license intellectual property and other technology in that office. The TLO staff has grown to 20 people, including the director, seven licensing specialists, a paralegal, a communications specialist, fiscal managers, and nine other supporting staff. TLO is funded from a "tap" of 15% of gross licensing income, which covers the office's salaries and expenses except for patent filing expenses. The TLO has been self-supporting since 1996. Patent-filing expenses to protect the innovations of faculty and researchers are provided by the system component from which the invention arose. For TAMU, the chief research officer allocates funds and approves expenditures to protect TAMU-generated inventions.

A significant incentive to support faculty participation in technology transfer is the license income distribution policy, which, after deducting 15% to operate TLO, provides 50% to the inventor's college and department or unit, and 50% directly to the inventor. The incentive to TLO, however, has been to maximize license income in order to support the operation. This has kept the operation focused on licensing to established companies able to pay licensing fees as well as royalties on sales. The strategy raised license income to $5.26 million in FY 1999, a royalty return on investment of 1.3%. License income increased to $6.05 million in 2000, and continued growth is expected in future years as recently executed licenses and options show potential for business growth and public benefit. The university's performance is good. License income ranks in the 84th percentile, and royalty ROI ranks in the 69th percentile of the 142 academic institutions that participated in the *AUTM Licensing Survey: FY 1999*.[8]

The office is a leader in state and national efforts to promote university technology transfer, as evidenced by its director being elected president of AUTM, and chair of the Committee on Technology Commercialization of the National Association of State Universities and Land Grant Colleges. In addition, two TLO staff members serve on the board of the Texas Technology Transfer Association.

The university is relatively new at encouraging start-ups. As noted later in this chapter (see Entrepreneurial Development), the venture capital and entrepreneurial community is underdeveloped in the Bryan/College Station area and there are not many role models for licensing university technology and building a company around it. Furthermore, certain state laws have restricted the ability of the university to participate in the development of start-up companies. These factors are reflected in a number of performance indicators constructed using AUTM Report data.[9] TAMU reported a total of 28 new licenses to start-up companies in fiscal years 1998 and 1999 combined, placing it in the 38th percentile in the total AUTM licensing survey population for this measure. TAMU reported a total of two new start-ups formed, one of which was in-state. TAMU ranks in the 41st percentile for total start-ups formed and in the 34th percentile for in-state start-ups formed.

In an effort to make working with start-ups easier, TAMU and other state universities worked with the state legislature to enact legislation which removes some critical legal barriers to working with and transferring intellectual property to small and start-up companies. The new law (S.B. 1190) permits public universities to establish technology transfer centers with more flexibility and authority to participate in the creation of start-up companies, including making deals for equity stakes in licensees, forming incubators and accelerators and other tools for support of entrepreneurs, and managing inventors' conflicts of interests if they wish to work with the start-up. The law also protects state universities from assuming fiduciary duties as equity shareholders in companies. S.B. 1190 passed in the spring of 2001 and took effect September 1, 2001.

A venture fund is being contemplated (see Entrepreneurial Development) to take advantage of the new opportunities that S.B. 1190 will make available. TAMU is moving purposefully to structure its technology transfer program to become as instrumental in entrepreneurial development as it is currently in supporting industry research partnerships. This also will support the *Vision 2020* imperatives for economic development and support of the growth of the state. In fact, *Vision 2020* sets a goal to "quadruple the number of spin-off industries associated with the University."[10]

INDUSTRIAL EXTENSION/TECHNICAL ASSISTANCE

The principal TAMU industrial extension agency is The Texas Engineering Experiment Station (TEES). Other extension and technical assistance programs are the Texas Transportation Institute (TTI) and the Texas Cooperative Extension. TTI generally works with public transportation agencies (state and local) but also works with companies involved in various aspects of transportation such as highway construction, transportation planning, and transportation systems management. Texas Cooperative Extension includes agribusiness and food processing firms in its array of clients.

In addition to educational and training assistance to in-state companies (see Industry Education/Training Partnerships below), TEES staff will do limited and focused engagements to help client companies develop business plans, adopt new technologies, improve methods and operations to increase productivity, and enhance competitiveness. Often these engagements are partially supported by federal Manufacturing Engineering Partnership funds.

Extension engagements often include "regular" TAMU faculty from the College of Engineering or other units. Short-term extension engagements often lead to longer research relationships, which is one reason faculty willingly participate. One TAMU official reported that most engineering faculty members consider extension work to be "pleasant, and a good addition" to everyday teaching and research duties. "They will do it unless it becomes burdensome," he said.

As a land grant institution, extension has been a traditional role of the university. Notably, although a number of organizations within the University System conduct extension and technical assistance efforts as part of their missions, these activities appear to be closely coordinated with teaching and research functions so that each benefits from the strength of the other.

ENTREPRENEURIAL DEVELOPMENT

The state of Texas has strong entrepreneurial traditions. The petroleum industry has a rich heritage of entrepreneurial activity that continues today, particularly in the exploration, development, and oil field service components of the industry. In new technology areas, companies such as Texas Instruments, Compaq, and Dell Computer started and grew in Texas.

TAMU has remained open to working with new and growing companies and has participated in recent ventures to develop incubator programs in the Bryan/College Station area. There is a general-purpose incubator operated by the Bryan-College Station Economic Development Corporation (EDC), and the Software Commercialization and Innovation Center (SCIC), an incubator program for software development companies. SCIC was established by two TAMU computer science professors as a nonprofit activity. It has incubated 20 companies, 10 of which have "graduated." Support for the SCIC was raised from a number of public agencies. The EDC's general-purpose incubator has also been staying busy with many new companies started by recent TAMU graduates with graduate degrees. Faculty start-ups are still rather rare but should increase as faculty culture changes take hold and recent legislation empowering more creative deal making with start-ups goes into use.

Any faculty-driven start-ups up to this point also would have been hampered by the lack of capital. Capital resources in the state are concentrated in the large cities; Houston, Dallas, and Austin — all of which are a two-to four hour journey away. Venture investors are more likely to organize a company in one of the major urban areas than in College Station. This has significantly limited the degree to which faculty entrepreneurs could participate in new ventures.

In 1994, TechCom, a company owned by TAMU, TEES, and TAES, opened a venture fund, the AM Fund I, to exploit early-stage innovations in Texas, particularly ones coming form the university. Investors raised $14.5 million and ultimately invested in 10 ventures, three of which were TAMU spin-offs. The University System was not a cash investor in the fund but, as a "special limited partner," was allocated a 40% equity stake in any AM Fund ventures. In return for this generous share, the fund managers had a right to review each invention disclosure. If the fund desired to invest in any technology, a license agreement was then negotiated between the fund and the University System. Additionally, the fund could acquire a one-year option for the cost of filing a U.S. patent application. The fund is due to liquidate by 2004.

TAMU leaders have been participating in and nurturing the Brazos Valley Technology Alliance, a membership organization of technology-based companies in the Bryan/College station area. This group is obviously interested in more entrepreneurial development in the community. The membership is young, growing, and enthusiastic. The alliance has monthly luncheon meetings focused on aspects of high-tech business development. The alliance also participates in events such as the annual technology expo and the business fair.

Although the essential elements for a flourishing entrepreneurial community are not yet fully in place, the *Vision 2020* priority to participate actively in developing these elements makes it reasonable to expect entrepreneurial activity to grow in the rich intellectual climate provided by the university.

INDUSTRY EDUCATION/TRAINING PARTNERSHIPS

TAMU has a broad approach to outreach to industry, carried out through a variety of interrelated and well-coordinated activities and organizations. The TAMU System Engineering Program includes the Look College of Engineering, the Texas Engineering Experiment Station (TEES), the Texas Engineering Extension Service (TEEX), and the Texas Transportation Institute (TTI). In the agriculture and life sciences field, the College of Agriculture and Life Sciences at TAMU is closely linked with the Texas Agricultural Experiment Station (the second-largest in the country) and the Texas Cooperative Extension.

TEEX is focused on the needs of Texas industries, and reflects the industrial characteristics of the state. TEEX provides more than 6,500 classes each year, taught at five training centers, the TAMU campus, and in many cases at company sites. In 1998, these courses reached more than 125,000 people and involved 2.1 million student hours. Two thousand seven hundred companies sent employees to TEEX courses. Course subjects ranged from management training in technology businesses to industrial fire protection (a world-class program). In addition to on-site courses, training is delivered via CD-ROM, the Internet, and remote television.

The TEEX training centers are in business and population centers around the state where students are likely to be working (Dallas, Houston, San Antonio). Many were organized and financed jointly with community economic development organizations.

Although Texas Cooperative Extension is focused on farming, it has become more involved in working with agribusiness in the state, including food processing and packaging. Agricultural Extension provides its statistics in a way that makes it impossible to identify industry or business participants precisely. It is clear these offerings are a plus for Texas-based food businesses.

The Look College of Engineering has developed two distance-learning delivered graduate programs: a master's in engineering management and a master's in petroleum engineering. In addition to Internet instruction, these programs bring students to residential centers in Houston, New Orleans, and Venezuela for part of their instruction. Participation is usually supported by students' companies.

TAMU is launching a global joint venture to develop work-oriented graduate training in petroleum engineering. Other educational partners are the University of Oklahoma and Heriot-Watt University in Scotland. The business partner is Schlumberger, the petroleum industry service company. Content will be delivered worldwide via the Internet and by satellite video links. Schlumberger will offer the courses to its clients as an added-value resource.

The TAMU Distance Education Program offers graduate degree programs in agriculture, industrial engineering, and education in addition to the engineering offerings noted above. A cooperative doctorate in agricultural education is offered in collaboration with Texas Tech University. The distance format allows extension agents across the state to pursue advanced study. The program has won acclaim from the Texas Higher Education Coordinating Board because it demonstrates effective use of resources from two universities.

The TAMU distance education master's programs in education (human resource development, educational technology), agriculture (agricultural development, wildlife/fisheries, plant pathology), and industrial distribution were developed in response to demand from industry and public education after a yearlong study in 1996. These programs fulfill workforce development needs, particularly requests from students and organizations. Additional programs under development that the Texas workforce has requested are a master's in mathematics for secondary school teachers, public administration master's programs in the George Bush School of Government and Public Service, a multi-disciplinary master's program in environmental engineering, and a Web-based global business certificate program. The College of Education is preparing to launch a major effort in continuing education with a focus on alternative certification for teachers.

Offerings are both Internet-based and by two-way interactive video feed via the Trans-Texas Videoconference Network to 106 sites throughout Texas, plus locations in Mexico City and San Jose, Costa Rica. The Office of

Distance Education has identified seven "peer university" distance education programs, four of which are offered by institutions participating in this study.[11]

CAREER SERVICES

The Career Center provides a variety of services to students and former students as well as Texas and national employers. The center includes the offices of Experiential Education, Career Education, and Placement Services as well as specialized services for alumni and student athletes. The center also serves some of the constituent colleges through Career Service Coordinators (CSCs) in these units. The center employs approximately 40 professional and support staff members, plus graduate assistants and student workers. The executive director reports to the Office of the Provost. Assisting in the oversight of the center is a career center advisory council comprised of 20 employer representatives and 21 faculty and staff members from various units of the university.

The Office of Experiential Education offers work-integrated learning experiences through a cooperative education program and domestic and international internship coordination. Its co-op program is one of the largest in the country with nearly 1,000 student participants annually. Approximately 85% of these students are placed in Texas locations. More than 300 employers seek to hire Texas A&M co-op students each year. Approximately 50% of the co-op students accept permanent positions with their co-op employers after graduation. At any given time during the school year, more than 2,500 students are registered with the Career Center in seeking internship opportunities. Many are with Texas employers because work often parallels class assignments. However, a significant number opt for out-of-state opportunities in cities such as Washington, D.C. During the 2000-2001 school year, 204 employers sought to interview prospective interns through the Career Center.

The Office of Placement Services provides services for seniors and graduate students completing their study. The Office of Placement Services operates the largest centralized interviewing operation in the country. The number of on-campus interviews has exceeded 30,000 per year for the past several years. Employers consistently compliment Texas A&M on its "one-stop shopping" concept versus the laborious task of working with several decentralized campus locations to interview students from various academic disciplines. During the 2000-2001 school year, 939 companies participated in student recruitment on campus. Many more have utilized the Center's Internet-based job posting and resume referral services.

The Office of Career Education assists students with defining appropriate and satisfying career goals. This unit also assists students to acquire job search skills. The office presents a variety of programs and activities such as career management courses, relevant seminars, advisory services, information dissemination, and promotion of activities and services of the various other entities on campus involved in career education, such as college-level career fairs. For example, in the most recent school year nearly 450 students enrolled in credit courses designed or taught by Career Center professionals. Student attendance totaled 13,558 for center seminars and special events. Nearly 19,000 students visited and toured the Career Center Resources Library. Career advising interactions with students numbered 24,234, which included appointments, walk-ins, e-mail, and telephone.

In an effort to personalize services for specific groups of students, college service coordinator (CSC) positions were created in cooperation with specific colleges who requested them. Though these CSCs are Career Center staff, they spend much more of their "career education" efforts at the colleges' locations in order to maximize exposure and convenience for students. This service concept was recently recognized at a Southwest Association of Colleges and Employers Annual Conference as a winner of a best practices award.

In addition to the Career Center as a recruiting resource, companies have been recruited to share resources to enable the center to be more effective in providing access to well-prepared graduates. Business and public agency representatives are invited to assist in presenting Career Center seminars and in making mock interviews more realistic. Employees of the consulting firm Accenture have provided an endowment to assist in the operation and maintenance of the Career Resources library. The Ford Motor Company has provided funding to install "Aggielaunch," a state-of-the-art software program to manage all data and scheduling activities of the Career Center.

A large majority of TAMU students are from Texas (95% of the undergraduates and 47% of the graduate students). As expected, most stay within the state as they graduate. The university maintains a balance between its efforts to place students in a national or global labor market and working with in-state employers.

FORMAL PARTNERSHIPS WITH ECONOMIC DEVELOPMENT ORGANIZATIONS

TAMU takes seriously its responsibility to play a role in economic development. Imperative 12 of *Vision 2020* is entitled "Meet our Commitment to Texas." Its introduction includes the following statement: "Texas A&M University must ... honor its heritage of enhancing the economic development of all regions of the State."[12]

On the local level, TAMU is the major force in the Bryan/College Station economy. The university faculty and staff and the large student body drive the community's economy. As such, the university needs to be active in community economic development and planning activities. In fact the university plays this strong role with intent and care. A university officer is a nonvoting member of the Bryan/College Station Economic Development Corporation (the community economic development organization). A university officer also serves as a member of the Metropolitan Planning Organization, is involved in chamber of commerce efforts, and serves on committees.

The Economic Development Corporation is active in recruiting "new economy" companies to the area. Success with the Compaq Design Center, the FMC Design Center, and similar university-related recruitments has served as role models for success. The large, well-prepared student body available for part-time work and the increasing number of faculty spouses provide a growing labor pool for new business prospects. Major employers in the economy are still the university, the state prison system, and agribusiness, so wage rates are relatively low, a short-term advantage.

The TAMU Research Park was created using university lands in College Station to create a business community that would benefit from proximity to TAMU's scientific and engineering resources. In addition to companies, the Research Park is the location for federal government research agencies, the Texas Transportation Institute, and several TAMU research programs. Long-term leases are made directly to tenant organizations or to developers who will build and lease facilities. The Research Park has strict rules about the nature of activity tenants can engage in at park facilities. The Research Park is managed as a component of the office of the vice president for research.

Transportation is a major planning agenda item. Improving access to the major population areas (Houston, Dallas, Austin and San Antonio) is paramount. The community has generally embraced *Vision 2020,* and community leaders have been included in the follow-up review and oversight panels.

The university has been a resource for community economic development throughout the state through the programs of TTI, Texas Engineering Extension Service, and the Texas Cooperative Extension. However, university leaders see a problem in enlisting meaningful support for *Vision 2020* at the state capitol and the governor's mansion. One TAMU official noted that the political leadership "dreams about the University of Texas and TAMU being leading academic institutions, but they don't understand the true cost of getting there."

INDUSTRY/UNIVERSITY ADVISORY BOARDS AND COUNCILS

TAMU is proud of its graduates who have achieved leadership roles in business, especially the industrial mainstays of the state and region: petroleum, chemicals, electronics, and communications. The university taps into the network of alumni, research collaborators, and assistance clients at many levels.

The Vision 2020 Task Force and working groups included alumni, research partners, and sources of employment for graduates from the business community. The Texas office of consulting firm McKinsey and Co. helped with the extensive benchmarking portion of the *Vision 2020* report.

TAMU is partnered with Texaco as members of the National Academy of Sciences Government-University-Industry Research Roundtable. This national policy-analysis group includes academic institutions as full members only if linked with a business co-member. TAMU is one of 13 university/business pairs.[13]

The vice president for research is organizing an advisory group that will review and monitor progress toward *Vision 2020* goals and objectives related to research and other relationships with the business community. Membership will include members of the entrepreneurial community (venture investors and entrepreneurs) as well as executives at larger companies. All participants will have an interest in the university's research and educational strengths.

At the college level, advisory groups with business and industrial members are common. In the Look College of Engineering, the dean has a Business Advisory Council, and each department in the college has a counterpart group. Members tend to be corporate CEOs or vice presidents, and either the company or the individual has a relationship with TAMU. Information flows both ways: Business members hear about the college's (or the department's) educational and research activities and progress, and faculty members and leaders get valuable feedback about employment trends and the real-world scientific and technical problems for which solutions are needed.

The Department of Chemistry in the College of Sciences is one of the largest and most distinguished departments at the university. In 1980, the department, which already had extensive relationships with chemical and energy companies, organized a formal consortium: The Industry-University Cooperative Chemistry Program (IUCCP). There are currently 12 company members, 10 full members, and two associate members. Member companies maintain long-term relationships with chemistry faculty members. As with other such groups, the intent is to have information of mutual interest flow both ways. Full members participate in support of research projects. The member companies specify the general area of interest for such projects but the specific projects are proposed by faculty members and reviewed by the IUCCP Steering Committee. In return for support, the full members get an early look at research results and a lead on licensing any intellectual property produced. An important IUCCP event is an annual research symposium for staff from member companies. Included in the program are student research presentations that are judged by the industry participants. Prizes are given to the best presentations, and members get to know promising graduates who are prospective employees.

This array of advisory and interaction opportunities helps strengthen the ties between the university and the business world at a variety of levels and keeps the needs of business for the university's "products" at a high level throughout the institution.

FACULTY CULTURE AND REWARDS

As in any research university, the TAMU faculty is heavily involved in teaching, research and service. In addition,

TAMU, as a land grant institution with a variety of applied-research and outreach responsibilities and a problem-oriented approach to science and research, is naturally engaged and interactive. TAMU officials mentioned a willingness by faculty members to participate in multidisciplinary projects and to work with companies and mission-oriented public agencies. As the university's research program grew and matured in the 1970s and 1980s, TAMU scientists often competed successfully for support when they collaborated with each other. This culture of outreach and collaboration is often missing at other research universities, even public universities.

As TAMU moves toward its *Vision 2020* goals, how to sustain these values will be at issue. Promotion and tenure guidelines emphasize the traditional values of high-quality, highly regarded research and teaching. One respondent reported that tenure is not as dependent now on getting National Science Foundation or other competitive federal grants as it was 10 years ago but tenure still depends on research success measured by publications in "high-impact" journals and peer perception ("having good people at good places say good things about the candidate").

"Departmental mix" is important at TAMU when considering faculty members' contribution, in keeping with the land grant tradition. This may mean that a candidate for tenure might survive review with a sub-optimal research portfolio if the department had outreach and extension responsibilities but a strong research faculty with little interest and resources to do extension and outreach duties. At the end of the day, however, the quality of the candidate's research is usually paramount. Said one respondent, "quality always trumps quantity."

TAMU is overcoming what one respondent called the traditional absence of a "culture of developing intellectual property." In an effort to change this, review committees are encouraged to consider the value and scientific impact of patents and to look for follow-up publications of merit (both in print and in preparation) based on the protected inventions.

TAMU's decentralized faculty performance review system is closely monitored by the Office of the Provost for consistency and uniformity. This will help as the culture continues to change as outreach and extension broaden to include relationships with business and enhancement of economic development.

Endnotes

[1] Texas A&M University Fact Sheet (http://www.tamusystem.edu)

[2] National Science Foundation Division of Science Resource Studies. (2001). *Academic research and development expenditures, FY 1999.* Washington, D.C.: National Science Foundation. Table B-33.

[3] Texas A&M University. (2000). Vision 2020. College Station, Texas: Texas A&M University (http://www.tamu.edu/new/vision/index2.html)

[4] Interestingly, six of these institutions are also among this study's 12 institutions.

[5] National Science Foundation. Division of Science Resource Studies. *Op. cit.* Tables B-33, B-36, B-38.

[6] The participating universities are University of Texas-Austin, University of Texas-Arlington, University of Texas-Dallas, Texas Tech University, and TAMU. The participating companies are: Advanced Micro Devices, Alcatel, Fujitsu, Motorola, Nokia, Nortel Networks, SBC, Texas Instruments, and WorldCom

[7] *Vision 2020. Op. cit.* p. 72.

[8] Association of University Technology Managers. (2000). *AUTM Licensing Survey: FY 1999.* Chicago, Ill.: Association of University Technology Managers.
Association of University Technology Managers. (1999). *AUTM Licensing Survey for Fiscal Year 1998.* Norwalk, Conn.: Association of University Technology Managers.

[9] *Ibid.*

[10] *Vision 2020. Op. cit.* p. 72.

[11] They are Georgia Institute of technology, Ohio State University, Pennsylvania State University, and the University of Wisconsin. See the Web site http://www.tamu.edu/ode/

[12] *Vision 2020. Op. cit.* p. 72

[13] In addition to TAMU, the university members include: North Carolina State University, Ohio State University, Stanford University, University of California-San Diego, and University of Utah (all participants in this study). Other university members are: Florida State University, Massachusetts Institute of Technology, University of California-Los Angeles, University of Illinois-Urbana-Champaign, University of Texas-Austin, University of Washington, and Washington University.

UNIVERSITY OF WISCONSIN

Since its founding as a public land grant institution in 1849, the University of Wisconsin-Madison (UW-M) has earned an international reputation for its dedication to academic excellence and its commitment to service. Outstanding faculty and innovative educational and research programs place it among the best universities in the United States.

The university has an exemplary record as a research-intensive institution. In the National Science Foundation[1] FY 1999 survey of academic research and development, UW-M reported research expenditures of $462.7 million, which ranks fifth among all U.S. universities and fourth among public universities. Five current or former UW-M faculty members have won Nobel Prizes, 10 have been awarded the prestigious National Medal of Science, and 45 faculty members are members of the National Academy of Science. Recently, two faculty members have received McArthur Foundation Genius Awards, and three have won Alexander von Humboldt awards for work in the biological sciences. Throughout the years, its faculty has been at the forefront of research in many fields. Researchers there discovered Vitamin D, synthesized the gene, and drafted the first social security legislation. Currently, faculty, staff, and students are engaged in more than 5,000 separate research projects, and there has been a massive growth in biotechnology research and other areas of considerable relevance to the technology-based knowledge economy.

The student body of 40,000 includes more than 26,900 undergraduates, 10,950 graduate and professional students, and 1,950 nondegree students from every state and 119 countries. A large fraction of students are Wisconsin residents (73% in the College of Engineering). The university's faculty numbers 2,284, and with 4,571 course offerings in 117 departments the university is comprehensive in scope. Its library system provides 5.5 million volumes and nearly 50,000 serial titles.

A long history of partnership connects the UW-M to the social and economic development of the state of Wisconsin. For example, nearly 10% of the content of former Governor Tommy Thompson's 2000 State of the State Address was devoted to plaudits about the promise of UW-M advances in biotechnology, and to announce new initiatives to help (e.g., a $317 million Biostar program, a master's degree in biotechnology, 100 new faculty members being recruited).[2] The following quote captures the general flavor of the relationship between the University of Wisconsin and the state:

> New discoveries in science and technology will create high-skill, high-paying jobs in Wisconsin. These jobs will provide a higher quality of life for our families and a brain gain for our state. A driving force behind this new economy will be the New Wisconsin Idea, a bold new partnership between the University of Wisconsin and the private sector.

Wisconsin is the story of an extraordinarily successful research university that has also nurtured a long-standing mission of service to its state, while at the same time creating a very entrepreneurial culture and some novel approaches to technology transfer.

MISSION, VISION, AND GOAL STATEMENTS

Since the early years of the 20th century, the university has operated under the general mission rubric of "The Wisconsin Idea," which places a considerable premium on outreach to various communities in the State, in the context of teaching, research, and service. Several campus informants suggested that the current and previous chancellor have both been an advocate for outreach, community linkages, and the historical legacy of the Wisconsin Idea. A guide to The Wisconsin Idea[3] states:

> ...the value of the interaction of theoretical knowledge and actual practice is translated into and embodied by the myriad of outreach activities of the university community.

The general principles underlying the Wisconsin Idea have been interpreted within many of the colleges and academic units on campus, and there is ongoing discussion of how to update and expand them in the context of a technology-based economy. Nonetheless, that updating process will be, in the words of one senior campus administrator, more akin to "a long successful marriage, in which the partners renew their vows from time to time." For example, in a recently developed strategic plan for the university,[4] one of the five strategic priorities was to "amplify the Wisconsin Idea."

The university does take special efforts to inculcate members of the campus community in the Wisconsin Idea. For many years the university has organized a Wisconsin Idea Seminar, a five-day professional development experience for approximately 35 carefully selected participants. The Office of Outreach Development, a permanent unit of seven staff members in the Provost's Office, organizes this and other events dealing with outreach. The office solicits nominations for participation in seminar from chairs, deans, and directors, and the senior faculty in general. Preference is given to recently tenured faculty, new chairs and associate deans, and new members of the Faculty Senate. There is also an attempt to get a good cross section of schools and colleges in the group. Once selected, seminar participants literally get on the bus and spend several days in activities such as meeting colleagues at other

UW system campuses, visiting with Wisconsin Native American groups, touring inner-city schools, meeting with alumni groups, visiting historically and ecologically important sites, and meeting with state businesses involved in technological innovation. Typically the seminar is oversubscribed and participation is only limited by available space and resources. Each participant's school or college covers room and board. A foundation grant covers other seminar costs.

To further illustrate the extent to which the university takes seriously the Wisconsin Idea and the outreach function, one can point to a recent project[5] also coordinated and partially funded by the Office of Outreach Development. This survey of UW-M faculty included 888 responses and assessed faculty activities in and attitudes toward outreach. Among the more interesting findings were the extensive involvement in outreach (87% of faculty indicated some participation), the impact of outreach on changing the direction of faculty research (53% said it did) and improving its quality (66%), the endorsement of faculty for the Wisconsin Idea (49% "strongly agree"), and support for the university using its knowledge to address societal issues (54% "strongly agree"). Also, the report stated that results suggesting a "disconnect between the value faculty place on outreach and their perception of the value the university places on it." In addition to the results themselves, it is notable that a large university took the time to examine these issues and got such widespread faculty participation.

INDUSTRY RESEARCH PARTNERSHIPS

National Science Foundation data[6] show that UW-M's industry-sponsored research expenditures in FY 1999 were $14.2 million, or 3.1% of total research expenditures. In 1992, they were 3.7% of total research expenditures. During this same period, overall research expenditures increased by 31% while industry-sponsored expenditures increased by 10%. In FY 1999, the percent of industry-sponsored expenditures was below the national average of 7.4% and ranked 83rd among the top 100 U.S. universities. To some extent, the percentage share data on industry research support reflect the huge success that the university has had in securing federal grants and contracts.

IN A NOVEL DEPARTURE FROM TYPICAL PRACTICE, UIR ALSO RUNS TWO GRANT PROGRAMS FOR FACULTY MEMBERS TO SUPPORT PROJECTS WITH POTENTIAL INDUSTRY APPLICATIONS.

Nonetheless, there is an active Office of University-Industry Relations (UIR) located in the Graduate School that facilitates these relationships, as well as plays important roles in technology transfer. The UIR coordinates the Community of Science database of faculty members' experience and areas of expertise, and a publicly available UIR database. The latter enables an external person to search free of charge for particular faculty expertise; about 80% of faculty members participate. It enables a user to pull up an abbreviated vita of a faculty member that describes educational background, research interests, publications, and contact information. UIR also publishes a monthly newsletter (*In the News*) that informs readers about UW-M research projects (particularly those that are prime for industrial collaboration), the growth and development of UW-M spin-off companies, and university-industry interactions. This is published monthly on UIR's Web site (http://uir2.uir.wisc.edu/news.html) and distributed via hard copy to university and state offices involved in technology transfer and economic development.

In a novel departure from typical practice, UIR also runs two grant programs for faculty members to support projects with potential industry applications. The Industrial and Economic Development Research Program (I&EDR) disburses about $900,000 of state money annually, in the form of small grants ($5,000 to $50,000) for support of early stage applied research. About 30-40 awards are made each year, and all must involve a Wisconsin industry or company. The assumption is that these awards will likely lead to follow-on industry or agency support, patents, and technology commercialization. A survey[7] in 1996 of recipients over the previous 10 years confirmed those expectations, with 31 patents, nine spin-off companies, and a 10-to-1 leverage ratio of subsequent funding attributable to the awards.

Another grant program administered by UIR is the Robert Draper Technology Innovation Fund (TIF). Approximately $400,000 is available each year for support of projects "to bring new concepts and inventions to the patent and licensing stage." Funds for the program are derived from the university share of royalty revenues from the current portfolio of licensed technologies. Proposals go to UIR and a committee of campus scientists and administrators reviews them. There is considerable latitude in the size of awards, although they average around $30,000. The projects generally involve proof-of-concept research, prototype development, creation of samples, and the like.

In addition to one-on-one industry projects, UW-M also is home to 21 research consortia, many of which have extensive industry involvement, both substantive and financial. Some have been operating for several years, such as the Wisconsin Electric Machines and Power Electronics Consortium (WEMPEC), which includes 50 Wisconsin companies, large and small, as members. UIR works with the various consortia to expand and maintain industrial participation. It also maintains on the UW Web site descriptions and contact information for each consortium (http://www.wisc.edu/uir/consortia).

It should be emphasized that the large size of the UW-M research enterprise and the decentralized entrepreneurial nature of the campus culture also tends to encourage industrial linkages within colleges and units. For example, the Food Research Institute (FRI) is the oldest and probably the largest consortium on the UW-M campus. Started in 1966, FRI now has forty-seven sponsors, including 39 companies (14 of which are Wisconsin-based) and eight associations, institutes, or councils. Within the College of Engineering there are currently 15 consortia, involving 197 companies, with 94 of them Wisconsin-based.

TECHNOLOGY TRANSFER

The University of Wisconsin has one of the oldest and most successful technology transfer functions in the country. License income was $18.01 million in FY 1999, a royalty return on investment (royalties divided by total research expenditures) of 3.97%. License income ranks in the 94th percentile, and royalty ROI ranks in the 89th percentile of the 142 academic institutions that participated in the *AUTM Licensing Survey: FY 1999*.[8] UW-M reported a total of 49 new licenses to start-ups in fiscal years 1998 and 1999 combined, placing it in the 91st percentile of the AUTM survey sample. UW-M reported a total of seven new start-ups formed, five of which were located in Wisconsin. UW-M ranks in the 82nd percentile for total start-ups formed and in the 77th percentile for in-state start-ups formed. Clearly, Wisconsin has been very successful in fostering entrepreneurial approaches to technology transfer, for reasons that will shortly become apparent.

Technology transfer and licensing responsibilities are shared between two organizations. The Office of University-Industry Research (UIR) works with faculty members to facilitate the invention disclosure process. It receives all disclosures, ascertains ownership and inventorship, and advises inventors on basic issues of intellectual property. Thereafter, responsibilities lie with the Wisconsin Alumni Research Foundation (WARF). WARF was established in 1925 as an outgrowth of research and technology development related to Vitamin D, and was the initial model of an independent but university-linked technology development organization. WARF reviews submitted inventions, and obtains necessary patents, or other protection for promising inventions, and then works with the inventors to implement a licensing and commercialization plan. After royalty distributions to inventors and others, WARF earmarks the balance of revenues for support of faculty research. This support has amounted to more than $220 million over the past 15 years. According to the AUTM data for 1999, WARF received 278 invention disclosures, received 79 patents, executed 106 licenses or options, and received over $18 million in licensing revenues in that year.[9] WARF gives 20% of the first $100,000 gross income per license to the inventor(s) and 70% to the inventor's research program or laboratory. Income greater than $100,000 is distributed 20% to the inventor(s) and 15% to department or unit where the work was performed.

In recent years WARF has been involved more frequently in licensing arrangements involving new companies. For example, WARF will now take an equity stake in a company rather than a straight licensing deal, which has enabled spin-offs to gain quicker access to their intellectual property and get a head start on business development and capitalization. This approach has reflected the increasingly robust entrepreneurial culture on campus, with a concomitant growth of allied support programs and services (e.g., incubators). This is likely to accelerate in the foreseeable future, given national trends described by AUTM and the growing expectation on the part of Wisconsin state government that UW-M will be the door to the knowledge economy for the state. Nonetheless, technology transfer policies at UW are already flexible and supportive of new company formation. For example, there is generally a "can-do" approach to managing conflicts of interest. To illustrate, it is permissible for faculty-owned companies to support research on campus in the faculty member's own laboratory. These arrangements involve serious oversight and review, but they happen.

Reflecting the increased emphasis on state-focused technology transfer activities that lead to economic development, a new initiative was built into the UW-M 2001 *Strategic Plan*: "Provide Opportunities that Encourage High Tech Businesses and Employees to Locate in Wisconsin." It calls for a number of actions, many of which are not traditionally construed as technology transfer. Nonetheless, it touches upon many of the themes enunciated throughout this book.

This initiative includes providing opportunities for businesses to interact easily with faculty, staff, and students at the university (job fairs, collaborative research, and consulting activities); developing academic programs (master's degrees, certificates, capstones, minors) supportive of current and future employees in high-tech businesses; helping to recruit alumni involved in those businesses to Wisconsin; building school/college expertise in technology transfer; exploring options of reducing out-of-state graduate student tuition and loan forgiveness to recruit a greater work force to Wisconsin; and educating students about the opportunities, challenges, and ethical issues involved in technology transfer.

INDUSTRIAL EXTENSION/TECHNICAL ASSISTANCE

The College of Engineering does not operate a formal extension program in the same sense as one finds at other land grant universities, but it reaches out to Wisconsin industry in a variety of ways. It devotes a full-time engineer to the Wisconsin Manufacturing Extension Partnership (WMEP), and its assistant dean for industrial research and development serves on WMEP's board of directors. The college's Office of Engineering Research and Development and Technology Commercialization is headed by an assistant dean. The office operates as the primary point of contact for companies seeking technical assistance, cooperative research, and access to the college's consortia and centers. It brokers relationships between companies and college faculty, staff, and students. The college's Department of Engineering Professional Development program has operated for more than 50 years and is one of the largest such programs in the United States. It offers short, specialized courses for industry, involving annually more than 400 seminars, workshops, and courses. More than 15,000 professionals attend the courses annually, and about 30% of attendees are from Wisconsin. The Office of Engineering Outreach specializes in courses in graduate and continuing education delivered by videotape, satellite, instructional television, and computer-based distance learning. The college also operates Wisconsin TechSearch, located at the Wendt Engineering Library. This is a fee-based outreach service for business and industry, offering access to university libraries and information resources. The college also produces a magazine called *At Work for Wisconsin*, which highlights interactions between college faculty members, staff, and students and Wisconsin business and industry. The publication is sent to Wisconsin companies and is made available through the Department of Commerce, industry organizations, and various university offices.

ENTREPRENEURIAL DEVELOPMENT

A recent university-commissioned study of UW-M-related high-tech business growth[10] identified a total of 178 spin-off or start-up companies with links to the university. According to the study, the majority of these were established in the last 10 years, and the number of new spin-off and start-up companies is now averaging around 13 per year. These firms currently employ nearly 7,000 people in Wisconsin with aggregate gross revenues of over $1 billion. The majority (57% overall, and 68% within last 10 years) derive from the biological sciences, a key strength of the university.

Several interrelated organizations help faculty through the process of starting a company. The Office of University-Industry Relations (UIR), which has responsibilities in the invention disclosure process, also advises faculty on overcoming administrative hurdles, business plans, and Small Business Innovation Research/Small Business Technology Transfer (SBIR/STTR) grantsmanship (since 1983 about two-thirds of the $57 million in SBIR and STTR funds awarded to Wisconsin involved UW-M-linked entrepreneurs).

The University Research Park, adjacent to the campus, is also a home for much of the programmatic activity related to entrepreneurial development.[11] Originally launched in 1984, it had had middling success in attracting larger, established companies as tenants. By 1987, the park had refocused its efforts on developing multi-tenant buildings particularly suited for technology-based start-up and early stage companies. The park worked out an arrangement with a local private contractor for the design and construction and private financing of a nine-building multi-tenant University Science Center. The buildings were to range from 10,000 to 40,000 square feet and were not originally designed as sites for technology incubators. In 1989, incubation services were added to the fifth two-story building in the Science Center. This involved an important role by a local utility, Madison Gas & Electric (MGE), which agreed to master-lease the facility and then sublease to start-ups. Incubation services were provided through a contract with a seed capital firm, Venture Investors. This generally consisted of business planning advice plus access to a network of business professionals. Companies also received common office equipment, office space, and flexible albeit rudimentary laboratory facilities. Nonetheless, within a few years the failure rate of tenant companies proved to be quite low, many companies graduated to larger space elsewhere in the Park, and the occupancy rate was such that the park released MGE from its master lease obligations. By the late '90s, the park itself was a huge success, growing to more than 904,000 square feet, with 88 (mostly small) companies, and more than 2,500 employees. There was also a need for a larger and more sophisticated incubator. The MGE Center, built in 1999, included the following upgrades: three times the space of the original incubator; better and more flexible mechanical services for laboratories, increased common space for meetings and interactions, and enhanced overall amenities. Venture Investors still provides most of the business development services to tenants, with assistance from UW-M and community organizations. Currently 21 companies are tenants in the enlarged MGE Center, all but one being linked to UW-M.

UW-M promotes entrepreneurship training and opportunities for students as well. The university's Technology Enterprise Cooperative (UW-TEC) is a campus-wide organization that permits students and faculty to test out ideas for entrepreneurial ventures. It provides formal course work and a seed fund. It also offers consultation and referrals for individuals with business ideas, and brokers partnerships with private-sector entities to commercialize technologies. UW-TEC also administers three competitions for students: The Schools Prize for Creativity, an undergraduate student invention contest; the Tong Prototype Prize, given for the best prototype of a student invention; and the G. Steven Burrill Technology Business Plan Competition for the best business plan. UW-TEC co-sponsors include the College of Engineering, the College of Agricultural and Life Sciences, and the School of Business.

CAREER SERVICES AND PLACEMENT

UW-M is quite active in linking to Wisconsin-based employers, and the experiences of two units are instructive. The Engineering Career Services (ECS) in the College of Engineering has more than over 650 Wisconsin employers in its database, and engages those companies before students graduate through internship and co-op opportunities, during placement prior to graduation, and as a service to UW alumni.

The Cooperative Education and Summer Internship Program places students in full-time employment for periods ranging from three to eight months prior to completing their degrees. Of the 349 students working in a co-op arrangement during the 1998-1999 school year, 57% completed their work terms in Wisconsin companies. The average student wage was $13.27 per hour.

Engineering Career Services (ECS) serves 650 Wisconsin employers seeking co-op and intern candidates, graduating students at the bachelor's, master's, and doctoral levels and experienced engineering alumni. Through the ECS Cooperative Education and Summer Internship Program, students work during summers and/or semesters prior to earning their degrees. Of the 618 students working as co-op and intern employees during the 1998-1999 school year, 57% completed their work terms at Wisconsin companies. The average student wage was $2,256 per month. The Cooperative Education and Internship program is not mandatory at UW-M, but students compete for employment opportunities.

While primary ECS activity focuses on the recruitment of new graduates in 10 engineering disciplines and programs, it also includes assisting Wisconsin employers in hiring recent graduates and experienced alumni at all degree levels. Approximately 39% of bachelor's engineering graduates annually accepted job offers in Wisconsin.

A recent ECS initiative provides a 50% discount to employers located in Wisconsin for purchasing online resumes. Over the past three years, ECS staff have visited 80 new Wisconsin employers to encourage program participation. During the spring of 2000, ECS sponsored a Wisconsin-only co-op job fair to assist Wisconsin employers in the hiring process. During prior years, mock interview programs have been offered by Wisconsin employers visiting the college through ECS sponsorship. ECS also markets services locally through the Madison Area Chamber of Commerce, the Wisconsin Association of Colleges and Employers, and through occasional ads in Wisconsin newspapers and professional engineering association newsletters.

Another fairly aggressive program of student placement outreach is found in the biological sciences. The Biotechnology Training Program (BTP), funded by the National Institute of General Medical Sciences of the National Institutes of Health, started in 1989. Several key faculty members wrote a grant proposal that was competitively awarded. It was renewed in 1999 for another five years. At more than $980,000 per year, the grant to UW-M is the largest of its kind in the country. The program supports 33 graduate students each year, typically for a period of three years. To date, more than 125 BTP trainees from dozens of different programs have been supported. Students may be nominated from any of 43 different departments in five colleges and schools. More than 154 faculty serve as trainers. The BTP Steering Committee strives to keep an equal mix of students from the physical and biological sciences. The program has an extremely strong interdisciplinary orientation.

The most innovative aspect of this program is the student internships with industry. Students design their own projects, or they may also elect to work on a project internal to the company. More than 60 biotechnology companies actively support the program by sponsoring interns, providing financial backing, or seminar speakers. BTP students have completed internships in 40 companies worldwide. Of the BTP trainees who have graduated, 15 work in the biotechnology industry (six in Wisconsin), one started his own company in Wisconsin, seven hold faculty positions, two work for federal research centers, one is at law school, and 18 are doing post-doctoral research around the country. A 1999 graduate of the program is now a vice president for research of a Wisconsin-based company. The on-campus collaborative research he did for his internship is the backbone of this new genomics company.

One of the integral elements of the program is active reciprocal involvement with industry. This includes the internships in industry; an annual winter banquet to which participating students, faculty, and companies are invited; a quarterly newsletter; and invited speakers from industry. All industry participants in the annual winter banquet are asked to complete evaluations of the event. Likewise, industry supervisors of BTP interns are asked to provide feedback on the internship experience, as are the students themselves. The BTP office continually tries to increase the number of industry scientists who provide information about internship and employment opportunities for BTP trainees. The industry speakers provide a window on the world of industrial research, and they spend individual time talking to the students about research in their respective companies.

Participating departments demonstrate their support of the BTP by sending their prospective students visiting campus to the BTP winter banquet. Since the banquet features many scientific posters prepared by BTP trainees, prospective students are exposed to the depth and excellence of doctoral research at UW-M, as well as the cross-disciplinary aspects. Many faculty have trainer status in other departments and have active collaborations, joint publications, or teach cross-disciplinary classes. The university administration has made several recent hires with the intent of bringing new but experienced faculty to campus with a background of cross-disciplinary research.

FACULTY CULTURE AND REWARDS

Consistent with the general thrust of the Wisconsin Idea, there are explicit recommendation in the faculty handbook concerning the Wisconsin Idea vis-à-vis tenure review. The handbook states, "Every tenure case should include evaluation of the faculty member's accomplishments in the context of the Wisconsin Idea. ...,"[12] meaning the involvement of the faculty member in outreach activities is to play some role in the tenure review and decision. Moreover, outreach is to be considered as encompassing service, research, and teaching. Outreach service "may include ... technology transfer," and evidence for excellence in outreach research may include "issuance of patents and evidence of intellectual property such as copyrighted materials." It is not clear how widely on campus these recommendations are implemented at the unit level. There has apparently been discussion, albeit inconclusive, about a formula or procedure for converting patents into publication credit. Nonetheless, the fact that these guidelines exist at all is notable.

Another unique attribute of the UW-M culture is related to faculty participation in start-up companies. At UW-M the presumption is that faculty own their own inventions. Unless there is a clear linkage to a campus research project, other innovations developed by faculty are considered outside the domain of intellectual property in which UW has a claim. In most other universities, there is a more restrictive interpretation of ownership, favoring the institution as a condition of employment. As an illustration of how this works at Wisconsin, there is a clear distinction made between UW-related companies that are spin-offs and those that are start-ups. The university considers spin-offs to be directly derived from campus-based research (typically supported by a federal agency and thus covered by Bayh-Dole). The university considers start-ups to be new companies that may involve UW-M faculty, staff, or students, but whose underlying technology is not attributable to campus-based research. This approach works as a major incentive for entrepreneurial activity. It is also believed to be a major advantage when recruiting new faculty. This presumption of faculty ownership is frequently undone when there is co-mingling of federal support, but the underlying cultural beliefs and values are important nonetheless.

University leadership has also done cultural advocacy in the area of entrepreneurial activities. A report produced on this topic in 1999, considerable effort has been devoted to documenting the long-term experience of the university in fostering start-up and spin-off companies. The resultant report,[13] produced in 1999, was extremely well researched, professionally packaged, and highly readable. The chancellor's office has distributed many copies with an appropriately enthusiastic cover letter to internal administrators, members of the governing board, and important friends of the university (including those in state government). This has served both to inform internal and external audiences about the role that the university is playing in building the Wisconsin economy, as well as to strengthen an already supportive organizational culture.

ENDNOTES

[1] National Science Foundation Division of Science Resource Studies. (2001). *Academic research and development expenditures, FY 1999.* Washington, D.C.: National Science Foundation. Table B-33.

[2] Governor Tommy G. Thompson. (2000) *State of the State Address.* January 26, 2000.

[3] Office of Outreach Development, University of Wisconsin-Madison. (1997). *Commitment to the Wisconsin Idea. A Guide to Documenting and Evaluating Excellence in Outreach Scholarship.* Madison, Wisc.: University of Wisconsin-Madison.

[4] Board of Regents of the University of Wisconsin System. (2001). *The University of Wisconsin-Madison Strategic Plan: To Sustain and Strengthen our Position of Preeminence in Research and Higher Education.* An alternative, somewhat condensed version of the plan is available from the chancellor's office as: Wiley, John D. (2001). *Connecting Ideas. Strategies for the University of Wisconsin-Madison.* Board of Regents of the University of Wisconsin System.

[5] The University of Wisconsin-Madison. (1999). *Faculty Outreach. Activities and Attitudes.* Survey Report.

[6] National Science Foundation. Division of Science Resource Studies. *Op. cit.* Tables B-33, B-36, B-387.

[7] Sobocinski, P.Z. (1999). *Creating High-Tech Business Growth in Wisconsin.* Madison, Wisc.: Office of University-Industry Relations, University of Wisconsin.

[8] Association of University Technology Managers. (2000). *AUTM Licensing Survey: FY 1999.* Chicago: Association of University Technology Managers.
Association of University Technology Managers. (1999). *AUTM Licensing Survey: Fiscal Year 1998.* Norwalk, Conn.: Association of University Technology Managers.

[9] Association of University Technology Managers. (2000). *Op. Cit.*

[10] Sobocinski, P.Z. (1999). *Op. Cit.*

[11] Hyer, G. R. (1999). Developing and Managing a Successful Technology Incubator. *Economic Development Commentary.* Vol. 23, No. 3.

[12] Office of Outreach Development, University of Wisconsin-Madison. (1997). *Op. cit.*

[13] Sobocinski, P.Z. (1999). *Op. Cit.*

VIRGINIA POLYTECHNIC INSTITUTE AND STATE UNIVERSITY

Virginia Polytechnic Institute and State University, popularly known as Virginia Tech, is one of the premier land grant research universities in the country. Founded in 1872, Virginia Tech is the largest of the four-year public universities in the Commonwealth of Virginia, with 27,869 students enrolled in fall 2000. In the FY 1999 National Science Foundation[1] survey of academic research and development, Virginia Tech reported research expenditures of $169.2 million, which ranks 50th among all U.S. universities and 33rd among public universities. Of this, a large fraction is concentrated in engineering ($53.5 million), the life sciences ($73.8 million) and environmental sciences ($21.4 million). Not surprisingly its College of Agriculture and Life Sciences is ranked fifth in the nation by the National Science Foundation in terms of total research expenditures among land grant institutions, as well as fifth in terms of funds for international agriculture research.

There is a strong tradition at Virginia Tech to conduct research through organized research units, such as centers or institutes. As a result, there are currently more than 100 research institutes, centers, and groups on campus, and many are explicitly organized around several disciplines (see http://www.research.vt.edu/interd/univresearchcenters.html). These include the Virginia Tech Transportation Research Institute, the Fralin Biotechnology Center, the Center for Self-Assembled Nano Devices, and the Optical Science and Engineering Research Center. A new Advanced Communications and Information Technologies Center is a state of the art facility to showcase and enhance Virginia Tech's capabilities in instructional technology, communications, and information technology. To illustrate the importance Virginia Tech places on an interdisciplinary approach to research, it created an Office of Interdisciplinary Program with objectives to define, enhance, and promote such activities. This office produces an informative and visually attractive annual publication describing the work of 87 centers, institutes, and laboratories, all of which have an interdisciplinary flavor.[2] Each entry follows a common format (Who We Are; What We Do; Contact Information) and the result is a very customer-friendly marketing document.

The institution is organized into eight colleges, and offers 61 undergraduate degrees and 114 graduate or professional programs of study. Several of these have achieved national prominence in terms of various ratings and rankings. For example, according to *U.S. News & World Report*, the College of Engineering graduate school is ranked 24th nationally, the graduate program in public affairs is ranked 10th, the Vocational Technology Program is ranked sixth, the Pamplona College of Business is 38th among undergraduate business programs, and Virginia Tech's overall undergraduate program is rated 26th. According to *Kiplinger Magazine*, Virginia Tech also ranked 18th as a "best value" among universities.

The institution is also expected to strengthen its national status through a number of new programs and initiatives that will unfold over the next few years. For example, the Harvey W. Peters Foundation is establishing a new school of osteopathic medicine in southwest Virginia. It is expected to be operational by 2003, with a possibility for some facilities to be located in Virginia Tech's Corporate Research Center. This development will have an impact on research and education in the fields of bioinformatics, biotechnology, telemedicine, and other life sciences.

Like many U.S. land grant universities, Virginia Tech is located in a relatively rural mountain area of Virginia. The town of Blacksburg has a population of 39,573, with a large fraction of residents being university-affiliated. Nonetheless, the University has been extraordinarily aggressive and effective in reaching communities and business partners throughout its region, the state, nationally, and internationally. Its motto, *Ute Prosy* (That I may serve), is reflected in its many outreach and partnering activities.

Illustrative of this orientation is the fact that there is a vice-provost for outreach, as well as an associate vice president for strategic partnerships. The intellectual rationale for the latter position was developed in a white paper[3] written four years ago by the current president of the university. There is also a director of economic development (http://www.vtconnect.vt.edu), who has a dual reporting relationship directly to the president and to the vice provost for outreach. This individual assists communities throughout the state in accessing the university's resources for economic development, markets the university's business-relevant services and activities to private enterprise, and resolves issues of cooperation among those activities.

The scope of outreach at Virginia Tech is regional, statewide, national and international. Regarding the latter, Virginia Tech has more than $24 million in international research and development, and projects in more than 40 countries. A more local approach to outreach is exemplified in its national reputation as the hub of an extensively "wired" local community. The Blacksburg Electronic Village (BEV), a partnership with Verizon, is a national model of how a university and a town can partner for the pervasive delivery of Internet services, and how such an effort can enhance a wide variety of community activities (see below).

Virginia Tech's story is that of a land grant university that has become very focused on an outreach and economic development mission — in addition to enhancing its research performance — and is in the process of making a host of organizational changes to align various activities and functions with those goals. All those changes have not yet been worked out, but nonetheless the institution is an excellent model of how significant cultural and structural change can be accomplished to accommodate an enlarged set of priorities.

Mission, Vision, and Goal Statements

Virginia Tech is trying to simultaneously enhance its national reputation as a center of research and scholarship while stepping up its activities in and impacts on regional economic development. Regarding the former, it has identified seven areas in which it wishes to attain or maintain "preeminence" and mounted major research and development initiatives in each of the following:

- Biosciences and biotechnology
- Computing, information, and communications
- Environmental sciences and energy systems
- Food, nutrition, and health
- Learning communities
- Materials science
- Transportation.

In some cases, the new initiatives cut across areas, such as in the new Virginia Bioinformatics Institute (VBI) and the new Institute for Information Technology. Nonetheless, a common theme in virtually all of Virginia Tech's major programs and plans is the potential for having an impact on the economy and citizens of Virginia, as well as being a national research power.

The university's motto, noted above, is elaborated in the mission, vision, and goal statements of a variety of campus-wide functional organizations, as well as within key academic units. A common theme emphasizes external partnerships and improving the economic development of the region and state through knowledge and technology. This is exemplified in the mission and vision statements (http://www.unirel.vt.edu/president/strategic/Mission010508.html) contained in the Strategic Plan adopted in August 2001:

Through its focus on teaching and learning, research, and outreach, the university creates, conveys, and applies knowledge to expand personal growth and opportunity, advance social and community development, foster economic competitiveness, and improve the quality of life.

Later on, in the same document under a heading entitled "The Virginia Tech Culture" is the following:

However, if there is one attribute that distinguishes Virginia Tech from all but a few of the nation's thousands of higher education institutions, it is the interconnectedness – the interactivity – of the university to the society and constituencies it serves. Virginia Tech is not a citadel of cloistered learning. We believe that universities are most viable when they are interactive, when they reflect and respond to the problems and challenges of their societies.

These ideas get restated and reformulated in a variety of descriptions of campus activities.

For example, the theme of "Putting Technology to Work" is prominent in Web-based materials describing the university, and that theme is expanded upon in the descriptive language of operating units. For example, the Research Division proclaims among its goals the two following:

- *Markets faculty talent and university capabilities within the university and to outside agencies and businesses in order to foster partnerships; and*
- *Transfers research results to the commonwealth, the nation, and the world.*

Similarly, the university's Program Development Office seeks:

> To facilitate communication and collaboration among the university, its faculty, and industry; thereby strengthening interactions with industry, encouraging corporate financial support of research, training, and outreach, leveraging these private funds with federal and state monies, and developing the economy of the Commonwealth of Virginia.

In the university's policy statement on intellectual properties, the first sentence under "Purpose" clearly enunciates the economic development role of the institution:

> Publicly (state) supported universities have the multiple missions of teaching, research, support of the public interest and fostering the economic development of the area/state in which they are located.

These perspectives are also reflected in the goals, visions, and missions of key academic units. For example, the current plan for the College of Agriculture and Life Sciences — building on its 90-year experience with Virginia Cooperative Extension in all parts of the commonwealth — begins with this poetic and stirring statement:

> Since the very first students set foot on campus, this institution has been foremost a college 'for the people' and a valuable part of Virginia's heritage and economic prosperity.

These sentiments are given a somewhat different voice using the metaphors of "outreach." To wit, the outreach vision statement of Virginia Tech (http://www.outreach.vt.edu/about.htm) states the following:

> Outreach is a critical form of scholarship of an effective university, particularly a land-grant university. It is neither an afterthought nor an appendage, but must be an integral, integrated part of the university.

In recent years, a new mission imperative has emerged around the issue of entrepreneurship. This has been a corollary of increasing activity and success in technology commercialization via start-up companies, as well as an increasing awareness on the part of key academic units that this is a key future strategy for the institution. For example, nearly half of the 65-page 2000 Annual Report of the Bradley Department of Electrical and Computer Engineering is dedicated to various articles on start-up experiences of faculty and students. Moreover, in an introduction to the report, the chair of the department advisory board comments that:

> Managing these entrepreneurial activities to best benefit the university, the department and the state is a key challenge for the coming year. The Advisory Board hopes to make a significant contribution by helping the university and the department create a new model for the future.

Echoing and expanding upon this sentiment, Bill Stephenson, dean of the College of Engineering observes in the same publication that:

> Unless we encourage entrepreneurship, we cannot attract the faculty we need in certain areas and run the risk of losing some extremely creative faculty members who are good teachers and good researchers.

INDUSTRY RESEARCH PARTNERSHIPS

National Science Foundation data[4] show that Virginia Tech's industry-sponsored research expenditures in FY 1999 were $13.3 million, or 7.9% of total research expenditures. This is slightly above the national average of 7.4%, and Virginia Tech ranked 34th among the top 100 U.S. universities. Between 1992 and 1999 overall research expenditures increased by 29% while industry-sponsored expenditures decreased by 7%. University officials suggest that these data are a function of two factors: the rapid growth of the federally funded portion of the research portfolio and the lower research and development intensity of Virginia-based industry.

Before getting into the nuts and bolts of university-industry research partnerships, it is worth noting here that the university tries very hard to manage relationships with companies via a "portfolio" approach. That is, since it is common for industrial partners of the institution to be engaged on several fronts at once (e.g., sponsored research, student recruitment, beta testing of a technology, technology licensing, making a donation of a capital facility), there is a corresponding need for coordination of those activities.

Virginia Tech has very recently put that responsibility into the hands of a single office, the associate vice president of strategic partnerships, that tries to stay abreast of the many activities involving a single company, avoid duplication of efforts, and maximize coordination across involved units. The job description for this associate vice president position states:

> *The position holder will work collaboratively with the leaders of the university's academic and administrative programs to develop and implement strategies that will attract corporate, foundation, and governmental support for its initiatives.*

One of the first tasks confronting the new position (filled in 2001) was to "develop and implement a comprehensive plan for the management of strategic partnerships." Virginia Tech does have in place a system of policies, procedures, and tools designed to make the university accessible for industry to engage in research partnerships. The Program Development Office (htttp://www.research.vt.edu/industry), an operating unit of the research division, fosters partnerships in research involving industry sponsorship. This mission is enabled via various practices, tools, and policies. One tool is the Virginia Tech Expertise Database (VTED) of faculty qualifications and experience that is made available both internally and externally via the Internet. The Database uses the Community of Science (COS) interface, and as a result faculty who are entered in COS are automatically listed with VTED. VTED provides unlimited access on the Internet to information that would normally be restricted to COS subscribers, mostly universities and larger corporations. The Virginia Center for Innovative Technology (CIT) provides some of the logistical and financial support for this effort. In parallel, with VTED, the Research Division also publishes online a monthly newsletter — *Virginia Tech Edge* — that contains timely short pieces about emerging research results, research programs, and newly available intellectual property.

Once some industry-university connection seems to be in play, the Program Development Office will play a role in facilitating the execution of a research contract, brokering the resolution of intellectual property issues, and generally providing the partnering company with an array of support services and information. As an example of the latter, the Program Development Office maintains, and publishes on its Web site, an ongoing database on various investment networks, venture capitalists, and public-private programs that address capitalization needs of industry.[5] As of summer 2001, two discipline-focused program development managers were are assigned to this effort — one focused on life sciences, agriculture, and information technology and the other focused on transportation, materials, energy, and the environment.

Another unit involved in fostering industry research partnerships is the Center for Organizational and Technological Advancement (COTA), which has "a special emphasis on connecting university research to the needs of Virginia industrial, commercial, governmental, academic, and professional organizations." COTA's mission seems to be much more in the economic development vein, and it operates a portfolio of projects that change in character over the years. Currently, the primary vehicles of COTA are: (1) the awarding of small grants for various organization to hold meetings, short courses, and conferences that deal with partnership topics; (2) the appointment of fellows — typically distinguished academic scholars and business leaders — who in turn develop educational programs. In FY 2000-2001 COTA sponsored about 100 programs at the Hotel Roanoke and Conference Center.

Another venue for extensive industry engagement is in Virginia Tech's award-winning[6] Corporate Research Center (CRC), which is a 120-acre research park located adjacent to the campus. The CRC is home to more than 100 companies that employ approximately 1,800 people. The CRC currently has 16 single and multi-tenant buildings, and operates as a for-profit subsidiary of the Virginia Tech Foundation. The current plan is to expand the CRC to 28 buildings in the future. The center is also making a concerted push to attract foreign companies wishing to expand in the United States, having recently joined a network of technology parks located in Hungary, Germany, Austria, and Japan. The CRC is much more than a real estate venture for the university. It is designed to foster extensive partnership relations with faculty, provide employment and internship opportunities for students, serve as a venue for university classes and laboratories, enhance the technology commercialization function of the university, and facilitate the institution's mission in regional economic development. Through the Business Technology Center, which is located in the CRC, there is also an acceleration of entrepreneurial ventures involving university faculty, university technology, and start-up companies with strong linkages to Virginia Tech.

TECHNOLOGY TRANSFER

Virginia Tech has one of the most active technology transfer functions among major public research universities. It is also one that is oriented toward entrepreneurial paths to technology commercialization, complementing its more traditional patenting and licensing functions. License income was $1.33 million in FY 1999,[7] with a royalty return on investment (royalties divided by total research expenditures) of 0.79%. License income ranks in the 60th percentile, and royalty ROI in the 54th percentile, of the 142 academic institutions that participated in the *AUTM Licensing Survey for FY 1999*.[8] Looking at licenses to start-up companies in fiscal years 1998 and 1999 combined, Virginia Tech reported a total of 12, placing it in the 52nd percentile in the AUTM Licensing Survey sample. During the same period, Virginia Tech reported a total of three new start-ups formed, two of which were located in the state. Virginia Tech ranks in the 57th percentile for total start-ups formed and in the 51st percentile for in-state start-ups formed. Among universities without a medical school, Virginia Tech achieved top-10 ranking in the number of licenses and options executed, the amount of new research funding related to licenses, and in the number of licenses to business start-ups.

Technology transfer is administered through Virginia Tech Intellectual Properties Inc. (VTIP), a nonprofit affiliate of the university. Virginia Tech assigns intellectual property to VTIP, which in turn organizes its evaluation, protection, and disposition. The roles of VTIP vis-à-vis inventors are spelled out in an extraordinarily clear set of guidelines ("Follow the Four Steps") on the VTIP Web site (http://www.vtip.org/ServicesforInventors.htm). Interestingly, these guidelines are very explicit and helpful about the situation in which "a new company is started to commercialize the intellectual property," which in turn may involve the faculty inventor as "a member of the management team," and where "equity interest may be part of the deal." Thus, in a few short sentences, VTIP legitimizes and provides a policy roadmap for some of the more contentious issues that have plagued many university technology transfer offices. VTIP policy on distribution of royalties is also fairly encouraging to faculty inventorship, as well as to their academic units. After VTIP deducts overhead and verified out of pocket expenses (e.g., legal assistance) from gross royalties, 50% of the balance goes to the inventor(s), 40% goes to and is retained by VTIP for the university, and 10% is allocated to the home department or unit of the inventor. Since FY 1994, VTIP has transferred $3.4 million to inventors, $2.7 million to departments, and more than $1 million back to the university.

In order that its policies and procedures stay abreast of changes in technology and the foci of invention, Virginia

Tech undertook a process of updating its Intellectual Property Policy. Virtually all of the proposed changes are in the area of software and courseware, and reflect the rapid development of the Internet and associated opportunities for copyrightable works. To its credit, Virginia Tech organized the change process as a very participative exercise, with online Q-and-A (http://www.rgs.vt.edu/opd/ipqa1.htm) and wide discussion within the university community.

As part of its own internal outreach and professional development agenda, every year VTIP sponsors an all-day workshop for the Virginia Tech community on intellectual property issues. Sponsors from industry and law firms typically defray expenses and provide some of the speakers. An event held in November 2000 was attended by more than 140 faculty members, graduate students, lawyers, and business leaders. It was also Webcast to an untold number of participants at remote campuses. The theme of the conference was "Reaching Over the Wall: University Intellectual Property and Outreach." It explored a variety of concerns that are associated with an aggressive technology transfer function, including conflict of culture between the university and industry, conflict of commitment with the academic and research mission, as well as more legalistic conflict of interest issues.

> **PERHAPS THE MOST SIGNIFICANT ASSET THAT THE UNIVERSITY POSSESSES IN THIS AREA IS THE ADMITTEDLY ENTREPRENEURIAL ORIENTATION OF ITS ORGANIZATIONAL CULTURE.**

Given the relative emphasis on outreach and economic development, there is an increasing emphasis within the technology transfer function in fostering start-up companies based in Virginia. This has resulted in a variety of initiatives, including a greater emphasis on technology business incubation services (see Entrepreneurial Development).

INDUSTRIAL EXTENSION/TECHNICAL ASSISTANCE

Virginia Tech has recently formalized the Technical Assistance Program (TAP), which provides short-term technical assistance to businesses, primarily in manufacturing industries. TAP is a component of the statewide Philpott Manufacturing Extension Partnership (MEP), which in turn is part of the national MEP network supported by the National Institute of Standards and Technology (NIST). President Steger serves on the board of the statewide program. Continuing Education administers TAP, and a mix of Tech faculty and graduate students staff the projects that are conducted with companies. The projects must involve less than $25,000 of direct services (usually much less), do not demand original research, and typically do not involve intellectual property concerns. Although TAP supports the national MEP network, the services provided to its client community extend beyond manufacturing. Started as a pilot project in 1998, more than 30 projects have been completed or are underway. All projects are fully funded by client companies.

ENTREPRENEURIAL DEVELOPMENT

Perhaps the most significant asset that the university possesses in this area is the admittedly entrepreneurial orientation of its organizational culture. This is bolstered programmatically by a technology transfer function (described above) that facilitates an entrepreneurial approach to commercializing faculty inventions, as well as the Business Technology Center (BTC) that is located in the Corporate Research Center to provide an array of direct services for early stage companies. Several on-campus organizations as well as units of government subsidize the BTC. These include the Virginia's Center for Innovative Technology, the towns of Blacksburg and Christiansburg, the Montgomery County Industrial Development Authority, the Corporate Research Center, the Pamplin College of Business, the College of Engineering, Virginia Tech Outreach, and Virginia Tech Intellectual Properties (VTIP). The BTC provides assistance in strategic planning, marketing, legal issues, personnel, financing, production processes, Internet technologies and business operations such as accounting. It has on-site staff in the Corporate Research Center but it primarily functions as a matchmaker or broker to a variety of business service providers elsewhere in the community or the state. Virginia Tech faculty and graduates provide some of that assistance but the BTC has access to a large cadre of consultants. Typically, BTC staff will work with a client to assess their needs and to develop a plan for the services that will address those needs. The client companies pay most of the cost of consultant services but in many cases this is often significantly reduced. In FY 1999-2000 it helped client companies with 277 projects. Projects can range from a few hours to several person-weeks of effort, and a client company is likely to average about 2.5 projects while working with BTC.

Some of Tech's many centers and institutes mentioned above are themselves hotbeds for entrepreneurial activity. For example, the Fiber and Electro-Optics Research Center (FEORC) has spun off 17 companies since its inception in 1985. These have been established by faculty, students, and combinations thereof. Luna Innovations, a Virginia Tech-related spin-off that has been involved in instrumentation, sensors, and advanced materials, recently made it onto the *Inc.* magazine list of fastest-growing small companies. From a public policy perspective, it is worth noting that FEORC was founded in part through support by Virginia's Center for Innovative Technology (CIT), a state program designed to foster technology-based economic development. Part of the CIT mandate to FEORC was to create new companies — and they did. It should also be noted that up until 1990, state conflict of interest laws tended to chill the environment for faculty involvement in start-ups. (Considering faculty as state employees meant they were subject to state conflict-of-interest rules that prevented their involvement in private enterprise.)

The Virginia Tech Foundation has played a significant albeit indirect role in fostering entrepreneurial development. Over the past few years it has made several investments in venture capital companies (currently totaling approximately $8 million), some of which in turn have reinvested in local enterprises. The foundation also played a financial role in the development of the Corporate Research Center, which, as noted elsewhere, serves small companies in a variety of ways.

The entrepreneurial orientation is also reflected in educational programs. For example, the Department of Electrical and Computer Engineering offers a "Virtual Corporation" option for its students. Participants "work within the structure of a commercial engineering firm, and design real products, systems, and technology, based on actual market conditions." Students are often involved over several semesters, and two of the original corporations are moving to closure on prototype products in the areas of medical imaging diagnostics and transit technologies. Regarding the latter, one team has developed a personal rapid transit system (PERTS) based on magnetic levitation technology. Small-scale prototypes have been developed, and a start-up company has been established.

In September 2001, Virginia Tech announced plans to establish a technology business "accelerator" in the Corporate Research Center (CRC). The new program — VT KnowledgeWorks — was formed with the leadership of the Virginia Tech Foundation and will be launched in cooperation with three private sector partners: eIncubator is an early-stage incubation company that works through a national network of service providers and investment companies; LaunchFuel, which is involved in the creation of new technology-based companies, primarily in IT; and Redleaf, another broker of incubation services and investments for technology start-ups. There will be a facility based in the CRC with each of the corporate partners contributing staff. The mix of start-up companies to be served is expected to consist of some based on Virginia Tech technologies as well as others with more diffuse ties to the institution. The accelerator will be managed by the CRC, with some portion of start-up costs coming from the Virginia Tech Foundation.

Industry Education and Training Partnerships

Virginia Tech has a large and comprehensive Division of Continuing Education that serves individuals and communities across the state. In a given year, it will provide more than 400 short courses, seminars, conferences and workshops that will reach more than 25,000 participants. The substantive foci of the programs tend to reflect the strengths of the university in life sciences, engineering, and other disciplines, but they also tend to be attuned to the demands of different regions in the state. Many of the programs are delivered at conference centers in Blacksburg or Roanoke. The latter is located at the Hotel Roanoke, an American Automobile Association four-diamond hotel that was gifted to the university a few years ago and subsequently underwent a $28 million restoration. It is on the National Register of Historic Places. A planned alumni and conference center on campus will significantly expand local lodging and meeting capacities within the next few years.

Separate from Continuing Education, there is also a network of 14 extended campus centers that are particularly important in the delivery of graduate coursework and entire degree programs (many available online), and in supporting regions and their economies. These are operated by Virginia Tech's Graduate School, and are gradually evolving to become more integrated with the main campus, while also being responsive to the unique needs of the communities where they are located. For example, operations in Northern Virginia have been structured around the Alexandria Research Institute, the Washington-Alexandria Architecture Center, and the Northern Virginia Center. The resultant interdisciplinary themes will concern development and applications of information technology, urbanization and built environments, policy and governance, and education and leadership.

The university also operates a statewide, broadband network (Net.Work.Virginia) that provides simultaneous transmission of voice, data, and video services. This is used in various programs. The Pamplin College of Business meets continuing education needs of the business and professional community through its Management and Professional Development office, which organizes faculty-led workshops and courses that are either tailored to the needs of specific clients or offered on an open-enrollment basis. Some programs are delivered on campus and others are offered at the company's site.

Career Services and Placement

The university has an active, highly visible career services function (http://www.career.vt.edu) that offers a variety of services to employers. These include a candidate referral service, on-campus interviews, and job-listing services. It hosts a number of events annually, such as job and career fairs, at which potential employers and students come together. One of these — "Connection" — is dedicated exclusively to encouraging internships and co-ops and is open to all students and employers. Specific colleges or academic programs organize a number of other fairs. In addition, through Career Services, potential employers can view resumes online, request that Career Services conduct a resume search to meet their hiring needs (candidate referral service), schedule dates to interview students in the Career Services offices, and make arrangements to present to student groups and meet with faculty. Career Services reports that for the class of 2000, 58% of graduates are employed in Virginia.

Formal Partnerships with Economic Development Organizations

Campus units and activities are closely aligned with both state and local economic organizations. Regarding the former, Virginia Tech cooperates closely with the Virginia Center for Innovative Technology (CIT), which operates a number of programs designed to enhance technology-based economic development. Several Virginia Tech Centers have also been sponsored in part by CIT. These include the Center for Wireless Communication, the Center for

Advanced Ceramic Materials, the Biobased Materials Technology Development Center, the Center for Coal and Minerals Processing, the Fiber and Electro-Optics Center, and the Center for Power Electronics.

Virginia Tech also participates in a number of regionally focused activities. Through its Public Services Programs (PSP) the university works closely with community agencies all over the state to attract and retain business and industry. For example, PSP conducts a Community Preparedness for Economic Development program. This assists communities with economic development courses and workshops, consulting services, and research intended to focus and improve their competitive advantages. The New River Valley Alliance and the Hampton Roads Economic Development Partnership are two regional economic development organizations that have partnered with Virginia Tech. The Southside Virginia Economic Development Initiative involves a partnership between Virginia Tech, two community colleges and various city and county agencies in the Danville, Virginia area. It will lead to the creation of an Institute for Advanced Learning and Research that is expected to be a locus for workforce preparation, education, and technology-based economic development. These regional partnerships continue to blossom. This year, the Southwest Virginia Regional Outreach and Economic Development Council met to set priorities on issues that it wants Virginia Tech's help to solve. These will generally be in the areas of education, technology enhancement, leadership, and economic development.

As a component of PSP, the university also hosts the Economic Development Assistance Center (EDAC), which was originally established in 1989 under a federal Economic Development Administration grant. The center provides assistance and staff training to local economic development organizations in the state. Assistance projects might include project feasibility studies, strategic plans, or market analyses that are conducted on a case-by-case basis. EDAC recently created a Virginia Institute for 21st Century Governance as a vehicle for presenting professional development event. A current offering is a course in Performance Measurement and Benchmarking, which is targeted toward state and local officials.

Perhaps the most visible and well-known example of a development partnership at a local level has been the Blacksburg Electronic Village (BEV). Launched in the early 1990s, the BEV (http://www.bev.net/project/brochures/about.html) has attempted to turn the city of Blacksburg, in partnership with the university, into a "virtual community" in which Internet access is pervasive. The BEV has succeeded along several lines. It claims to have the highest per capita use of the Internet in the nation (87% as of late 1999), to be the first community in the country to offer residential Ethernet services in apartments and townhouses, the first community in the country to have every school connected to the Internet, to have the highest per capita concentration of Internet service providers, and the highest business use of the Internet of any community in the world. More than 75% of Blacksburg businesses use the Internet for advertising and/or commerce, and nearly 500 businesses have electronic listings on the BEV Village Mall. Outcomes that are attributed to BEV include the establishment or arrival of more than 20 information technology-related businesses. It has also increased the quality of life for retired people and shut-ins, and enabled new kinds of K-12 applications and increased parental involvement therein. The services and programs of various nonprofit service or cultural organizations are much more visible to citizens, and participation has increased apace. While Virginia Tech spearheaded the establishment of BEV, some of the current operations and future development (e.g., network access) have been transferred to the private sector, with positive impacts on economic development. Nonetheless, the BEV continues to provide a wide range of services to Blacksburg's government, nonprofit organizations, and individual citizens.

INDUSTRY/UNIVERSITY ADVISORY BOARDS AND COUNCILS

The role of industry advisory councils at Virginia Tech is pervasive. It is typically an integral part of the dozens of research centers and institutes that pursue an industry-relevant research agenda. It is part of the governance and information input structure of several academic units and colleges. An internal study identified 33 university advisory boards, including several explicitly focused on external partnerships and economic development. Chief among the latter are the university-wide Economic Development Advisory Board, the College of Engineering Advisory Board, and the advisory board for the Department of Electrical and Computer Engineering. The Economic Development Advisory Board is structured into regional advisory councils so as to better serve the unique regional economies of the commonwealth. The Engineering Advisory Board is structured as a Committee of 100 and composed of distinguished alumni, all of whom have made significant contributions to the field. The advisory board for the department of Electrical and Computer Engineering has a number of high-powered industrial leaders, many from technology-based companies. It has been very influential in the development of new research and educational programs.

Faculty Culture and Rewards

Faculty "culture" and reward systems can operate in informal, subtle ways, or they can be expressed more visibly and officially. An example of the latter is Virginia Tech's explicit acknowledgement of the worth of outreach, external partnering, and economic development in the strategic goals of the university As enunciated by the president in 2001 (http://www.unirel.vt.edu/president/strategic/Goals010803.html), the following goal statements and objectives are directly relevant to establishing a campus culture that supports external partnering and involvement in regional economic development:

- *Require each college to have a well defined and articulated outreach program*
- *Include University Outreach in the new faculty orientation and college and administrative unit orientation session*
- *Maintain participation in Outreach activities as a criterion for promotion and tenure decisions*
- *Use University Outreach to expand non-credit programs, technical assistance and economic development*

And:

> *4.1 Create policy that encourages and nurtures faculty economic development efforts*
> *4.2 Increase partnerships with groups serving those who are typically underserved and underrepresented*
> *4.3 Create three new strategic partnerships with the private sector such as the Southside Initiative to benefit both the region and the university*
> *4.4 Increase by 25% student involvement with communities through internships, service-learning projects, and outreach projects*
> *4.5 Create more effective response mechanisms for evaluating input and needs to serve the private sector better*
> *4.6 Establish a senior level university economic development council to target efforts, formalize policy, and assess programs*

There are also symbolic events and activities that can have an effect on how faculty members construe their culture and reward environment. For example, in May of 2001, the university and VTIP jointly hosted the annual Inventor Recognition Reception honoring the 25 recipients of patents during 2000. Any faculty member who has ever received a patent was invited, as well as administrators and faculty from across the institution. The president and vice provost for research attended and spoke, and the former noted that patents "represent a significant resource for economic development." This has been an annual activity for several years, and while it is an informal, mingling kind of event, it nonetheless sends an important cultural message about outreach through technology transfer. All such VTIP acknowledgement activities are spotlighted in their newsletter and released to the media. In fact, press releases are organized whenever a Virginia Tech faculty member receives a patent or whenever a start-up company based on university technology launches. Tech frequently will buy spots on Virginia public radio to acknowledge faculty achievements and accomplishments. These kinds of public pronouncements by senior university officials are typically an excellent way to define the normative boundaries and informal rewards for faculty.

As another example, the College of Engineering is sending a clear cultural message to faculty and students alike on the importance of entrepreneurial activities. Located on its Web site is a section dedicated to Entrepreneurs of the New Millennium with bios and photos of Virginia Tech graduates who have successfully launched technology-based companies (http://www.eng.vt.edu/development1/entre2000.pdf). The message is clear: This is important and it can be done

Virginia Tech is very serious about creating expectations and rewards for faculty to be involved in outreach. Recently, there have been university-wide changes in the annual review process for faculty members that include a section on Outreach that must be part of a faculty member's activities portfolio. In this context the following conceptual guidance (http://www.provost.vt.edu/fhp/GPT100.html) is provided:

> *Faculty members are expected by the university and the public to make their professional knowledge and skills broadly available to society. Outreach is one of the principal responsibilities of a land-grant university. It entails skillful, knowledgeable, professional applications and extensions of academic fields and specialties. Outreach must be grounded firmly in university programs. It is an umbrella under which fall activities in continuing education, community and economic development, cooperative extension and other programs that extend the knowledge and expertise of faculty for the direct benefit of society.*

Also provided are the following suggestions for inclusion in a faculty member's dossier:

- *An account of the candidate's specific outreach responsibilities.*
- *Professional achievements in program development and implementation.*
- *Outreach publications, included numbered extension publications, trade journals, newsletters, other papers, web sites, refereed journals, multimedia items, etc.*
- *Results of participant and/or peer evaluations concerning the significance and impact of programs.*
- *Recognition and awards for outreach effectiveness.*
- *Other assigned outreach or extension activities.*

Clearly, Virginia Tech is developing a comprehensive approach to shifting its organizational culture and reward system, in both symbolic and specific ways, to one that more explicitly supports the increased emphasis on external partnering and outreach.

ENDNOTES

[1] National Science Foundation Division of Science Resource Studies. (2001). *Academic research and development expenditures, FY 1999*. Washington, D.C.: National Science Foundation. Table B-33.

[2] Office of Interdisciplinary Programs, Virginia Tech University. (2001). *Crossing the Lines*. Report.

[3] Steger, C. W. (1997). *Strategic Partnerships and the Future of Virginia Tech*. Unpublished paper.

[4] National Science Foundation. Division of Science Resource Studies. *Op. cit.* Tables B-33, B-36, B-38.

[5] htttp://www.research.vt.edu/industry/earlystage.html.

[6] National Council for Urban Economic Development. (1997). *Best Practice in Technology Transfer and Research Centers.* Report.

[7] Licensing income has increased to over $1.5 million for FY 2000.

[8] Association of University Technology Managers. (2000). *AUTM Licensing Survey: FY 1999.* Chicago, Ill.: Association of University Technology Managers.

Association of University Technology Managers. (1999). *AUTM Licensing Survey: Fiscal Year 1998.* Norwalk, Conn.: Association of University Technology Managers.

UNIVERSITY OF CALIFORNIA AT SAN DIEGO

The University of California-San Diego (UCSD) is both a relatively young research university and one that is nationally prominent. Founded in 1960 as part of the University of California system, UCSD reported research expenditures of $461.6 million in fiscal year 1999. This places them sixth among all U.S. universities and fifth among public universities in total research expenditures according to National Science Foundation data.[1] The institution was ranked 10th nationally by the National Research Council in the quality of its faculty, a level of perceived excellence shared by no other university established during the 20th century. Its neuroscience and oceanography programs are ranked first in the country. It has five Nobel laureates, 60 members of the National Academy of Science, and 83 endowed chairs on the faculty. In September 2000, *U.S. News & World Report* ranked UCSD seventh among public universities, and its Irwin and Joan Jacobs School of Engineering in the top 10 among public universities. The School of Engineering was also ranked 10th by the National Academy of Sciences, and the UCSD School of Medicine is ranked 23rd nationally. The latter is in the top tier of medical schools in terms research expenditures per fulltime equivalent faculty. Not surprisingly, UCSD is home to a number of prominent institutes and centers, including the Center for Wireless Communication, the Scripps Institution of Oceanography, the UCSD Cancer Center, the San Diego Supercomputer Center (SDSC), and the recently established California Institute for Telecommunications and Information Technology, which will have access to funding support of $356 million over the next four years.

The university enrolls approximately 20,000 students, and is planning to grow to 30,000 students within the next decade. UCSD is the most popular institution in the University of California system in terms of the number of undergraduate applications. The concept of a small college within a larger university undoubtedly attracts many of these applicants. Six unique undergraduate colleges are each focused around a particular theme and area of study. For the fall 2000 freshman class, the average high school GPA and SAT composite scores were 3.99 and 1259 respectively. Within five years of receiving their undergraduate degrees a commendable 60% of UCSD undergraduates have gone on to graduate study. The undergraduate program is heavily oriented toward engineering (20% of graduates) and the biological sciences (25%).

Several factors have contributed to this sparkling record of growth and accomplishment. For one, UCSD has had forceful and imaginative leaders during its history, which have always had a goal of national excellence. Second, it has been blessed with some significant faculty recruiting advantages for assembling a world-class faculty. The San Diego area is known for its climate, lifestyle, and amenities. In addition, the UCSD campus is in a beautiful setting. Many prominent researchers have come to UCSD, often to stay for decades, if not their entire career. Third, the UCSD academic culture was allowed to evolve in nontraditional directions, which in turn resulted in a healthy interdisciplinary and entrepreneurial tradition that was important in the development of many major research initiatives. Prospective faculty members are attracted to the university culture, particularly those with an itch to be entrepreneurial in either a business or an academic context. Finally, UCSD has been helped by its network of partnership relationships with the city and county of San Diego, which have had profound implications for the blossoming of the institution as well as for the establishment of San Diego as a major technology-based regional economy.

MISSION, VISION, AND GOAL STATEMENTS

It is impossible to understand the role the UCSD has played in the community without understanding the evolution of the San Diego economy over the past few decades.[2] When UCSD was established in 1960, San Diego was, in effect, a Navy town with a surfeit of tourists and retirees. To the extent that technology-based industry existed it was primarily aerospace and did contract work for the U.S. Department of Defense. For much of the next three decades San Diego's technology sector blossomed, primarily as a function of defense-related electronics, aerospace, and related industries, although there was a gradual growth in non-defense technology industry. During the same period, UCSD was focused primarily on building national research excellence in the physical and biomedical sciences.

Beginning in the 1980s the San Diego economy began to undergo more dramatic changes. There was a significant downturn in the defense work, both locally and nationally, which was at its worst between 1988 and 1992. In the early 1990s San Diego lost nearly 60,000 jobs, mostly concentrated in aerospace and manufacturing.[3] Paralleling these structural changes, in the 1980s San Diego also lost two bids to land major research and development centers, the Microelectronics and Computer Corporation and Sematech. The local post-mortem suggested that one important weakness of the San Diego bid was its poorly demonstrated ability to form coalitions across sectors and industries and to pull together as a technology community. These events served as a catalyst for examining new modes of university-industry cooperation and new approaches to economic development strategy.

The happy part of this story is that beginning in this period San Diego has been able to transform itself into an entrepreneurial, technology-based economy focused increasingly on commercial markets, and that UCSD has played an important and critical role in this process. In contrast to many world-class universities, UCSD came to see itself as very much a corporate citizen of San Diego, with an associated responsibility to build the economy and well being of the region. To a significant degree the vision that fueled these events, and the origin of the UCSD partnership mission, can be found in Richard Atkinson, who was UCSD chancellor between 1980 and 1995. He came to the university after a stint as director of the National Science Foundation, during which he took considerable credit for supporting and launching many of the Foundation's industry-oriented centers programs. The role that he played at UCSD in fostering external partnerships was both programmatic and inspirational. One of Atkinson's early initiatives was to push for the establishment of a new School of Engineering, which ultimately received significant endowing support from a San Diego-based technology entrepreneur. Atkinson also worked cooperatively with the local economic development organization to foster a greater degree of cooperation between campus researchers and industry, which resulted in the well known CONNECT program detailed later in this chapter. The initiatives and culture that Atkinson helped to launch in the '80s and '90s have been maintained and strengthened under the administration of the current UCSD chancellor, Robert Dynes. He joined the faculty as a professor of physics in 1991 after 22 years at Bell Labs, when he was named to the National Academy of Sciences. Obviously understanding the need for a healthy university-industry interface, Dynes came to UCSD and established a novel interdisciplinary research program that included a major role for industry partners. He has been a significant contributor many of the partnership initiatives that are described below, and has promoted the university's "responsibility to contribute to the quality of life and the economic health of the San Diego region" in his public comments.

Atkinson is currently president of the University of California system, and he continues to be an advocate for university-industry partnering. On March 10, 2000, in a message to the UC regents, he restated that position in a manner that is instructive for UCSD's history: [4]

> UC has had a long history of cooperating with industry to advance research, instruction, and public service. Industry and research universities have always had an intellectual partnership in the United States, especially in fields like engineering and medicine. This partnership has generated a vital give and take between science and technology, research and application. A classic example of the productive relationship between basic and applied science is the work of Louis Pasteur, who made fundamental discoveries in microbiology while trying to improve the French brewing industry. A more recent example is the radio telescope, an invention that evolved from efforts to reduce static in microwave communications.

> Cross-fertilization between academic and industrial research is what distinguishes science in the U.S. from that of most other nations and is one of the reasons that university scientific discoveries are so rapidly translated into new industries, companies, products, and services. It is also one of the reasons the U.S. is generating new companies, new jobs, new products and services that improve the lives of our citizens at a much faster pace than in the rest of the world.

This is the underlying philosophy that contributed to the establishment of many of the external partnering activities that will be described below. At a critical point in local economic history, Atkinson seized the opportunity to add new dimensions to UCSD's mission and orientation, while still building the core academic excellence of the institution, and Dynes has continued that tradition. This was no mean feat.

This spirit is reflected at the unit level as well, in both the backgrounds of individuals in leadership positions as well as in goals and mission statements. For example, the mission statement of the Jacobs School of Engineering states:

> Our mission is to educate young men and women to be industry and academic leaders, and to create new technologies that will fuel economic prosperity. Partnerships with industry are essential to both our education and research missions.

Not surprisingly, the dean of the School of Engineering has an entrepreneurial background, and the current chancellor has industry experience. This acknowledgement of the external role that UCSD plays is reportedly shared by the leadership structure throughout the institution (e.g., deans, department heads, the academic senate).

INDUSTRY RESEARCH PARTNERSHIPS

NSF data[5] show that UCSD's industry-sponsored research expenditures in FY1999 were $31.4 million, or 6.8% of total research expenditures. In 1992, they were 2.7% of total research expenditures, suggesting a fairly healthy increase. By illustration, during this 1992-99 time period, overall research expenditures increased by 64% while industry-sponsored expenditures increased by 319%. In FY 1999, the percent of industry-sponsored research was slightly below the national average of 7.4%, and ranked UCSD 46th among the top 100 U.S. universities. Nonetheless, this is a highly respectable figure given the large amount of federal funds garnered by the university. What are noteworthy, however, are the special programs that are operated to foster university-industry relationships.

For example, the CONNECT program — which is focused primarily on entrepreneurial activities (see below) — also hosts a periodic "Meet the Researchers" event. These are marketed heavily to local and regional technology-based companies and provide a venue in which UCSD professors can present their current research alongside industry researchers, many of whom are local. A series of seminars in 2001 was focused on bioengineering.

Another illustration is found in the Corporate Affiliates Program (CAP) in the Jacobs School of Engineering. With a school goal of "forging partnerships with industry in order to fuel the economy of the San Diego region and the nation," 50 companies currently are members of the affiliates program. The annual dues range from $2,500 to $25,000 depending upon a company's sales revenues. "Affiliate" status does not follow the model of more passive affiliate programs that existed at many universities during the 1980s. The UCSD version involves a much more active role for affiliate companies. For example, annual research reviews feature talks by faculty on their current work, poster sessions by graduate students, and displays by CAP member companies. A frequent outcome is a project or center-based research collaboration. Through an executive board CAP member companies also confer quarterly with the dean of the school on future research directions, the strategic mission, and various partnership issues. CAP members have preferential and facilitated access to meetings of research groups within the school, as well as one-to-one interactions with particular faculty members. To a significant degree CAP members also help define the research and educational directions of the school by their involvement in the planning of centers and other major initiatives.

The most significant industry research partnership at UCSD is the California Institute for Telecommunications and Information Technology (Cal – (IT)^2), which was launched in 2000 as one of three winners under the new state program of California Institutes for Science and Innovation. State commitments of $200 million over the next four years have already been matched by $140 million in industry support from more than 40 companies. Industry participation is expected to exceed $200 million within the foreseeable future. Cal – (IT)^2 will be a complex initiative involving more than 200 research faculty members from UCSD as well as the University of California at Irvine (UCI). The massive program will be organized in terms of five interdisciplinary "layers" (materials and devices; networking infrastructure; interfaces and software systems; and policy, management and socioeconomic evolution), while at the same time focusing on four "application drivers" (environment and civil infrastructure, intelligent transportation, digitally enabled genomic medicine, and new media arts). In each area, academic researchers will link closely with industrial partners and sponsors through a variety of innovative contexts, such as "smart environment test beds." Needless to say, the hope and expectation is that this program will firmly establish southern California and the whole state in a leadership role in this burgeoning technology area.

Technology Transfer

The Technology Transfer and Intellectual Property Service (TTIPS) of UCSD operates with an orientation that is similar to the activities described above (http://invent.ucsd.edu). Not only is the mission of TTIPS to "facilitate the transfer of UCSD technologies," and "enhance the research experience of UCSD researchers through technology transfer," but it also strives to "promote and target economic development by leveraging University technologies." One could paraphrase this as "do well for the university and its researchers, but also do right by the regional economy." Not surprisingly, UCSD has a relatively long-standing commitment to maintain an active, professionally staffed technology transfer office, which is sensitive to both its internal and external constituencies.

Its overall level of performance reflects this commitment, as can be seen from its most recent fiscal year of technology transfer statistics.[6] In FY 2000, the office realized 485 agreements and 48 licenses, received more than $9 million in income, and brought in $5.75 million in associated research support. An important part of the UCSD technology transfer story, however, is the office's willingness to accommodate entrepreneurial routes to commercialization, as well as to maintain a regional orientation toward licensing. Many licensees are in the San Diego/Orange County/Los Angeles region, and UCSD claims to have spun off 150 San Diego companies, including 63 in the biomedical industry. Using somewhat different criteria (startups that are significantly based on UCSD technology), TTIPS claims 12 startup deals in 1999 and 2000 combined. In the TTIPS newsletter, which is circulated extensively on campus and externally, a section is typically devoted to technology transfer and entrepreneurship, where licensing deals involving new or small companies are described.

To facilitate this entrepreneurial orientation, TTIPS has a director and staff that are familiar with the problems confronting technology start-ups. They also have developed and promulgated clear guidelines and procedures for faculty members with an inclination in this direction and have collaborated with CONNECT (see the next section) to broker entrepreneurial development services, funding, and the like. All of this is embedded in an office that does very well indeed in terms of traditional patenting and licensing activities. It is worth noting that TTIPS claims to be "mission driven rather than policy driven." That is, its core policies are virtually identical to those at all of the University of California. However, TTIPS at UCSD avows that "establishing a new biotech telecommunications industry is more important than $20 million in royalties and fees." To this end, policies are managed and interpreted so as to expedite the commercialization process, conflict of interest issues are managed promptly and at a high level of authority, and a variety of "virtual incubation services" are provided to faculty. To formalize this orientation, the TTIPS has established a License and Entrepreneur Assistance Program (LEAP) that helps small companies in the community as well as entrepreneurial faculty researchers access and commercialize UCSD technology. LEAP brokers a range of services that are essential for the technology-based start-up (i.e., legal, technology valuation, business planning, interim management). Local business service companies provide many of these gratis, or in anticipation of future revenues.

Entrepreneurial Development

San Diego County is a major center for entrepreneurial activity. In 2000 it ranked first in the state for Small Business Innovation Research Program grant funding and garnered $1.2 billion in private venture funding.[7] UCSD has been a significant and effective player in entrepreneurial development in the San Diego area, primarily through it CONNECT program. CONNECT was established in 1985, with administrative facilitation by then-Chancellor Atkinson, primarily as an economic development organization focused on technology-based entrepreneurship. It has a paid staff equivalent to 15 full-time employees and a large cadre of volunteers that donate time. While a program of UCSD, it receives no university funding, and secures its income from membership dues, event fees, and grants. Memberships are structured into sponsors ($3,000 to $25,000 per year, mostly major business service providers), company members ($100 to $2,500 per year, depending on size), and event sponsors (corporation or other entities that will provide major support for a conference or meeting). Nearly 1,000 companies participate in one or more class of membership. CONNECT sees itself as an "incubator without walls" that brokers access to the resources needed by new companies, and business opportunities and technologies for participating business service providers. In some cases, the resources being brokered derive from university research and development, but in most cases they do not. Annually, there are 50 to 60 events that serve groups ranging from a few dozen to more than a thousand.

One of its services includes providing various short courses for new companies or would-be entrepreneurs. Some are repeated annually or even more frequently. For example, Starting and Financing Technology Companies is offered twice a year, is taught by a successful technology entrepreneur, and draws a healthy audience of scientists and engineers in the early "thinking about" stage of starting a company. The courses are frequently coupled with various conferences that are in turn organized around themes of interest to local technology entrepreneurs. Recent events included Cal Bio Summit 2000 and Emerging Markets in Telecommunications.

Another example, Springboard, is oriented toward early stage entrepreneurs and selected companies. Participants receive four to eight weeks of coaching in business plan development by experiences technology executives. Then participants prepare a formal presentation to a feedback panel, typically consisting of an investor, an industry executive, an accountant, a lawyer, and one or more other business service professionals. Springboard has helped more than 150 companies raise more than $200 million in capital. Variations on the Springboard program now include a thrust focused on telecommunications start-ups as well as a "graduate" event for telecommunication companies that have received at least one round of investment.

A natural complement to Springboard is the Technology Financial Forum. This is held annually, and is oriented toward young companies that have already received some seed investment. During the forum entrepreneurs have an opportunity to present their current business plans to venture capitalists and other investors. As a precursor to the actual forum event, they receive extensive coaching and mentoring from business experts.

Events are often jointly organized with local industry associations, such as the San Diego Telecom Council. For example, CONNECT also hosts an annual Biotechnology Corporate Partnership Forum. The provides a venue for San Diego biotech companies to introduce their technologies to pharmaceutical companies, venture capitalists, and larger biotech and biomedical companies. Last year this was part of the CALBIOsummit co-sponsored with Biocom.

CONNECT also serves as a facilitator of several ongoing networking activities oriented toward the local community. These include Biotech Business Development CONNECT, which involves biotech business executives in periodic events and activities; Athena, a network of women technology executives; and HR CONNECT, an association of human resource executives from local technology companies.

In addition to community-oriented activities, CONNECT also provides or brokers assistance to UCSD technology transfer activities that involve start-ups. CONNECT's role lies in fostering linkages to business service providers, capital, or other "virtual incubation" activities, and these are performed on a case-by-case, as-needed basis. There is no formal administrative linkage between CONNECT and the UCSD technology transfer program, however.

CONNECT is also linked to various entrepreneurial programs in academic units on campus. For example, the School of Engineering has launched a Technology Management and Entrepreneurism Program with three major components: (1) an entrepreneurism curriculum for engineering students; (2) campus-wide educational events to inform students about entrepreneurism; and (3) a technology incubator housed in the Jacobs School. CONNECT has been significantly involved in the planning of these initiatives. Recently, CONNECT and the School of Engineering agreed to co-fund and staff a position that would be located in the school and be dedicated to fostering entrepreneurial activities involving engineering faculty. Under the rubric of "translational medicine," CONNECT and the School of Medicine have launched a venture fund to support faculty who are developing interventions that have commercial potential.

INDUSTRY EDUCATION AND TRAINING PARTNERSHIPS

While not focused exclusively on industry, UCSD provides a rich menu of educational and training offerings through its extension program, which annually serves 35,000 adult students. Courses are taught on the main campus, as well as at a permanent North County Center, another site at Sorrento Mesa next to QUALCOMM, and at several more ad hoc locations throughout San Diego County. Some programs are offered at corporate sites on a contract basis. Content ranges from traditional academic courses to cultural samplings and the latest in knowledge economy topics. Each quarter about 450 classes are offered, many of which are bundled into one of more than 100 certificate programs (e.g. e-commerce; drug discovery and development). Approximately two-thirds of participating students work in high-tech industries, and about half of these are subsidized by their employer. These programs are not traditional degree offerings but post-baccalaureate continuing and professional education.

FORMAL PARTNERSHIPS WITH ECONOMIC DEVELOPMENT ORGANIZATIONS

As described above, the CONNECT program of UCSD is in itself an economic development organization, with a host of partnership relations with San Diego-based organizations involved in business development. In addition, UCSD has been the lead organization for San Diego Dialogue, a regional consortium of 150 individuals representing organizations on both sides of the San Diego-Tijuana border. The dialogue fosters public policy analysis and discussion on how this international region can thrive in the global economy. It examines issues such as regional integration and cooperation, school reform, and global linkages. The dialogue identifies specific issues, and reports and analysis may be commissioned. A mix of corporate and foundation contributions, as well as revenues from events, support the work of the dialogue. To illustrate the continuity of UCSD's orientation toward community partnering, a former UCSD chancellor, Will J. McGill, played a key role in the founding of the dialogue in 1991 and the involvement of UCSD leadership has been strong ever since. The San Diego Dialogue staff operates as a unit within UCSD Extension (as does CONNECT).

CAREER SERVICES AND PLACEMENT

The many ties that have been established between UCSD and the San Diego have paid off handsomely in terms of the movement of graduates into the area workforce. Since its inception, UCSD has graduated 80,000 students, and more than half of them are currently working in the San Diego job market. Many of these graduates end up working for companies in the San Diego high-technology economy. For example, by the university's statistics, "… 40% of the people who work in the San Diego biotech/biomed industry work for UCSD spin-offs."[8] Given the rigorous entry standards and the high quality of admissions noted above, it is clear that the university is brokering a highly positive balance of trade in human resources for the region.

FACULTY CULTURE AND REWARDS

At first glance, the organizational culture and informal rewards of UCSD seem very focused on traditional scholarship and cutting-edge science. In fact, there is no administrative structure to coordinate or manage the activities described in this chapter as a coherent whole. However, in a parallel and less formally, there is pervasive cultural support for external partnerships, entrepreneurial activities, and involvement in regional economic development. The mission and vision language of units reflects this duality, saying in various ways: We will be world class, but we are also a part of and contributor to a regional economy. On the opening page of the "Who we are" page of its Web site, UCSD lays claim to a "tradition of innovation and risk-taking," which is expressed in research and educational excellence as well as economic impact.

While oriented more toward the external San Diego community, CONNECT is also involved in symbolic, culture reinforcing events. These include an annual award event in which faculty members' various innovative accomplishments in product development are acknowledged. These are organized by industry category (e.g., electronics, general business, Internet/software, and life sciences), although there is also an award for "a product that transcends all categories in its ability to transform our region." These awards are presented at a luncheon that is highly publicized and well attended, and the recipients encompass a wide range of companies in terms of size and stage of development.

Much of the prevailing culture of UCSD follows from the leadership of recent chancellors, who have legitimized entrepreneurial activities and industry partnerships. A significant number of early successes have reinforced this direction, which in turn has attracted faculty who are so oriented. In effect, the culture is well established and mutually reinforcing. The culture of the university also reflects organizational development strategies that were selected early in the game. That is, build on strengths and hire "name" people, invest heavily in a relatively few areas of science instead of trying to be all things to all people, and open the university to external partnerships with industry and the community.

ENDNOTES

[1] National Science Foundation Division of Science Resource Studies. (2001). *Academic research and development expenditures, FY 1999*. Washington, D.C.: National Science Foundation. Table B-33.

[2] For an excellent overview see: Palmintera, D., Bannon, J., Levin, M., and Pagan, A. (2000). *Developing High-Technology Communities: San Diego*. Produced under contract to Office of Advocacy, U.S. Small Business Administration by Innovation Associates Inc., Reston, Va.

[3] Palmintera et al, *op. cit.*

[4] Available online at http://www.ucop.edu/ucophome/pres/comments/industry.htm.

[5] National Science Foundation. Division of Science Resource Studies. *Op. cit.* Tables B-33, B-36, B-38.

[6] These are based on UCSD data as opposed to the University of California system-wide statistics that are reported to the Association of University Technology Managers, and summarized in other chapters in this book.

[7] Walshok, M. L. and Lee, C. W. (2001). *Innovation Metrics: How to Measure a Region's Success*. Presentation to the UCSD Division of Extended Studies and Public Programs.

[8] http://www.er.ucsd.edu/who/index.htm.

UNIVERSITY OF UTAH

Recently celebrating its Sesquicentennial year, the University of Utah has evolved into a distinguished research university, the flagship of the Utah system of higher education. Located on a 1,494-acre campus in Salt Lake City, total enrollment was 26,182 in the 2001 academic year, with students coming from every Utah county, every state in the nation, and 102 foreign countries. The institution is organized into 16 colleges, served by 3,404 faculty members and 10,940 staff. The University of Utah offers 75 undergraduate programs, more than 50 teaching majors and minors, and 96 graduate majors.

The university has a long tradition of service and outreach to the state and the mountain region. As stated by President J. Bernard Machen:

> *But we choose to measure our success at this 150-year juncture in terms of the service we provide to all the people of Utah. There is not a single citizen in the state – and most surrounding states – whose life is not better because the University of Utah is here.*

In the National Science Foundation (NSF) survey of academic research and development,[1] Utah reported total research expenditures of $153.8 million in fiscal year 1999, which ranks 60th among all U.S. universities and 41st among public institutions. A large fraction of the research program is organized and delivered through more than 40 centers and institutes, and over half of university research involves the College of Medicine. Eleven of the existing centers are state-supported centers of excellence, which are explicitly designed to maximize industry partnering and technology commercialization. Based on recent internal data from FY 2000, research awards totaled $237 million, of which industrial support accounted for more than 14%.

INDUSTRY RESEARCH PARTNERSHIPS

According to NSF data[2] the University of Utah's industry-sponsored research expenditures in 1999 were $8.9 million, or 5.8% of total research expenditures, compared to the national average of 7.4%. In 1992, the comparable figure was 3.8% of total research expenditures. Between 1992 and 1999, overall expenditures increased by 42% while industry-sponsored expenditures increased by 117%. For FY 1999, Utah ranked 53rd among the top 100 U.S. universities in the percent of industry-sponsored research expenditures.

In assessing the University of Utah's strengths in industry partnering the geographic and economic context of the state must be taken into account. Utah is a typical western mountain state, large in area and small in population. With slightly more than two million residents statewide, and about half of those located in Salt Lake City, Utah has not historically been a national center for industry or finance. Nonetheless, as indicated above, the university has rapidly increased industry research partnerships and has been in the vanguard of a burgeoning Utah technology economy. However, because of the economic geography of the state, much of its industry-sponsored research involving larger companies has been with out of state businesses. In contrast, the university has been quite successful with new or small technology companies based in Utah, many of which represent spin-offs from its own research. In 1997 *U.S. News & World Report* ranked Salt Lake City sixth in the world on an indicator of new technology development, and since then it is frequently on various rankings of technology-oriented metropolitan areas.

To facilitate various partnerships with industry, the university has established a robust and customer-friendly set of policies and procedures coupled with an enabling organizational culture. As an example, the College of Mines and Earth Sciences operates an industrial liaison program in which a company-specific liaison manager works to ensure that the appropriate resources and services are brought to bear upon company needs. Services might include seminars and conferences, consulting with individual faculty, and various collaborative research relationships.

A useful conduit for university-industry relationships has been the 320-acre University Research Park, which was established in 1968. The University of Utah Research Foundation, a corporate subsidiary of the university, operates the park. There are 34 buildings, with 44 resident companies employing 6,100 people and contributing $600 million to the state's economy. Components of 37 university departments are also housed in the park, and not surprisingly, many park-based companies open their facilities for research and educational access to academic departments, use student interns, and interact with on-campus organizations in a variety of informal ways. More than 80% of companies in the park use faculty members for consultants, 60% participate in research proposals with the university and 85% use either faculty or students in research projects. Approximately 40 of the companies represent start-ups with University of Utah lineage. The university is very open and proud of its relationship with these companies.

The Colleges of Engineering, Mines and Earth Sciences, and Pharmacy strongly encourage and support industry interaction and involvement through industry affiliates programs. These are membership-based programs that recruit industries into a technology-based consortium or partnership. A basic membership fee is set and the benefits for that fee may include early announcements of research progress, first options for licensing technologies, a set number of consulting hours from faculty and a seat on the board of directors for the affiliates program. Generally, the industry members are invited to two meetings annually to discuss current research. The University of Utah currently supports six such programs.

The Utah Engineering Experiment Station also has a Web site (www.utah.edu/eees/) to notify its client companies of collaborative research opportunities. Assistance in this area includes organizing industry and academic partnerships, developing sources of industrial research support, and preparing proposals to obtain federal funds to match industrial research dollars.

TECHNOLOGY TRANSFER

License income was $3.26 million in FY 1999, a royalty ROI (royalties divided by total research expenditures) of 2.19%. License income ranks in the 76th percentile, and royalty ROI ranks in the 79th percentile of the 142 academic institutions that participated in the *AUTM Licensing Survey: FY 1999*.[3]

In fiscal years 1998 and 1999 combined, Utah reported a total of 35 new licenses to start-ups, placing it in the 93rd percentile in the total AUTM licensing survey population for this measure. Looking at new start-ups formed, Utah reported a total of 13, all of which were located in the state. Utah ranks in the 96th percentile for total start-ups formed and in the 97th percentile for in-state start-ups formed.

The University of Utah technology transfer office has a reputation of being one of the most outstanding in the country. Based on AUTM data[4] from its 1998 survey, the institution ranked in the first (top) quartile of performance on invention disclosures per $10 million of research, in patent applications per $10 million, in patents per $10 million, in licenses per $10 million of research, and in the rate of start-up companies based on university technologies. More recently, *Technology Access Report* has ranked the office second in the country on the basis of a six-factor performance measure.[5] The six factors are start-ups, licenses executed, new patent applications, research funding related to a license, industrial research, and gross license income.

Additionally, a recent internal study[6] documented the size and geographic focus of pre-production induced investment in licensed technologies arising at the University of Utah. A survey of the university's portfolio of 114 active, exclusive licenses revealed that $137.4 million has been invested in bringing these technologies to market, and that 293 jobs are created and maintained each year. Start-up companies create 75% of this investment. This figure represents only pre-production investment, not the additional investments made in the production and sale of licensed products. Furthermore, $109 million of the $137.4 million in induced investment flowed into the state of Utah, creating and maintaining 271 jobs a year in the state. This translates into the state receiving 77% of the total investment and 92% of the total jobs. Finally, the study demonstrated that $48.4 million is invested in the state of Utah for every $1 million the university receives in revenue from a license.

Other data demonstrates how prolific the University of Utah is in the technology transfer arena. The number of disclosures to the office has increased steadily over the years, reaching 181 in FY 2000. The University filed 144 patents and had 37 patents issue in FY 2000. The number of licensing agreements rose from 25 in FY 1999 to 39 in FY 2000, and licensing income reached a new high of $4.55 million.

About six new start-ups based on University of Utah technology are founded each year. These start-ups invest over $25 million annually in the development of new products. Nationally recognized companies such as Evans & Sutherland, Sarcos, ARUP Laboratories, Idaho Technology, Iomed, Myriad Genetics, Anesta, and Theratec all were start-up companies located in the University Research Park.

Three of these companies are of special note because of their active involvement with the University of Utah. Myriad Genetics is a genomics company focused on the identification of genes that cause common diseases. Myriad, in addition to licensing technology from the university, also sponsors in excess of $1.5 million in research at the University of Utah. Sarcos has developed multiple products including integrated silicon-based microsystems, programmable drug delivery microsystems, interactive telecommunication systems, and tele-robots. The founder of this company still remains a faculty member at the university. Idaho Technology is a faculty-student venture. The team created a rugged, portable lab that can be used by soldiers in the field to identify biological weapons such as anthrax. The device is only the size of a hefty suitcase but can identify deadly DNA in minutes. The company is moving beyond its first client, the United States Air Force, to the larger market of the food processing industry. Here the challenge will be to identify bacteria such as E. coli and salmonella.

A variety of policies and practices enable technology transfer to thrive. For example, the university is actively involved in bridging the gap between faculty inventions and companies looking for new technologies. The university's Web site (www.tto.utah.edu/welcome.htm) provides researchers with information and funding sources for commercializing their technologies. Additionally, it provides an array of downloadable forms to make the process easier. The Web site also provides a detailed listing for companies of technologies the university has available for licensing. These listings include hyperlinks to published papers, patents, and Web sites explaining the faculty's research interests. Companies can also electronically submit a technology questionnaire, in which they specify technical areas of interest. The university then keeps them abreast of inventions in those areas.

Faculty, as well, are enabled through fairly flexible policies and practices. The university has a generous royalty sharing policy to encourage faculty to formally disclose intellectual property. Faculty can simultaneously hold equity in a company and be a full-fledged member of their academic unit, although conflict-of-interest disclosures are expected. Moreover, companies owned by faculty can contract with the university for research projects, including the participation of the faculty member and his/her laboratory. Again, oversight and management of these relationships is required.

The University of Utah Research Foundation (UURF) also funds both a small intramural seed grant program and a Technology Innovation Program. The intramural seed grant program supports projects that might lead to the commercialization of a faculty invention, either via a start-up or a license to an existing company. The Technology Innovation Program provides up to two years and $70,000 of funding to faculty members for the purpose of commercializing university inventions. Faculty members are required to get matching funds, and consultants are hired to help the faculty members find potential licensees. The goal of this program is to help the commercial development of promising technologies at the university and to find a licensee to further commercialize the technology within two years.

As a recent enhancement of its technology commercialization efforts, the University of Utah has become a founding member of the T2M (technology-to-market) organization that networks entrepreneurs with venture capitalists, bankers, technology industry executives, and business service providers, mostly in the West. Entrepreneurs can participate in evaluation and mentoring services, and a variety of seminars, meetings, and networking events are offered to member. The T2M focus is on developing a community of informed entrepreneurs and managers who can develop new technologies and accelerate their time to commercialization. Equally important, T2M provides a platform and educational workshops to assist in developing a stable core of managers who can help the new company to thrive and expand, and to stay in the Salt Lake region.

INDUSTRIAL EXTENSION/TECHNICAL ASSISTANCE

One element of the University of Utah that focuses on industrial extension and technical assistance is the Utah Engineering Experiment Station. The mission of the Utah Engineering Experiment Station (UEES), as defined by the state legislature, is to serve as a technological bridge between the University of Utah and private and public sector organizations in the state. To accomplish this goal, the UEES facilitates the exchange of ideas and acts as a forum to advise university faculty of private and public-sector needs. The UEES, which promotes university problem-solving resources for Utah's industries, reports to the dean of the College of Mines and Earth Sciences, and, thus, the UEES outreach program has focused on the mining and mineral-processing industries. Utah does not have the same type of manufacturing industries, such as metal fabrication, as do states with more mature manufacturing sectors.

The UEES recently received a grant from the U.S. Department of Energy to support its efforts relating to mining, metals, and mineral processing industries. The objectives of this grant were to improve the energy efficiency, pollution prevention, and productivity of Utah's mining, metals, and processing industries. The UEES also works closely with the federally funded Manufacturing Extension Partnership, which supports small and medium-sized manufacturing companies.

Another important program in the UEES is the Industrial Liaison Program (ILP). The object of the ILP is to facilitate industrial extension and technical assistance to target industries. The ILP helps promote the exchange of ideas and increase faculty members' awareness of private and public sector needs and issues. It also assists in providing industry-relevant workshops and conferences, facilitating industry-supported collaborative research, and enhancing problem-solving efforts by university faculty members.

One key element of the ILP is the institution of a company-specific liaison manager, who informs the company about relevant university resources and programs. The liaison manager facilitates the use of these resources by focusing on the specific needs and issues of the individual company. The liaison manager is also made aware of the broader industry vision and direction as defined by relevant industrial and professional organizations, and is closely supported by the UEES staff. Services offered by the ILP include seminars, conferences, and smaller focused technical meetings.

ENTREPRENEURIAL DEVELOPMENT

Along with its focus on technology transfer, the university strongly supports the creation of start-ups based on university-developed technologies. This entrepreneurial orientation is fostered in several ways. For example, the state-sponsored Centers of Excellence Program (COEP), while not focused exclusively on the University of Utah, has been a major programmatic asset. COEP funds later stage research in order to mature innovative technologies that might be commercialized via new products and new companies. Established in 1986, the projects are conducted by university faculty, with substantive and financial participation by private sector partners. Each center is organized around a domain of technology, and during the 1998-99 fiscal year $1.98 million was distributed through the 16 active centers (11 at the University of Utah). State investments were matched by $11.77 million in private sector and other support. Since the inception of the program, more than $30 million in state funds has leveraged $332.7 million in matching support. More importantly, since the inception of the program, the centers have contributed to the creation of 2,155 jobs, 123 spin-off companies, 96 patents, 161 licenses, and nearly 900 companies receiving technical assistance. In a typical year, the 11 centers directly affiliated with the University of Utah typically produce five-to-six new companies and a similar number of patents, and deliver assistance to well over 100 companies. The only major obstacle to an even greater degree of technology-based entrepreneurial activity is a relatively small local venture capital industry.

The university also had some early culture-developing experiences in a programmatic sense. During the early 1980s, the National Science Foundation supported the Utah Innovation Center, headed by Wayne Brown. This was an early experimental precursor to the technology business incubators that are now found in many university communities.

Entrepreneurial development is also encouraged in the instructional programs of the institution. For example, the College of Business has recently launched a Technology Management Program, in which entrepreneurship is an important component. An Undergraduate Research Opportunities Program (UROP) involves students in real research projects with faculty, and many of these also involve collaboration with technology businesses in either the Research Park or the Salt Lake area.

Industry Education and Training Partnerships

The University of Utah has numerous programs that enhance the undergraduate and graduate experience and promote interaction with industry and economic development of the region. The Executive MBA program brings to campus the leaders and future leaders in industry and business around the region. One focus within the program is an emphasis upon building networks and expertise in starting and building new companies. Also, set within the David Eccles School of Business is the Utah Technology Entrepreneur Center.

The College of Engineering also fosters interaction through an Industry Graduate Fellows program in Engineering and an Undergraduate Clinic Program. The Industry Graduate Fellows Program offers industry an opportunity to support a graduate student for $25,000 annually. The funds are used to develop a project of interest to, but not directed by, the industry sponsor. The Undergraduate Clinic Program supports projects carried out by the students. The student selects the projects but the industry sponsors are invited to participate in project reviews and to provide assistance, as needed, to the student.

Career Services and Placement

The university has the usual array of placement services and activities, but some units have adapted their placement activities to reflect the heavy entrepreneurial orientation of the institution. For example, the College of Business has a program for undergraduate students that places them in start-up companies, generally in the Salt Lake City area. The students get an opportunity to participate in early-stage business planning and development and rub shoulders with scientist and engineers developing cutting-edge technology products.

Because the culture at the University of Utah promotes individual entrepreneurial activity among faculty, this value is passed along to graduate and undergraduate students. Students in many fields are immersed in research specifically directed towards product development with a start-up company in the region. Students get hands-on experience with technology commercialization by associating with faculty start-ups, most of which are located in the University Research Park. Because of the tremendous experience and intellectual stimulation provided to the students involved in start-up companies, the university has made the decision to support these activities. The university is very cognizant of the potential for conflict of interest and by policy requires close monitoring of these relationships.

Another avenue for student involvement in entrepreneurship is the newly evolving Utah Entrepreneur Center (Utec), a unit within the David Eccles School of Business. There are three focus areas within Utec. The first area is curriculum, including a speaker series. In its first year, more than 150 students enrolled in the entrepreneur classes. Already underway is the creation of a new undergraduate major and a specialty track in the MBA program. Secondly, Utec is coordinating the Utah Entrepreneur challenge. The Challenge is a student business plan writing competition. Over 200 student groups have entered the competition and over 100 have submitted executive summaries. The award is $70,000 cash. In addition, the center has aggressively pursued involvement with community and campus including an Inventions to Commercialization conference, T2M, and the Governor's Silicon Valley Alliance.

FORMAL PARTNERSHIPS WITH ECONOMIC DEVELOPMENT ORGANIZATIONS

As the flagship university in a small state, the University of Utah is an active and frequent partner with the state's Economic Development Corporation, which is the agency charged with business development, recruitment, and technology-oriented initiatives. The university also actively participates in the Utah Partnership, a consortium of businesses and institutions of higher education, which facilitates and promotes government-industry-university initiatives.

However, as noted earlier, the primary vehicle of economic impact for the university has been through its orientation and activities in entrepreneurship. This orientation builds from a cadre of excellent faculty, which in turn has developed a critical mass of commercializable technologies, and is recognized and encouraged by political support and legislative mandates.

INDUSTRY/UNIVERSITY ADVISORY BOARDS AND COUNCILS

The university has dozens of formal industrial advisory boards that serve a variety of roles. Commonly these are associated with formally organized research units (e.g., centers or institutes) where industrial board members are drawn from the appropriate industry sector. In some cases, board members as representatives of specific corporations, pay an annual fee for the privilege of a board position. In most cases, boards are purely advisory to the research and educational missions of the unit. In a few instances, the board/council is advisory to an academic unit (e.g., the College of Science).

FACULTY CULTURE AND REWARDS

The University of Utah's cultural support of its entrepreneurial outreach mission is of relatively long standing. During the 1980s, the then-president coined the term "academic capitalism" and sent a letter to faculty encouraging them to pursue active relationships with business and industry, particularly in areas that would have an impact on state economic development. This long-stated goal has manifested itself in a variety of practices and policies at institutional and unit levels. For example, the College of Engineering confers an annual patent award for the best patent issued to someone in the College. However, much of the institutional culture and formal and informal reward systems are focused on the entrepreneurial successes of the university.

For example, there were early major successes in the establishment of entrepreneurial technology companies that are part of the culture and folklore of the university. Out of Evans and Sutherland, a University of Utah spin-off company, a lineage extends to the following: Netscape, Novell, WordPerfect, Silicon Graphics, and Adobe. All were founded or co-founded by alumni or former faculty of the University of Utah. Clearly this history has contributed to the growth of a positive entrepreneurial culture in Salt Lake and within the university community.

One more formal way in which the university champions entrepreneurial activities is through its Web site, where one will find a listing of companies that are based on University of Utah technology and/or are Utah-based (http://www.tto.utah.edu/companies.lic_link.htm). The list also has links to the home pages of those companies. In another section of the Web site there is text titled "Research and Enterprise: The University and New Industry," which presents in concise summary form many of the activities described in this chapter and argues for the importance of university involvement therein (www.research.utah.edu/enterprise/index.html).

The university promotes individual entrepreneurship through flexible policies, intramural grant support and a regional and campus culture. The "Utah culture" encourages individuals to transfer bench scale research to the private sector, particularly in the form of new start-up companies. In some departments, faculty inventorship is lauded and rewarded, though this is not consistent among all colleges on campus. While many institutions have taken a centralized approach to economic development by establishing programs specifically targeted to enhancing local development, for the past 30 years the University of Utah has actively encouraged and supported entrepreneurship among its faculty as its primary contribution to economic development. The university works in close partnership with local organizations and agencies such as the state Department of Community and Economic Development, the Wayne Brown Institute, and the Technology to Market (T2M) program.

ENDNOTES

[1] National Science Foundation Division of Science Resource Studies. (2001). *Academic research and development expenditures, FY 1999.* Washington, D.C.: National Science Foundation. Table B-33.

[2] National Science Foundation. Division of Science Resource Studies. *Op. cit.* Tables B-33, B-36, B-38.

[3] Association of University Technology Managers. (2000). *AUTM Licensing Survey: FY 1999.* Chicago, Ill.: Association of University Technology Managers.
Association of University Technology Managers. (1999). *AUTM Licensing Survey: Fiscal Year 1998.* Norwalk, Conn.: Association of University Technology Managers.

[4] These are based on an STC re-analysis of the most recent national data (*AUTM Licensing Survey: Fiscal Year 1998. Survey Summary.* Association of University Technology Managers Inc., 1999)

[5] Odza, M. (1998). Technology Access's Six-Factor Tech Transfer Rankings. *Technology Access Report* (May, 1998, pp.7-11).

[6] Jansen, C., and Jamison, D. (1999). *Technology Transfer and Economic Growth— A University of Utah Case Study.* Salt Lake City, Utah: The University of Utah.

CARNEGIE MELLON UNIVERSITY

Carnegie Mellon University (CMU) is a small private university of 7,500 students and 3,000 faculty and staff located in Pittsburgh, Pennsylvania. Founded in 1900 as Carnegie Technical Schools by industrialist and philanthropist Andrew Carnegie, it was initially designed as a vocational training school for the sons and daughters of working-class Pittsburghers. While CMU is now considered one of the nation's premier research universities, it has maintained a pragmatic orientation that is consistent with its modest roots.

Although CMU is now primarily known as a technical university, its research roots can be traced back to the social sciences, involving pioneering work on job placement rating scales carried out by its Division of Applied Psychology in 1916. In addition, it offered the nation's first degree in drama in 1916. The size and reputation of its research programs grew gradually under the leadership of a series of talented presidents including Thomas Baker (1920s and '30s), Robert Doherty (1940s), and John C. Warner in the (1950s). The growth of CMU's research infrastructure accelerated in the mid-1960s when CMU was formed by the merger of Carnegie Institute of Technology (the name adopted in 1912) and Mellon Institute, increasing its endowment and adding world-class facilities and research personnel. Significant growth was also experienced between 1972 and 1990 when CMU's research program leaped from $12 million to $110 million under the leadership of Richard Cyert. In spite of its small size, CMU reported research expenditures of $142.2 million in fiscal year 1999, and ranks 67th among all U.S. universities and 21st among private universities in total research expenditures in the FY 1999 survey of academic research and development expenditures of the National Science Foundation (NSF).[1]

CMU has a well-deserved reputation for innovation and a pragmatic approach to education. The Carnegie Plan for Professional Education, which required engineering majors to take a quarter of their courses in humanities and social relations and emphasized problem-solving skills, was developed in the 1940s and was eventually adopted by virtually all engineering programs at universities around the country. Other educational innovations to which it can lay claim include the mini-seminar format of executive education and the use of the "management game." Both have become standard practice in management programs in the United States and abroad.

CMU is made up of seven colleges and schools: Carnegie Institute of Technology (Engineering), College of Fine Arts, College of Humanities and Social Sciences, Mellon College of Science, the Graduate School of Industrial Administration, School of Computer Science, and the H. John Heinz III School of Public Policy and Management. A variety of national rankings attest to the quality of its programs. CMU was ranked 23rd among undergraduate institutions by *U.S. News & World Report* in 2000 and 2001. Nationally ranked departments or programs include: computer engineering (first); business (second); computer science (third), and public affairs (seventh).

CMU is located the Oakland section of Pittsburgh. Pittsburgh and surrounding Allegheny County have a population of about 1.3 million. The six-county western Pennsylvania region has about 2.4 million people. As with many of the so-called "rust belt" regions, the Pittsburgh metropolitan area has faced a variety of economic challenges over the past several decades as traditional manufacturing industries were forced to downsize or sometimes close down because of increased foreign competition, outmoded production facilities and other factors. In fact, the Pittsburgh metropolitan area was the only one among the country's top 30 to lose population in the last decade, declining 1.5 percent. Population has grown slightly over the past few years, although at a slower pace than comparable metropolitan areas.[2]

However, high technology activity has been one of the bright spots for the region. Major technology clusters in the region include: information technology, biomedical and biotechnology, and advanced manufacturing. According to statistics compiled by the Pittsburgh Technology Council, technology workers have grown by 12% between 1996 and 1998. In addition, venture capital investment in the region reached $57 million in 1998 an increase of 439% since 1995. Pittsburgh's major research universities, in particular CMU, have been major contributors to the region's strong technology-based economic growth.

Since most of our exemplary institutions are very large public universities, one might be tempted to conclude that smaller institutions can have only a limited role in technology-based economic development. However, the experience of CMU and greater Pittsburgh suggests that this need not be the case. While CMU does not have great size or even a huge endowment, its commitment to excellence in a variety of technical and scientific areas, supportive culture, and enhanced commitment to local economic development have allowed it to become a major regional asset.

Mission, Vision and Goal Statements

While some private universities have a tradition of remaining aloof from outside interests and the local community, CMU's historic roots, both as a technical institution and as an institution established to meet the educational needs of a blue collar population, have fostered a tradition of engagement. CMU's unique spin on what it means to be engaged can be seen in its current vision, mission and values statements.

Its vision statement says:

... will be a leader among educational institutions by building on its traditions of innovation, problem solving and interdisciplinary collaboration to meet the changing needs of society.

Its mission statement says:

...to transfer intellectual products to society

The same statement says this about its values and traditions:

Responsibility to Society:
We serve society through transfer of technology, continuing education programs, public service and enrichment of the community through arts.

These statements not only signal the centrality of technology transfer to CMU's engagement with the outside world but also highlight the importance of certain values including innovation, problem solving, and interdisciplinary collaboration to achieving this goal.

Another public and official manifestation of CMU's engagement can be seen in its current strategic plan. Regional impact is one of three areas of focus highlighted by the plan.[3] The regional impact component of the plan acknowledges the symbiotic relationship that exists between CMU and the region and asserts the university's intention to address local and regional issues. Sample language includes:

Our ability to attract and retain the best faculty, staff and students is dependent on the educational, economic, cultural and social vitality of our regional community.

[CMU will] use our strengths, in collaboration with other Pittsburgh institutions, to advance the educational, economic, social and cultural opportunities of the region for all its citizens.

Strategies proposed to address these goals include (1) expand its technology commercialization efforts, (2) use research and inquiry to directly address regional problems and (3) provide regional policy leadership and strategic planning. In order to ensure follow-through in these areas, CMU President Cohon has appointed Don Smith, director of the Center for Economic Development, to the position of special assistant to the president for economic development.[4] In this capacity, Smith chairs the university's Economic Development Council.[5] The council meets at least quarterly to share information, respond to opportunities, and advise the president and provost.

While there is no denying the importance of official mission statements and changes in its organizational chart, many CMU officials preferred to talk about the focus on engagement as an integral part of CMU's culture. A great deal of the credit for establishing and reinforcing that culture can be attributed to the vision and leadership of two men: former President Richard Cyert and Professor Herbert Simon.

Cyert, president from 1972-90, was one the first university CEOs to truly embrace a business model for running a university. He was a pioneer in the use of strategic planning and, because of CMU's small size, stressed the importance of achieving a "comparative advantage," a focus on excellence in certain fields so that CMU could outdistance its "competitors."[6] Although CMU's historical strengths as a pragmatically oriented technical institution helped dictate some of its focus, the specific choices made by Cyert and his colleagues and successors were nonetheless visionary. Early and significant entry into emerging fields like robotics and software engineering, encouragement of entrepreneurial activities and, later on, development of "Andrew," one of the nation's first campus-wide computer networks, were by-products of this approach. The payoffs from these investments are easy to see: CMU's robotics and computer/software programs are ranked among the best in the country and are vehicles for intensive interaction with industry. In 2000 and 2001, *Yahoo!* magazine ranked CMU as the most wired university in the nation.

Dr. Herbert Simon also had a profound and lasting impact on CMU's culture. Simon was an intellectual giant whose interests and curiosity about human decision-making and problem-solving processes could not be confined to a single field or discipline. A political scientist by training, Simon received the Nobel Prize for economics and major national awards for his work in cognitive psychology, automation, computer science, political science, management, and operations research. Simon is also considered one of the founders of the field of artificial intelligence. Simon influenced CMU in several ways. First, he played a major role in the formation of the Graduate School of Administrative Science, the School of Computer Science, and the College of Humanities and Social Science's Psychology Department. In addition, he was a supporter of the university's commitment to entrepreneurship. At least as important, he became a role model for the CMU scholar: a problem solver of unbounded curiosity who works at the intersection of various disciplines yet simultaneously achieves the pinnacle of scholarly recognition.

> THE ECONOMIC STRUGGLES OF PENNSYLVANIA AND PITTSBURGH DURING THE PAST DECADE APPEAR TO HAVE CONVINCED UNIVERSITY LEADERSHIP HOW CLOSELY INTERTWINED CMU'S FUTURE IS WITH THE HEALTH OF ITS LOCAL INDUSTRY AND COMMUNITY.

As we will discuss below, CMU's commitment to innovation, problem solving, multidisciplinary focus, and engagement have been reinforced by an ongoing investment in strategic planning and self-assessment over the past 30 years and have been reaffirmed by current President Dr. Jared Cohon. At the same time, the economic struggles of Pennsylvania and Pittsburgh during the past decade appear to have convinced university leadership how closely intertwined CMU's future is with the health of its local industry and community. This recognition appears to have resulted in an expanded, more deliberate, more focused commitment to impacting local and regional economic development outcomes.

INDUSTRY RESEARCH PARTNERSHIPS

The National Science Foundation data[7] show that CMU's industry-sponsored research expenditures in 1999 were $17.6 million, or 12.5% of total research expenditures. In 1992, they were 17.2 % of total research expenditures. This decline appears to be driven by a rather dramatic increase in non-industrial funding. During this time period, overall expenditures increased by 25% while industry-sponsored expenditures decreased by 7%. Nonetheless the scope of industry-sponsored research is well above the national average of 7.4%, ranking 10th among the 100 largest U.S. research universities.

A number of factors appear to have contributed to CMU's strong performance in industrial research. First, CMU has historically emphasized programs that appeal to industry. It has maintained that focus to the present with its three largest colleges, engineering, computer science, and business, having direct relevance to industry. In addition, the quality of CMU's engineering, science, and business programs serves as a magnet for industrial involvement and sponsorship. A long list of programs in engineering, science, computer science, and business are ranked among the best in the nation. Undoubtedly, when firms want to interact with a university they want to interact with the best, and CMU can lay claim to that mantle for quite a number of its programs.

Another factor that contributes to CMU's active program of industrial research is its long-standing and well-deserved reputation for a multidisciplinary or interdisciplinary approach. It can boast more than 50 technology or economic development-focused research centers, institutes, and consortia, including 14 industrial consortia. Among this number it can count some of the most prestigious center programs, including two NSF Engineering Research Centers, one NSF Science and Technology Center and two of the 18 Sloan Industry Centers. It has also been home to one of NSF's industrially focused Industry-University Cooperative Research Centers. Perhaps the crown jewel among its centers is the Robotics Institute (RI). Started in 1979, RI is the world's largest robotics lab. In 1998 it was home to more than 150 faculty or staff scientists (including tenured and tenure track faculty), 80 graduate students, and 40 undergraduate students. Its total annual research volume exceeds $30 million.

In order to enhance interaction with corporate partners, CMU is planning a new project in an area called Panther Hollow — a valley that abuts the western edge of campus. Phase I will result in a 120,000-square-foot facility that will house the Digital Greenhouse (described below). It will also provide space for technology companies, many of which are new to the Pittsburgh region but have quickly become research partners of the universities.

Access to CMU's research centers and researchers is encouraged and facilitated by the university's Office of Corporate and Foundation Relations. This office supports a "research directory" that catalogs faculty, departmental, and center research interests and expertise. It also interacts with firms via student recruitment, executive education, and philanthropic support. While these mechanisms are certainly valuable, a great deal of the industrial involvement and investment in CMU seems to be driven and sustained by the efforts of individual faculty, departments, and centers, and by the quality of its programs.

TECHNOLOGY TRANSFER

The Technology Transfer Office (TTO) includes nine professionals and is responsible for commercializing the ideas and products produced by CMU faculty and students. License income was $5.9 million in FY 1999, a royalty return on investment, (royalties divided by research expenditures) of 4.21%. License income ranks in the 85th percentile, and royalty ROI ranks in the 90th percentile of the 142 academic institutions that participated in the *AUTM Licensing Survey: FY 1999*.[8]

CMU reported a total of 28 new licenses to start-ups in fiscal years 1998 and 1999 combined, placing it in the 83rd percentile among the AUTM licensing survey sample. CMU reported a total of 10 new start-ups formed in 1998 and 1999, seven of which were in-state. CMU ranks in the 89th percentile for total start-ups formed and in the 88th percentile for in-state start-ups formed.

Activities for the 2000 fiscal year continue to show a strong performance including: 106 disclosures, 39 patent applications, 27 patents granted, and 21 new license agreements. One reason for this high level of activity may be that CMU gives faculty inventors 50% of revenues from licenses, one of the more generous sharing formulas offered by major research universities. According to TTO records, 48 new companies have been formed based on CMU technology since 1993. According to recently compiled records, roughly 120 local firms can trace their origins back to the work or efforts of CMU faculty, students, or alumni. The vast majority of these companies were started in the 1990s.

Many of the outputs of CMU's technology development activities have been commercialized in and benefited Pittsburgh and the state economy. Six (out of 21) of the new license agreements executed during 2000 were with local companies, including four start-ups. The range of local companies started over the years is quite diverse and includes companies in life sciences, educational software, transportation, medicine, and software, among others. In spite of its success in this area, the university is trying to become more proactive in increasing the likelihood that those benefits will accrue locally[9] To this end, the TTO mission statement has added to its list of beneficiaries "the Pittsburgh community."[10] The TTO's 2000 annual report indicates "we have recently added a new focus to our mission: an emphasis on contributing to the local economy" and reports it will accomplish this goal by:

- *Assisting in the creation of more start-up companies by establishing and facilitating new guidelines for company formation by faculty;*
- *Improve the accessibility of the office to the faculty community;*
- *Enhance our leadership role in community organizations which are focused on regional economic development.*

The University Research Council in 2001 to address changes to the technology commercialization and entrepreneurial efforts of the university. Its report is being reviewed now, and the new "Innovation Network," a revised suite of services available to CMU faculty, will be based upon the URC recommendations.

INDUSTRIAL EXTENSION/TECHNICAL ASSISTANCE

CMU does not have a formal extension service. However, many faculty are involved in providing technical assistance and consulting assistance to local firms on an ad hoc and personal basis.

ENTREPRENEURIAL DEVELOPMENT

CMU's cultural emphasis on innovation, problem solving, and a multidisciplinary focus have been a fertile environment for entrepreneurial activity. While traditional academic expectations and standards remain very high, norms and procedures (e.g., leave-of-absence) have traditionally been supportive of faculty entrepreneurship. As a consequence, the typical technical, scientific, and business department can lay claim to its fair share of successful entrepreneurs. Perhaps the most widely known corporate name to trace its roots to CMU is Lycos. However, it would be a mistake to attribute CMU's recent successes to culture alone. Over the years, CMU has taken a number of steps to promote and support entrepreneurship within the university and the local community.

As in other areas, CMU has reaped the benefit of being an educational innovation "first mover." Formal courses in entrepreneurship have been offered at CMU since 1972. These offerings gradually expanded during the '70s and '80s until the creation of the Donald Jones Center for Entrepreneurship (DJCE). Founded in the 1990s by John Thorne and named after one of Pittsburgh's most successful entrepreneurs, DJCE not only provided a university-wide scope to these activities, it also helped target regional entrepreneurs, professors, and research staff at CMU and the University of Pittsburgh. DJCE offers graduate, undergraduate, and continuing education programs in entrepreneurship education; it also conducts research on entrepreneurship.

DJCE is housed in the Graduate School of Industrial Administration and includes three full-time (two chaired) and eight adjunct faculty. It has an endowment of about $5 million and receives about $250,000 each year in gifts and grants. Perhaps the one thing that sets DJCE apart from other entrepreneurial programs is the amount of entrepreneurial experience possessed by its faculty. Virtually all of its faculty are founders, co-founders, CEOs, presidents, and/or board chairs of a long list of successful high-technology start-up firms.

Over the years, DJCE, its faculty and students have won a number of awards, including a seventh place ranking among entrepreneurship centers by NASDAQ in 2000, four "Entrepreneur of the Year" awards for faculty from *Inc.* or Arthur Young & Company, and seven of 12 prizes at a regional Venture Capital Investment Competition in 2000.

However, the most impressive testament to the center's success is the growing list of successful start-up ventures it has spawned. For instance, STC Technologies (an outgrowth of SolarCare Inc.), a developer of medical tests and diagnostic products based in Bethlehem, was sold for $255 million in 2000.

Although CMU does not have its own incubator center, entrepreneurs have easy access to facilities at the Pittsburgh Technology Center located near the campus. The university is also planning to set aside space for start-up companies in the new Panther Hollow development. Plans are also underway to establish an "Innovation Network" that will provide a suite of services to would-be CMU entrepreneurs.

The efforts of the DJCE reach outside CMU in several ways. With a mission to "provide instruction, guidance, and support to potential and current entrepreneurs who plan to start or continue to grow a business in southwestern Pennsylvania," DJCE provides continuing education programs to the local and regional community. In addition, MBA courses often involve a consulting arrangement with local entrepreneurial companies. Scholarships for courses are available through the Pittsburgh Technology Council. Further, faculty are heavily involved in community and economic development efforts. Finally, although its only ties to CMU are through members of the board of directors, the Enterprise Corporation of Pittsburgh [11] founded by John Thorne serves as a "nonprofit spin-off" of these activities targeted at local and regional entrepreneurial activity.

INDUSTRY EDUCATION AND TRAINING PARTNERSHIPS

As discussed earlier, CMU has a long tradition of innovation in education starting as far back as the Carnegie Plan in the 1940s. In fact, many of its educational innovations have been designed to meet the needs of industry. For instance, in the 1950s the university developed the widely used "management game" and the mini-seminar series format used in many executive education programs. It also offered the first degree in e-commerce in the country in 1997. CMU continues that tradition today by offering a wide selection of highly focused, industrially relevant executive education and distance education offerings.

The Program for Executives is an intensive, rigorous, selective four-week program offered by the Graduate School of Industrial Administration (GSIA) for upper-level managers, which is designed to broaden their overall perspective and strengthen their skills in the art and science of general management. It allows intensive interaction between students and the program's 10 full-time staff and 25 affiliated faculty. The program is run by its non-faculty instructional staff. Technology-focused specialties offered as part of its executive education programs include: e-commerce, management essentials for information technology, technology-driven supply-chain management, and human resources for e-business.

Other industrially focused educational programs offered include the Institute for Technology & Management (IT&M), an advanced educational center focusing on the needs of the financial management, securities trading, software, and other information-based industries; the Program For Technical Managers, which provides an overview and development program for senior and upper-middle managers who oversee the technological and innovation functions of the organization; the Donald Jones Center for Entrepreneurship (described in the previous section); and the Green Engineering & Management short course for executives in civil and environmental engineering. The Software Engineering Institute also offers courses and seminars to help improve software engineering practice.

The Carnegie Bosch Institute (CBI) for Applied Studies in International Management is another example of CMU's willingness to partner with industry. CBI is a unique alliance between the Graduate School of Industrial Administration at Carnegie Mellon and the Robert Bosch Group, one of Germany's largest international corporations. The Institute was established in 1990 with a major endowment provided by Bosch. The institute's mission is to initiate and support research in international management, to educate and develop globally minded managers, and to foster international cooperation. In addition to its executive education programs, CBI funds a series of research projects and conferences focused on improving the management of international corporations.

Beginning as early as 1996, CMU has offered distance-learning programs through the School of Computer Science, the H. John Heinz III School of Public Policy and Management, and the Graduate School of Industrial Administration. Some of the more prominent industrially relevant offerings include: certificate in software engineering, a five course program adapted from the master's curriculum; a master's of science in information technology-software engineering, which includes an industry-based practicum project; a customized master's of software engineering (MSE) designed for professionals working for CMU corporate sponsors with at least six co-located students; and the information technology management track within its master's of sciences in the information technology program.

Students also can earn a master's degree in industrial administration via distance learning courses. CMU is in the process of developing an engineering master's program in the Washington, D.C., area that will rely heavily on distance learning. In a new twist on distance education CMU has created "Carnegie Technology Education," a nonprofit subsidiary focused on software system development education, to "mass-market career education needs by creating and delivering profitable education programs that will enable graduates to begin and sustain financially rewarding careers."

Career Services and Placement

Because of its national reputation, CMU attracts employers from all around the country. In fact, the records for the 2000-2001 school year from the university's Placement and Career Services indicate that only about 10% of on-campus recruiting organizations come from Pennsylvania. Consistent with its focus on regional economic development activities however, the university has taken a number of steps to help meet the needs of local and regional employers. For instance, local employers can now post job openings on the university's Jobtrak.com web site for free (a $20 saving per listing). Further, the Career Center and its staff have increased their involvement in local economic groups like the Western Pennsylvania Career Services Association (WestPACS) and the Pittsburgh Technology Council. WestPACS is a consortium of 34 four-year colleges in Pittsburgh and Western Pennsylvania and organizes job fairs for local employers. Finally, CMU participates in the Pittsburgh Technology Council's job fair that focuses on software, engineering and other science and technology fields; "@pghcafe" (pronounced "at Pittsburgh café").

Formal Partnerships with Economic Development Organizations

Over the past 10 years, the partnership between CMU and state and local economic development interests has grown and strengthened. On the one hand, CMU has been actively involved in a variety of Ben Franklin initiatives. The Ben Franklin program is Pennsylvania's economic growth-focused science and technology initiative with a regional arm known as Innovation Works. However, CMU has been more than a passive recipient of state science and technology largesse. CMU played an important role in the Regional Revitalization Initiative, a blueprint for the revitalization of southwestern Pennsylvania. It also has been an active supporter of and even a tenant at the Pittsburgh Technology Center. CMU was instrumental in attracting Union Switch & Signal to the center. The university played an important role in the siting and development of the state- and NASA-supported National Robotics

Engineering Consortium building in the Lawrenceville district of Pittsburgh, an economically challenged community. More recently, the university and one of its prominent researchers worked closely with the Pittsburgh Regional Alliance to convince Seagate to locate its research and development facility in Pittsburgh.

The Pittsburgh Digital Greenhouse (PDG) is another example of the growing partnership between CMU and regional and state economic development interests and other local universities. Started in 1999, PDG is a partnership between CMU, the University of Pittsburgh, Penn State University, the commonwealth of Pennsylvania and local economic development organizations. It was designed to facilitate the development of an industry cluster around application of system-on-chip technology in the digital multimedia and networking markets. PDG offers industrial members access to pre-competitive research, educational programs, expansion or relocation support, and recruitment assistance. PDG has about 25 industrial members and has supported several million dollars of research activity at local institutions. CMU played a critical role in PDG's development: key faculty helped plan its focus; it incubated the initiative as a nonprofit subsidiary before it was spun out to become community owned; and CMU's special advisor for economic development served as its interim president. Plans are now under way to create a life science greenhouse built on the PDG model. This will build on BioVenture, a partnership between CMU and University of Pittsburgh.

Ties between the local technology-based economic development community and CMU go beyond these fairly high profile initiatives. For instance, the Pittsburgh Technology Council provides scholarship support for some local participants in CMU's highly regarded entrepreneurship programs. In fact, the Entrepreneurial Management Program is co-sponsored by the Fay-Penn Economic Development Council and Pittsburgh Technology Council, among others. While the focus in this case study has been on technology-based economic development, it is worth noting that CMU has been very active in developing a variety of educational and social linkages with local schools and local community groups such as the Squirrel Hill Urban Coalition. One factor that contributes to these efforts is the plethora of local foundations. Pittsburgh has more foundation money per capita than any other major U.S. city. These foundations can often be tapped to help support worthwhile initiatives that have the potential to impact local economic development.

The H. John Heinz III School of Public Policy and Management serves as a critical resource and linking mechanism for regional economic development activity. This school and its faculty have a great deal of expertise in technology-based economic development. For instance, one of CMU's two Sloan industry centers, the Software Industry Center, is actually housed in the Heinz School. More importantly, the Regional Technology Policy Group within the Heinz School's Center for Economic Development is also heavily involved in the study, development, and dissemination of policies and practices that promote technology-based economic development. For instance, one of the school's regional benchmarking initiatives helped highlight some of the region's problems and served as a catalyst for the development of a number of local initiatives, including the Regional Revitalization Initiative, the Working Together Consortium, and ultimately the Pittsburgh Regional Alliance.

INDUSTRY UNIVERSITY BOARDS AND COUNCILS

Unlike most universities, CMU has a very centralized and very powerful system of advisory boards. Originally conceived as a mechanism for developing and refining strategies during the strategic planning process, advisory boards were institutionalized to become a critical part of CMU governance about 1990.

These advisory boards help the university by:

- Assisting the departments in assessing strategic direction, solving problems, achieving goals, and rising to new levels of excellence through counsel

- Ensuring that each department periodically conducts a self-assessment of its goals and directions by imposing a regular schedule of visits
- Providing independent assessment of the departmental strategic directions and objectives to the president, the provost, and the board of trustees

Each advisory board is chaired by a member of the board of trustees and typically includes some of the biggest names in that particular field. Roughly every three to four years, an advisory board will go through a cycle of meeting with departmental representatives, reviewing goals and objectives, reviewing and benchmarking progress toward achieving those goals, and preparing a final written report of its findings and recommendations, which is shared with the president, provost, trustees, the respective dean, and the department head. These reviews are also used with service units like computer services. While many universities have embraced strategic planning as an important tool for university advancement, few equal CMU in the thoroughness and comprehensiveness of its benchmarking and follow-through efforts. Industry is well represented on the advisory boards for business, science and engineering departments and ensures that these programs are high quality and responsive to its needs.

Industry also plays a major role in many of CMU's multidisciplinary centers. Obviously, industry is well represented in all of the university's industrial consortia where they play an active role in guiding the research. However, they also are well represented in the many academic centers spread throughout the university. For instance, all of the advisory board members for the Center for Entrepreneurship are former entrepreneurs or venture capitalists.

FACULTY CULTURE AND REWARDS

As described throughout this chapter, CMU's "culture" plays a significant role in the success and dynamism of its partnering activities. There is substantial evidence that faculty have embraced and internalized organizational norms and values of innovation, problem solving, interdisciplinary focus, and engagement. For example, although CMU does not have an official policy that requires new faculty appointments to be endorsed by other academic departments, that is exactly the way most appointments are made. CMU officials explain, "That's just the way you do things at CMU." Similarly, in spite of little official policy attention to the matter of leaves of absence, faculty appear to have no problem securing leaves to get involved in start-up companies. As another CMU official reported, "When your current department chairperson spent several years as a principal in a start-up, you figure out that asking for a leave isn't going to be a big deal."

Interestingly, a culture that appears to be very supportive of partnership-based economic development does not appear to be incompatible with more traditional academic values. Faculty tenure and promotion decisions appear to still require outstanding scholarly productivity. To further reinforce this point, a recent survey of CMU students found that the most frequently cited reason for attending CMU was its "academic rigor."

ENDNOTES

[1] National Science Foundation Division of Science Resource Studies. (2001). *Academic research and development expenditures, FY 1999*. Washington, D.C.: National Science Foundation. Table B-33.

[2] *Pittsburgh Post-Gazette* Benchmarks. http://pittsburgh.about.com/cs/facts/ .

[3] The plan includes three domains: CMU's foundation (community success, financial strength); CMU's core activities (education, research); and CMU's areas of focus (strategic areas of leadership, international initiatives, regional impact).

[4] The position changed to university director of economic development in 2001.

[5] Other members of the council include the directors of the Don Jones Entrepreneurship Center, the Technology Transfer Office, the Center for Economic Development, deans from business, policy, computer science and the CIT.

[6] See CMU Web link "History of Carnegie Mellon" (www.cmu.edu/home/about/about_history.html)

[7] National Science Foundation. Division of Science Resource Studies. *Op. cit.* Tables B-33, B-36, B-38.

[8] Association of University Technology Managers. (2000). *AUTM Licensing Survey: FY 1999.* Chicago, Ill.: Association of University Technology Managers.
Association of University Technology Managers. (1999). *AUTM Licensing Survey: Fiscal Year 1998.* Norwalk, Conn.: Association of University Technology Managers.

[9] An internal CMU report says approximately 150 local start-ups that can trace their origins to CMU's faculty and students, but it is difficult to evaluate the accuracy of this estimate.

[10] The other listed beneficiaries include: "Carnegie Mellon and its units, its scientists, engineers and other innovators, participating licensees and investors and society in general."

[11] Enterprise Corporation of Pittsburgh is now a part of Innovation Works.

STANFORD UNIVERSITY

Stanford is the cause of Silicon Valley ...

It's impossible to list the ways Stanford interacts with Silicon Valley. The University is a huge pool of talent that supplies the Valley with many of its engineers, lawyers, bankers, and venture capitalists. In addition to the odd billionaire entrepreneur. It's a source of fresh technology as well as a neutral ground where industry types mix with faculty, students, and even competitors.

What sets Stanford apart from other intellectual centers isn't that it contains extremely smart people with big ideas; it's that there are so many smart people in the one part of the world tailor-made to take their ideas and turn them into something real – and often profitable.[1]
— Fortune *magazine*

Stanford University was established in 1891 by Leland and Jane Stanford in honor of their only son, Leland Stanford Jr., who had died of typhoid fever. Leland Stanford Sr. was an entrepreneur who had made his fortune in supplying goods to gold prospectors and in building railroads. The Stanford bequest mandated the development of a "university of high degree." In addition to money, the bequest included 8,800 acres in Palo Alto, California. The availability and use of this "private land grant" has played a significant role in Stanford's impact on the regional economy. The Stanfords also mandated that the university be nontraditional relative to the norms of that era. It was co-educational, nondenominational, and it emphasized a "practical education to produce cultured and useful citizens." Given this mandate, the university developed strong educational programs in engineering, business, medicine, and the natural sciences. As with many institutions, its history has had impacts other than curricular on today's university.

Stanford has evolved into a research university of the first rank. Its undergraduate and graduate education programs are highly competitive, and Stanford students are among the best and brightest. Stanford reported research expenditures of $426.5 million in fiscal year 1999, which ranks eighth among all U.S. universities and second only to Johns Hopkins among private universities in total research expenditures in the FY 1999 survey of academic research and development expenditures of the National Science Foundation.[2]

Stanford's intellectual reach is broad. The School of Engineering, founded in 1925, now enrolls 21% of all Stanford students and spends more than $90 million for research annually. *U.S. News & World Report* ranks it second in the U.S. only to the Massachusetts Institute of Technology in overall quality. The School of Medicine was founded as the Cooper Medical College. It was merged into the university in 1908, and moved from San Francisco to Palo Alto in 1959. The medical school also has a strong research emphasis, receiving more than $230 million for research and claiming the highest research expenditure level per faculty member. The Graduate School of Business was organized in 1925, and enjoys a national reputation. *U.S. News & World Report* ranks it first in the nation. A number of other graduate departments are highly ranked by *U.S. News & World Report*: In the biological sciences, Stanford ranks second overall, with no sub-specialty ranked lower than eighth. In the chemical sciences, second overall. Stanford graduate programs appear in the top 25 in all fields ranked by *U.S. News & World Report* except two. Stanford is top-ranked in computer science, physics, and psychology, is ranked second in mathematics, and is ranked third in geology[3]

A review of the history of Stanford and the conversion of the Santa Clara valley from an agrarian area to the Silicon Valley, and the consequent outcomes of steps the university took indicates three critical factors led to Stanford's leading role in the economic development of its region.

The Stanford "land grant." Made as part of the bequest, the Stanford family recognized the land's value beyond providing a venue for the university campus, specifying that it could not be sold and that its value would only increase. The Stanford family donated 8,800 acres of land, which subsequent boards of trustees and campus leaders have substantially preserved. The university is now the largest private owner of undeveloped land in Santa Clara County[4] Stanford University land holdings are parts of one other county, two cities, and two towns. An important benefit of having available land was the university's ability to create an industrial/research park in the early 1950s. The idea of the park developed when Varian Associates, an early technology spin-off company, approached the university with a proposal to build its facility on leased university land in order to be adjacent to the intellectual resources of the institution. Dr. Fredrick Terman, who was then dean of the School of Engineering and a supporter of the Varian Brothers' venture, built on this proposal with a concept that other companies with technological interests complementary to Stanford's would be interested in locating near the university. Subsequently, the university planned and developed an 800-acre park, known first as the "Stanford Industrial Park," then later as the "Stanford Research Park." Consistent with the original vision of the Stanford "land grant," companies could not buy building sites but could get long-term leases. Early occupants, in addition to Varian, included Hewlett-Packard (whose world-wide headquarters are still in the park), Eastman Kodak, Beckmann Instruments, Syntex Pharmaceuticals, and Xerox Corporation. The park, although modest by today's standards, served as a prototype for later ventures such as North Carolina's Research Triangle Park and became the incubator for the Silicon Valley. The Stanford lands also include a major shopping center, which is an important revenue source for the university and the city of Palo Alto, and large preserves of undeveloped open space in a region where open lands add materially to the quality of life.

Dr. Fredrick Terman. Possibly the single most important individual in the development of the university's role as an engine of economic growth, Terman received his undergraduate education at Stanford following World War I and went to MIT for graduate work. Terman returned to Stanford to teach electrical engineering and during his tenure became a leader in that field. In addition, he tirelessly worked to link the university's research and education efforts to the interests of business and government. He was continually concerned that there be jobs in the region for Stanford graduates, as the contiguous Santa Clara valley of that era was a sleepy small town and a rural region. He encouraged students like Hewlett, Packard, and the Varian brothers to start businesses and helped them with advice, contacts, and even what would now be known as angel investments. He is credited with such programmatic innovations as the research park, the Engineering Honors Cooperative Program (see Industry Education and Training Partnerships later in this chapter), and the concept of building academic "steeples of excellence" (see Faculty Culture and Rewards later in this chapter). Terman served as dean of the School of Engineering and chief academic officer of the university before his retirement. No other person could more legitimately claim the title of father of Silicon Valley.

The Cold War. In the 1950s, as tensions increased between the United States and the Soviet Union, the federal government actively looked for new defense technologies, and encouraged the private sector to develop technologies and build devices that would help make the nation's military strong enough to secure dominant world leadership for the United States. Dr. Terman's doctoral advisor at MIT, Dr. Vannevar Bush, had laid out a blueprint for the growth and development of America's scientific enterprise in his report to President Truman, *Science, the Endless Frontier.*[5] This report proposed an intensive effort to advance technology in the service of the nation's foreign policy and welfare. A key issue in the 1950s was national security in a nuclear age. World War II had demonstrated the importance of technology in the conduct of war and in deterring the possibility of war. The government defense and intelligence establishments were the sole markets for these new communications, computing, and electronic products. Defense contracts for both research and development and procurement fueled the growth of these industries in the 1950s and 1960s. Somebody had to design, test, and build the instruments that the government was buying to assure the nation's strategic advantage. Stanford and the newly founded businesses spun out during the pre-war and post-war years were the right companies at the right place at the right time. What better opportunity for an institution like Stanford, which had built a strong academic research position in engineering and sciences underlying these technologies and where well-prepared students could be found? The demands of the Cold War for new technology and high-technology products fueled the development of the Stanford region's businesses such as Fairchild Semiconductor and Varian Associates in the 1950s and 1960s, and formed the basis of what has become Silicon Valley's basic industries.

In summary, the Stanford story is not about a formal, deliberate approach — buttressed by mission and vision statements — to being a player with industry. Rather it is a story of timing, leadership, and the triumph of a robust entrepreneurial culture.

MISSION, VISION AND GOAL STATEMENTS

Stanford has traditionally followed a vision to be a research university of the highest rank. The Stanford bequest sets out the vision that the university would be "a university of high degree." It has sought the most accomplished faculty and the students with the greatest potential. Its mission and vision statements speak of its academic and educational role and ambitions but not of an economic development mission per se. Stanford's historical and current impact on the regional economy has instead come from a complex set of interrelated situations and circumstances just outlined. It has always been subordinate to the university's goal of academic excellence.

Dr. Frederick Terman, while serving as university provost, coined the metaphor of "steeples of excellence"[6] to describe the Stanford approach. As a steeple rises far above the general skyline and appears unique in architecture, the academic "steeple" enjoys a unique visibility and reputation. Academic steeples are built by recruiting and retaining a "critical mass" of faculty members in a selected niche or sub-discipline. In doing so, an institution must make choices in order to focus resources and attention toward the selected "steeple" areas often at the expense of other opportunities. Despite this risk, many of the steeples on the U.S. academic skyline carry the Stanford logo, and the strategy has worked well. The institution has developed and maintained excellence in many academic areas while the overall faculty has increased to only 1,368 — a sign of the validity of this concept focusing on the best and brightest in well-defined areas.[7]

> **STANFORD'S EXCELLENT RESEARCH IN A NUMBER OF "PRACTICAL FIELDS," COMBINED WITH A WILLINGNESS TO PURSUE INTERDISCIPLINARY RESEARCH, HAS BEEN A MAGNET FOR COMPANIES LOOKING FOR COLLABORATIVE RESEARCH RELATIONSHIPS.**

Ironically, the university has avoided formal statements of vision, mission, goals, and objectives. One university official reported that the board of trustees in the early 1990s requested a strategic plan and mission statement and were told by the then-president and other administrators that such an effort would be unnecessary. Their argument was, in effect, that the mission and goals were well understood by the university community, so why engage in a redundant exercise.

President John Hennessey's recent inaugural address[8] not only emphasized heavily undergraduate teaching and the humanities, but also noted the constant role of research in the financial and intellectual future of the university, implying that a continuing renaissance in undergraduate instruction in the humanities was built on the existing base of science and technology.

INDUSTRY RESEARCH PARTNERSHIPS

Stanford's excellent research in a number of "practical fields," combined with a willingness to pursue interdisciplinary research, has been a magnet for companies looking for collaborative research relationships. In the greater scheme of things, the industry share of support is not unusually high. The NSF data[9] show that Stanford's industry-sponsored research expenditures in 1999 were $31.5 million, 7.4% of total research expenditures. In 1992 they were 4% of total research expenditures. During this time period, overall expenditures increased by 16% while industry-sponsored expenditures increased by 88%. In FY 1999, industry-sponsored expenditures were equal to the overall national ratio of 7.4% and ranked 36th among the 100 largest U.S. research universities using this measure.

While Stanford has been a leader in technology transfer for many years (see Technology Transfer below), research relationships with industry were not always well managed. A 1995 faculty study of industry relationships in the medical sciences painted a grim picture. The report mentioned "a growing mutual distrust ... [based on] ... perceived differences in motives and mission that are not based on fact." The report said, "Stanford is perceived as one of the worst American universities to deal with, especially on the topic of ownership/patent status of intellectual property."[10]

Until 1995, Stanford followed the practice of linking the administration of industry-sponsored projects with the administration of government research grants. This was coupled with episodic advice and guidance obtained from the Office of Technology Licensing (OTL) on matters of disposition of intellectual property, managing conflicts of interest, and publications. Nonetheless, the flexibility required to organize and get an industry-sponsored project underway and managed while in progress was not compatible with government grant administration, and working through these issues was often frustrating for both the professor and the company.

OTL was given subsequently the responsibility for managing industry-sponsored research. The Industrial Contracts Office is now located with OTL but reports to the dean of research. This new organizational step at the institutional level, combined with a concerted effort to train research administrators at all levels of the university, appears to have made the growth of industry-sponsored research possible and positive relationships easier to develop and maintain.

Stanford uses the Internet extensively and effectively to provide a helpful "gateway" for companies to access expertise. Information on faculty research interests is readily available and searchable, and information is available about industrial affiliate programs and others. Much of this is at the site maintained by the University Office of Corporate Relations.[11] The Office of Corporate Relations appears to serve as a "network manager," providing links to a variety of campus resources of interest to business. A link to the Office of Technology Licensing site (http://otl.stanford.edu/flash.html) includes information on technologies available for licensing and a user's guide to information on policies and agreement provisions.

TECHNOLOGY TRANSFER

Stanford University has long been a leader and benchmark institution in technology transfer through patenting and licensing. In keeping with the university's laissez-faire approach to faculty entrepreneurism and innovation, its intellectual property policies have given the faculty inventor more latitude than most institutions. A faculty inventor has the option to place an invention in the public domain when there is no agreement between the university and a sponsor to the contrary. Therefore, the technology transfer program has had to provide value to the faculty inventor, who is not obliged to assign rights to the university by the sponsor of his or her research.

Stanford's Office of Technology Licensing was established in 1970, 10 years before most universities were encouraged to take similar steps by the Bayh-Dole Act. OTL was a pioneer of the "marketing approach" to technology transfer. Rather than waiting for a technology pull, reacting to requests for licenses from interested companies, the OTL encouraged faculty to promptly disclose inventions, then quickly and carefully evaluated the market value of inventions, obtained protection of intellectual property, and looked for licensees for those inventions with the highest potential. This approach began at Stanford at a time when such an approach was viewed as unseemly by some of Stanford's peer institutions. A successful outcome of this approach was the patenting of recombinant DNA technology and a successful program to license the technology widely. This program returned $255 million over the life of the patent estate to Stanford, the University of California (where a co-inventor worked), and the inventors.

Stanford's technology transfer program has followed the pattern of most programs that have returned handsome financial rewards. Of the almost 2,000 licenses granted by September 2000, only eight generated more than $5 million. In total, 31 technologies to date have generated more than $1 million each.[12] This pattern is common among institutions that post large royalty revenues. Most come from a limited number of "blockbuster" technologies.

Stanford's policy for the division of license income reflects the university's decentralized nature but also demonstrates how licensing success and the incentives that derive from these successes can have a positive effect on the academic culture. OTL retains 15% of the gross license income. The balance (85%) is split evenly between the inventors, the inventors' departments, and the inventors' schools or colleges. This has the effect of returning most of the proceeds to the academic units where inventors work. If OTL can operate on less than the 15% retained, any remaining sums go to the university's dean of research (chief research officer), to be used for purposes related to research and education. Even for an institution the size of Stanford, this can be a sizable sum of undesignated money, and can accrue.

Even without recombinant DNA (the patent estate expired in December 1997, and royalty income ceased a year later), the Stanford licensing program remains healthy. An emphasis is placed on making license deals and on building lasting relationships with licensees, not necessarily on maximizing royalties. OTL awarded 265 new licenses in 1998 and 1999, approximately seven licenses per $10 million of research expenditure. Net license income (license income after deducting income paid "off the top" to other institutions that share rights to the licensed intellectual property) remained a healthy $28 million in 1999, or 6.5% of research expenditures that year.[13] Stanford is in the 95th percentile of those institutions participating in the AUTM licensing survey on net licensing income, and the 94th percentile on licensing income as a percentage of research expenditure.

Stanford as a matter of policy does not give preference or actively seek local licensees. However as a practical matter, the strong ties between Stanford faculty and students and local businesses and venture entrepreneurs means that a strong regional market exists for new inventions. Stanford reported a total of 83 new licenses to start-up in fiscal years 1998 and 1999 combined, placing it in the 98th percentile in the total AUTM licensing survey population for this measure. Stanford reported a total of 28 new start-ups formed, all of which were in-state. Stanford ranks in the 99th percentile for total start-ups and in the 99th percentile for in-state start-ups.

Beyond the biomedical realm where patent rights are paramount and can be quite valuable for their entire life (recombinant DNA is a good example), the licensing relationship may be as valuable as any formal rights licensed, for both the university and the licensee. OTL recognizes this and seeks to do deals in support of existing relationships.

INDUSTRIAL EXTENSION/TECHNICAL ASSISTANCE

Stanford is a private university with a strong vision to excel as a research university known for quality undergraduate and graduate education. As such, there is no institutional mission or organization to provide outreach and extension services.

However, Stanford has an entrepreneurial culture and an entrepreneurial faculty. Companies in the Silicon Valley are staffed with Stanford graduates, founded on Stanford technology, and run by Stanford graduates. So long as interaction with companies will promote their academic research and teaching goals and objectives, there are few policy constraints on providing the equivalent of extension services to local companies. When this is layered with access to Stanford education and training, the university's support of entrepreneurship and the technology business community and the rich capital resources in the region, the impact is powerful. In effect, by offering faculty members the opportunity to work with companies for their own best interest or because they find the issues intellectually challenging, Stanford is able to operate a no-cost industrial extension program for the general San Francisco Bay area.

ENTREPRENEURIAL DEVELOPMENT

Stanford's experience with entrepreneurship runs long and deep beginning with Frederick Terman's concern with encouraging students like Hewlett and Packard to start technology businesses in the 1930s. Terman continued to see the need to promote business development through the post-war 1950s and 1960s in order to provide work opportunities close to home for Stanford graduates and to build a competitive edge for the region in the ongoing electronics revolution.

An important step was the creation in 1951 of the Stanford Industrial Park (which later became the Stanford Research Park). The park was created by leasing land from the original Stanford farm on a long-term basis. The first tenant was Varian Associates, a graduate student start-up. The park has flourished but not as an incubator. Land is too costly, and other independent business incubators have sprung up near the campus.

The string of Stanford start-ups continues, including successes such as Symantec, 3Com, Logitech, Sun Microsystems, Silicon Graphics, Netscape, MIPS Computer Systems (now-President John Hennessy was involved with this one), Cisco Systems, and Yahoo!. From 1973 through 1993, more than 300 companies were founded by Stanford faculty and students. This activity continues. In 1997, 1998, and 1999 Stanford reported 43 new start-up companies based on licensing of the university's technology.

The Stanford Entrepreneurship Task Force is an on-campus grass roots effort to coordinate activities of a variety of entrepreneurship-oriented groups across the University. Although it is university-based, members of the Silicon Valley entrepreneurial community with similar interests participate in many of the task force's activities. Like a number of university activities, it has evolved "bottom-up" out of a need by a number of university organizations to keep informed, coordinate activities, and jointly work on "events" of common interest. The effort is about 18 months old, and appears to be working. The task force provides a vehicle for venture capitalists, attorneys, and others in the area to stay in touch with activities in Stanford's laboratories and classrooms. Other connections are multi-layered and include alumni entrepreneurs, "returned faculty" who have worked in businesses but are now back on campus, faculty consultants, and student-workers. There appear to be few barriers to close and continuing engagement.

The core organizational and logistical support for the task force has been provided by the Stanford Technology Ventures Program, a teaching and research effort of the School of Engineering to train engineers and scientists in entrepreneurship skills. STVP is supported by the Kaufmann Foundation, and works closely with a student group, the Business Association for Stanford Engineering Students (BASES). Stanford has supplemented a rigorous engineering curriculum with formal and experiential education in entrepreneurship, drawing on the local alumni base and faculty role models. This program, and perhaps more importantly the underlying culture of the institution, has a strong influence on students and graduates. One faculty member pointed out a watch phrase of Stanford's engineering school: "If you want to be an engineer, go to MIT; if you want to be an entrepreneur, come to Stanford."

Stanford benefits from a solid history of entrepreneurial success that has produced many role models; both faculty and student cultures reward entrepreneurship in both the academic and business worlds. *Fortune* magazine reports on this student culture by quoting graduate engineering students attending a "show-and-tell" with venture capitalists at the university. When one student pointed out that he could always get a job with McKinsey (the consulting firm) one of his colleagues replies: "What, and waste a perfectly good education?"[14]

This foundation of activity supports continuous, up-to-date activity in teaching and research, and facilitates coordination with the local entrepreneurial infrastructure that sustains the impact and maintains what analysts have called the "Silicon Valley edge."

INDUSTRY EDUCATION AND TRAINING PARTNERSHIPS

Beginning in the 1950s, Stanford saw opportunities in the need for advanced continuing education for engineers at some of the pioneering Silicon Valley companies. The transistor and the semiconductor were coming on the scene, and the firms had to deal with rapidly changing technologies to remain competitive. The School of Engineering started a unique graduate program called the Honors Cooperative Program, which allowed working engineers to take courses at night and earn advanced degrees. Dr. Terman encouraged the development of this program to support new and growing companies in the area (at the time, the term "Silicon Valley" was not used). The Honors Cooperative Program continues with strong support from the Stanford Center for Professional Development.

The use of video to aid the Honors Cooperative Program began in 1964 and rapidly grew both on-campus and to other locations in the area. Off-campus links to Silicon Valley companies began in 1969. Stanford's reputation and quality drove demand, and as the initial client companies grew beyond the valley the need for wider transmission of offerings grew as well. The Stanford Instructional Television Network (SITN), run by the School of Engineering, became a leader in the emerging field of distance learning.

In 1995, SITN became the Stanford Center for Professional Development (SCPD), still run from the School of Engineering. In addition to television, the preferred medium has become the Internet. The center is a leader at using the Internet, and it reaches more than 6,000 students a year through more than 250 courses offerings. The center is also experimenting with "on-demand" presentation of content and subdividing courses into smaller chunks of learning information. The center employs 50 people and has the technical capability to have course sessions on the Internet or on the air within one hour of the original presentation. SCPD is successful enough to pay for itself and for faculty time through tuition revenues. SCPD supports distance learning and Web-based instruction for all Stanford academic units on a charge-back basis. SCPD has also considered joint ventures with for-profit organizations and other academic units but is closely tied to its primary mission to promote Stanford education.

The Graduate School of Business does not offer online courses or evening or part-time executive MBA programs. It does offer a range of brief, problem-oriented executive courses, the Executive Education Program, and has a one-year residential master of science in management program for mid-career managers.

CAREER SERVICES AND PLACEMENT

Like most universities, Stanford operates a comprehensive career center for both undergraduates and graduates. In addition to the institutional program, the graduate School of Business has a placement program for MBA graduates. Eighty percent of all graduating graduate students have had at least one encounter with the center. The center relies heavily upon a computer-based and Web-accessible "dating service" to make matches, rather than relying upon campus recruiting visits by companies.

The Career Center sees its mission as supporting Stanford's overall mission by helping well-prepared students get into the right work situations to support their continued growth and learning. Geography does not play a factor any more than geography plays a factor in business-sponsored research and technology licensing.

It appears from Career Center statistics, however, that Stanford creates an inflow to the region. The center estimates that in-state students are a minority of Stanford's student body. Forty-four percent of undergraduates are in-state. Graduate student data is not as precise, but estimates are that 35% come from California, and graduate students comprise 52% of the student body. However, more than 50% of Career Center placements are at jobs in California, demonstrating a positive effect on the local economy, which was not measured by the 1995 Economic Impact Study.

Companies in the valley have various relationships with Stanford faculty and students that create visibility and positive perceptions for students looking for jobs. This campus presence gives local companies an advantage when other more traditional advantages of the region are fading: The cost of living is increasing; the "livability" and quality of life is diminishing; there are companies working with challenging technology elsewhere in the world.

Stanford graduates are in demand in the global market, and established companies from outside the region have often lost out to smaller, newer companies with a larger campus presence. This changed in 2000 and 2001 as the information technology and Internet economy slowed down.

One aspect of placement that cannot be overemphasized is the formal and informal roles played by Stanford alumni. For example, the Alumni Association runs an Internet service that links up alumni with potential employers. The School of Business newsletter is a well-known resource for finding MBAs with an itch for the next deal. This presents unique opportunities for entrepreneurial, technology-savvy grads to tap into a strong network for their second, third, or later job placement.

Partnerships with Economic Development Organizations

Stanford's important role in the economic development of the Silicon Valley and the San Francisco Bay area is evident, as is its continued pivotal position as a source of educational services and new ideas essential in a knowledge economy region.

This impact was initiated and sustained without formal relationships with economic development organizations but rather with a web of continuing relationships at many levels. The university has been able to see ways that close relationships with business can promote its educational and research interests and companies can readily see the benefits of university on their bottom lines.

This was not always the case. As professor of engineering and Dean of the School of Engineering in the late 1930s and the post-war 1940s and '50s, Dr. Terman was concerned that Stanford graduates in the newly important fields (electrical engineering, physics, and mathematics) had to go east or at best to the Los Angeles area to find work. Terman began by encouraging graduate students like Hewlett, Packard, and the Varian brothers to build companies nearby, and by encouraging leading corporations like Fairchild, IBM, and Xerox to locate research and development centers nearby. Using Stanford land for an industrial research park helped. As defense spending grew and the demand for the products and services based on these scientific areas grew, the local economy was off to the races.

As Silicon Valley has flourished, economic development attention has shifted from promoting growth to managing growth. Stanford lands comprise the largest parcel of undeveloped land in Santa Clara County, and Stanford, with more than 14,500 employees,[15] is one of the largest employers in the county. The university must be careful about adding people, which will mean more cars, a more congested roadway system, and more demand for housing in an area where costs are quite high.

Industry/University Advisory Boards

Stanford has more than 100 research centers organized in its various schools and departments. It is common for these centers to have industry affiliate programs or industry advisory boards. For example, the School of Engineering has 28 affiliate programs, and the School of Earth Sciences has 16.

Advisory boards function absent any detailed institutional policy. There is, however, considerable practice history to draw on, and deans have considerable latitude to innovate within their schools.

In addition to affiliate programs and industry advisory boards, general advisory councils or boards of visitors at each school include strong representation from business. Deans, who are concerned about graduate employment opportunities, research support, and donations, are aware enough of the for-profit sector of their constituencies to includ business people — often alumni — on these advisory groups.

The liberal use of advisory boards and industry affiliates programs provides another mechanism that ties Silicon Valley companies (as well as other companies) to the university. They provide another means to strengthen lasting relationships.

FACULTY CULTURE AND REWARDS

On the surface, Stanford's faculty culture appears to be quite traditional. Given the "steeples of excellence" approach, Stanford recruits the top candidates in those fields where it has built its "steeple." Expectations for continued academic achievement are high, and for the most part tenure and promotion are based solely on academic achievement and building an outstanding academic reputation among the national "invisible college" of scholars. Outside activity, including working with companies or starting a company, are neutral factors. Tenure and academic promotions are granted solely on academic achievement.

There is another important aspect to Stanford's academic culture, however. Faculty members are expected to support themselves and their research activities with little help from the institution beyond start-up support for new faculty members. In a word, the Stanford culture rewards the academic entrepreneur. As a result, there has been an open environment in which doing research with a company or a new venture is not considered in a negative light, provided it enhances the education of students and provides or contributes to opportunities to conduct important, nationally visible research. There appears to be little "either/or" attitude about business sponsorship of research versus government support.

In past years, taking time off to work in a company generally did not happen until a faculty member got tenure. It was pointed out in the interviews that President Hennessey took his time off to work in his company after receiving tenure. However, this pattern began to change in the late 1990s as non-tenured faculty are considering this route as well. The cost of living in the area is such that younger faculty members with marketable skills are interested in supplementing their university income, and the lure of a potential equity share in a start-up is powerful.[16] Faculty are encouraged by the fact that Stanford would select a technology entrepreneur and scientist to be a dean, a provost, and most lately the president to lead it into the new century. Dr. Hennessey's experience and that of other faculty leaders present strong role models and many opportunities simply cannot wait. So far, according to university officials, those who have taken time off have worked very hard to stay on time in the university's seven-year tenure track, and appear to be making the expected progress on schedule.

The talented faculty has in turn proved to be a strong magnet for business in many areas of technology. These relationships move beyond working with established companies to working with start-ups. Here again, Stanford has a rich tradition dating back to the 1930s when Dr. Terman, as professor of engineering, encouraged graduate students to commercialize their discoveries. Hewlett-Packard began in Palo Alto in 1938 with Terman's encouragement and a $500 loan. The list of successive business start-ups is long and impressive. Today, although it is neither favored nor precluded, taking time off from an academic career to work in a company, owning a piece of a company, or developing your own inventions, is not atypical of a Stanford professor's career in the sciences and engineering. Although the medical school is more traditional on these matters, faculty there have also been involved in similar activities. Continued and frequent examples of this activity provide strong and plentiful role models for both junior faculty and students.

ENDNOTES

[1] Aley, J. (1997). The heart of Silicon Valley: Why Stanford. *Fortune.* (July 7, 1997, pp. 68-69).

[2] National Science Foundation Division of Science Resource Studies. (2001). *Academic research and development expenditures, FY 1999.* Washington, D.C.: National Science Foundation. Table B-33.

[3] Ranking of university graduate programs. (2001) *U.S. News & World Report.* (http://www.usnews.com)

[4] Pacific Partners Consulting Group. (1997). An Economic Impact Study of Stanford University (1995). Stanford, Calif.: Pacific partners Consulting Group.

[5] Bush, V. (1948). *Science – the Endless Frontier.* Washington, D.C.: National Science Foundation, (1961 reprint).

[6] Terman, F. (1968) *Steeples of Excellence.* Report to the State of South Carolina.

[7] Counting faculty members at a university is difficult at best. The 2000 Stanford Fact Book presents this number with the following definition: "Includes tenure-line faculty, non-tenure-line faculty and senior fellows at specified policy centers and institutes. Academic staff-teaching, center fellows, and Medical Center-line faculty are not members of the Academic Council."

[8] Hennessey, J. (2000) *Stanford in the 21st Century.* A speech at his inauguration as Stanford's 10th president, October 20, 2000 (http://www.stanford.edu/news).

[9] National Science Foundation. Division of Science Resource Studies. *Op. cit.* Tables B-33, B-36, B-38.

[10] The report is quoted by Schreiberg, D. (1998). The Matchmakers. *Stanford Today.* (Jan/Feb, 1998, pp. 49-54).

[11] http://corporate.stanford.edu/.

[12] Ku, Kathy. (2001). Stanford University Office of Technology Licensing, 2001.

[13] Association of University Technology Managers. (2000). *AUTM Licensing Survey: FY 1999.* Chicago, Ill.: Association of University Technology Managers.
Association of University Technology Managers. (1999). *AUTM Licensing Survey: Fiscal Year 1998.* Norwalk, Conn.: Association of University Technology Managers.

[14] Aley, J. *Op. cit.*

[15] Pacific Partners Consulting Group. *Op. Cit.* (Employment figures include employees at the university, the University Health System and the Linear Accelerator Center.)

[16] Lords, E. (2000). Being a Professor in Silicon Valley May Mean You Can't Afford a Home. *Chronicle of Higher Education.* (February 11, 2000, p. A-16).

SUMMARY AND RECOMMENDATIONS

What lessons do these case histories of 12 outstanding U.S. universities teach on how to make a difference regionally in the knowledge economy? Based on their examples, how might we instruct their peer institutions to operate more effectively in the new world of external partnering and involvement in issues of state and regional technology-based economic development?

The research team believes that the most important lessons can be grouped into three areas: (1) knowledge about policies and practices that seem to be working among our study sample of institutions; (2) some more general guidelines about implementing and maintaining such innovations in an organization as complicated and often political as a university; and (3) how both sets of lessons can be accelerated and supported by new directions in public policy at both state and federal levels. The reader should be forewarned that in commenting on categories two and three the authors are getting somewhat beyond the empirical observations of the case studies. Nonetheless, we believe there are important crosscutting themes that should be enunciated.

BEST PRACTICES AND INSTITUTIONAL POLICIES

As described in Chapter 1, our analytic and data-gathering approach focused on 10 domains of partnering activity. These were based on themes that seemed to dominate the existing research and practice literature in this largely undeveloped field. In fact, these 10 areas of inquiry seemed to be the right ones; very little that that we uncovered in the 12 case studies could not be subsumed under one of these categories. Returning to that structure, what were some of the types of novel practices and policies that we observed in our case studies?

Mission, Vision, and Goal Statements

We found many examples of mission statements — at various organizational levels within our sample of cases — that were rich with the metaphors and language of partnering. They included:

- The use of mottoes, program names, and slogans that served a rallying or branding function
- The use of thematic prose on economic development and industrial partnering in institutional strategy documents, goal statements, and objectives
- Comparable themes in college or unit level documents
- An extensive incorporation of all of the above into speeches, brochures, Web sites, and publications, many of which were particularly targeted for audiences outside the institution

Industry Research Partnerships

Based on national statistics, our sample of institutions was among the nation's leaders in the scope of industry-sponsored research and in the "customer friendliness" of relevant policies and practices. The latter included:

- Single points of contact and coordinating structures via which companies can explore potential research relationships
- Efforts to simplify research contract language and to use novel forms of packaging relationships (e.g., master agreements, strategic partnerships)
- Databases of faculty interests and competencies and associated Web-based search engines that help companies find faculty members that match their needs
- Hiring nationally prominent scientists — with industry and/or entrepreneurial backgrounds — into high-prestige endowed chairs
- Research parks, contiguous to campuses, to encourage permanent and ongoing relationships between tenant companies and faculty researchers
- Tying together graduate education and industry research partnerships

Technology Transfer

All of the case study institutions had excellent technology transfer functions, and many had novel features that were consistent with a larger partnering and economic development orientation. These included:

- Policies and procedures that were helpful to would-be faculty entrepreneurs, including concerted efforts to achieve legislative relaxation (for public institutions) of equity participation in licensing deals involving start-ups
- Extensive informational outreach to faculty members to familiarize them with principles and operations of the technology transfer function
- Close working relationships and physical co-location between the technology transfer function and the management of industry-sponsored research
- The availability of pre-seed, proof-of-concept money for the further development of research-based innovations

- Sensitivity to issues of economic geography and the migration of value-added development out of the state and a corresponding tendency to license to state-based companies

INDUSTRIAL EXTENSION AND TECHNICAL ASSISTANCE

Approximately half of the case institutions were heavily involved in technical assistance and outreach to established industrial companies. Some of the typical features of those programs included:

- State-subsidized technical assistance services, delivered statewide, via a network of regional university offices
- Extensive use of faculty and graduate students as outreach staff
- Operational linkages to colleges of engineering
- Ties to the federal Manufacturing Extension Partnership

ENTREPRENEURIAL DEVELOPMENT

Many of our exemplary institutions were involved in various facets of entrepreneurial development, with both internal and external community foci. Elements included:

- Technology business incubation services and facilities, either directly administered by the university or with a strong university linkage
- Entrepreneurial coursework and majors, for both technical and business students, that included both classroom and experiential components
- Research parks with appropriate space and services for new or small companies
- Outreach programs focused on community-based entrepreneurs
- University links to and nurturing of community-based venture funds

INDUSTRY EDUCATION AND TRAINING PARTNERSHIPS

Across the board, our cases spoke to a significant commitment to serve companies in a variety of educational and training roles. Some examples:

- Education and training offerings that are catered to the needs of key state-based industries
- Decentralized, statewide delivery of extension courses
- Special programs targeted toward state and local economic development officials
- Use of formal training needs assessment to drive the design of education and training programs

CAREER SERVICES AND PLACEMENT

The primary "product" of a university is embodied in its graduating students. Their placement or channeling into jobs can also be conducted in ways that contribute to state economic development. Some examples:

- Extensive use of internships and co-op programs, particularly in state-based companies
- Giving state-based companies a "first look" at emerging graduates via job fairs or Web-based services
- Career service discounts to state-based companies

FORMAL PARTNERSHIPS WITH ECONOMIC DEVELOPMENT ORGANIZATIONS

There were various ways that our sample of institutions became more directly involved in regional or state economic development activities, including:

- Hosting, or operating under contract, state technology programs
- Being involved in high-level recruiting of large technology-based companies
- Participation in local or state industry or technology councils
- Training economic development professionals
- Conducting economic development policy studies and evaluations

INDUSTRY/UNIVERSITY ADVISORY BOARDS AND COUNCILS

Advisory boards and councils represent another vehicle for welding together academic and external interests and perspectives. Various structures exist, with some examples being:

- Industry advisory boards for centers or institutes
- Presidential-level advisory councils, with significant involvement by industry
- Involvement of industry in unit-level strategic and curricular planning

FACULTY CULTURE AND REWARDS

Across our institutions there were many with policies in place to guide and encourage external partnering and involvement in regional economic development. Policies often also linked this activity to tenure and promotion. In addition, these universities provided many examples of less formal but no less significant cultural practices and supportive activities. They included:

- Formal awards and acknowledgement events to honor faculty inventors, entrepreneurs, and industry partners
- Efforts to redefine the service component of scholarship (e.g., for tenure or promotion review) to encompass industry partnering, technology transfer, involvement in economic development and allied activities
- Links and pages on university Web sites and media efforts that extolled partnering successes
- Hiring of senior institutional officials (e.g., presidents, chancellors, deans) with industry and entrepreneurial experience
- Developing and promulgating myths and stories of partnering or entrepreneurial success

ENABLING AND MAINTAINING CHANGE

After spending nearly two years documenting notable practices and policies among our sample of universities — juxtaposed against our much longer experiences with the many institutions that were not represented in the study sample — our team came to some strongly held opinions about how universities can and cannot become effective partners with industry and participants in regional economic development. First of all, we are struck with how tenuous or fragile the partnering business is in most university environments, and that the institutions described herein should be commended for their courage and perseverance. The typical campus environment is not modeled after the corporate world, in which singularity of purpose is easily maintained. Universities are very diverse and heterogeneous organizations on many dimensions — disciplinary, political, and cultural.

Moreover, in many universities there is a widespread belief (or myth) that industry and economic development partnering translates into academic mediocrity. For many institutions the activities described in this volume are not natural acts. While it is perhaps easier for land grant institutions to make the reach, it is nonetheless difficult for many of them as well.

The upshot is that unless influential, key university champions really believe in this stuff, and work it hard, it may be stillborn or quickly become part of the university's organizational archaeology — programs or centers with odd names and no purpose anyone can remember. Organizational innovations such as partnering and engagement have the same struggle to survive their early, enthusiastic stages of implementation and become an ongoing part of organizational life, as do many other discarded ideas.

Nonetheless, we believe that there are several organizational factors that can contribute to the development and maintenance of partnering activities. In the following sections we will discuss the roles of (1) leadership; (2) supportive conceptual and language systems; (3) organizational structures and policies; and (4) the state and regional policy and political context.

THE IMPORTANCE OF LEADERSHIP

A common theme among the cases, particularly in those schools that are relatively new to the world of external partnering, is the presence of a strong president or chancellor and senior leadership who are pushing this agenda. Universities are conservative organizations in terms of their basic orientations, structures, and priorities; it takes Herculean effort to move them off their center of gravity. For faculty members, university life goes on much as it always has, with the changing tones and directions of institution-wide initiatives tolerated as so much background noise. Moreover, most of the changes that are exciting from a faculty point of view — whether shifts in discipline-focused epistemology or research foci, or new approaches to graduate training — seem to occur at the unit (e.g., department, center, institute) level. The average faculty member lives in this world and generally isn't affected daily by the "bureaucracy" of central administration. Moreover, faculty members are often isolated from activities in other departments, colleges, or units, and may succumb to rivalry more easily than to collaboration.

Similarly, at the risk of offending a large number of brilliant and dedicated individuals, we would argue that the average university CEO has not historically been knowledgeable about or supportive of the activities described in this book. Few of these otherwise dedicated men and women have personal experience, for example, in being involved in a technology start-up company, or participating in a governor's economic development brain trust, or playing a key role in an industry sponsored research consortium. The more typical career path is to start as a productive discipline-focused scholar, to move to departmental administration, and then to dean and beyond. Relatively few CEOs bring another set of experiences.

However, some university CEOs (several among our cases) have been touched somewhere and somehow by a different agenda and have become champions of a larger set of priorities for their universities. For example, the president of Stanford was involved in a Silicon Valley start-up; the chancellor of the University of California-San Diego was nationally prominent in industry research; and virtually all of the CEOs among our study samples are strong and visible champions of partnering activities. There are parallel examples at the level of deans and vice presidents for research. Although all of these individuals remain fervent advocates for the traditional academic mission of excellence in education, research, and public service, they have come to believe in other goals as well. Moreover, in their writings and speechmaking, they argue that an increased emphasis on serving the regional economy and

173

partnering with industry *complements* the traditional goals. In effect, "partnered" faculty members are likely to be better scholars in terms of traditional criteria, a view that has increasing empirical support in the research literature.[1] Government leaders that have an interest in steering their state-based public institutions toward greater partnering need to mindful of the leadership issue and how important it is to make careful choices at this level. University CEOs and other senior leaders will typically be in their jobs five to 10 years. If they are hostile, inexperienced, or immune to this agenda nothing much will happen during their watch.

The criticality and importance of leadership changes over time. For example, in order to move a university away from it traditional ways and organizational center of gravity, a strong voice at a high level must call for change. Among our cases, Ohio State is perhaps the best example of a mission and vision "renewal" situation, one where the CEO played this very important role. Chronologically downstream from early implementation, there are other opportunities for leadership to make a difference. For those institutions that have been programmatic commitments to partnerships and then go through one or more changes in administration, there is often a need to renew and enhance the partnership mission, vision, and program structure. UCSD is an excellent example where current leadership has maintained and enhanced the gains realized by predecessors.

Aside from being a believer and a vocal advocate, what particular functions do innovative institutional leaders perform? On the basis of our cases we believe that there are two other broad categories of behavior that are critical: (1) creating an intellectual argument and local language system around the new activities; and (2) building and maintaining organizational structures and policies that will sustain the work of partnering.

VISION, MISSION, AND MYTHS

In every institution studied there was a supportive organizational "culture" that rested on a body of beliefs, values, and metaphors. In each university we found a dense thicket of words describing the whys and wherefores of partnering. Since universities live in the world of ideas, elegantly and forcefully expressed, this was no surprise. Nonetheless, it appears that every institution had put a great deal of effort into developing rationales for moving into novel domains of organizational behaviors.

These supportive arguments come in many forms: vision statements, mission statements, strategic planning documents, and mottoes (in Latin and/or English). They typically are developed concurrently at several levels within the university, including institution-wide language enunciated by CEOs and senior leadership, college-level statements, and in some cases at the level of departments or other academic units such as centers or institutes.

In fairness, these various statements should *not* be considered as having been created in whole cloth and simply handed down by leadership. Great universities do not work that way. In most cases, the language supporting partnerships was hammered out via a laborious and participative process of discussion, public comment, and occasionally formal actions by units of faculty governance such as an academic senate. Although difficult, these processes are worth undertaking; universities cannot be changed by fiat. This is another lesson of which external governance (boards of trustees) and political leadership (legislators and governors) need to be mindful, before they move too quickly and unilaterally to mandate the policies and practices discussed in this volume. A participative process of intellectual dialogue and self-discovery usually needs to take place.

There is another important role in the change process for the intellectually visionary and courageous institutional leader: targeted recruitment. In order to move an institution in these new directions, universities may have to seek a different breed of candidate to fill key positions. It is doubtful that traditional career paths will yield the experiential base for a candidate for president, provost, or dean that will lead the institution in a partnering direction. The commitment and perseverance displayed by leaders in our cases cannot be created overnight. It is our observation, with little hard empirical evidence outside of our small sample of cases, that these individuals have come to this juncture as a result of a long process of experiential learning and intellectual dialogue that is hard to replicate. Nonetheless, the process of learning could be accelerated among the current and upcoming cadre of institutional leaders. For example, one could visualize a series of learning experiences — led by campus CEOs and other administrators who are wise to the ways of partnering — for their peers at institutions that are just getting their feet wet in these areas.

To some degree, the partnering activities that are discussed and advocated in this volume represent, in part, the whole process of redefining scholarship. Much of this started a decade ago with the publication of the highly influential *Scholarship Reconsidered*[1] by E.L. Boyer. The largest impact of this volume, and the resultant series of intensive on-campus discussion, has been on reviving rewards for teaching and legitimating "outreach." Nonetheless, on some campuses and in some units, there has been explicit attention to many of the activities that we have described in industry partnering and contributing to economic development. Among our cases, Penn State and Virginia Tech have perhaps been the most articulate about making partnering and outreach — as described in this volume — an integral part of the overall mission of the institution, and in language that is reminiscent of the *Scholarship Reconsidered* arguments.

Finally, we would like to point out the apparent importance of what we would label as *local mythology* in support of the partnering agenda. In every institution there seemed to be a body of local lore and apocryphal stories that we heard repeated across informants and found throughout text materials that were supplied to the team. Sometimes these were about heroic (and now wealthy) faculty entrepreneurs. In other settings, the angle might be the job creation impacts (expressed via human-interest examples) of technical assistance to a regional manufacturing company. The metaphors and details of these tales seemed to energize the tellers, and we sensed that they were told and retold within the campus community. One organizational theorist has described the process of "management by storying around,"[3] and we think an analogous process is operating among our case institutions.

STRUCTURES, POLICIES, AND INSTITUTIONALIZATION

At some point in their life span, most organizations go through processes of innovation and change. However, all too often the impetus of positive change gets lost unless the new approaches are somehow made part of ongoing organizational life. Some years ago Robert Yin[4] described the process of "routinizing" innovation, a concept with considerable applicability for the study at hand. Yin recognized that many innovations are tried in organizations such as universities and there is great enthusiasm and visibility during the pilot or start-up phase. However, the key for making a sustainable contribution is to get beyond the pilot stage, and turn the most critical organizational features of the novel program into standard operating procedure through job descriptions, mission statements, and the like.

One thing that characterized our sample of institutions is that the language of mission, vision, and mythology was not just hot air. There were real people doing real jobs in structures, programs, and offices dedicated to various aspects of partnering. The important point is that organizational structures and activities that are relatively novel within the larger university community were put in place and maintained. For example, in several of the universities there was an office or senior position dedicated to outreach (or economic development) with administrative responsibility, a budget, and authority to move the partnering agenda. Similarly, many of the institutions created coordinating structures — often backed by the authority of the CEO or chief research officer — that tied together the different domains of partnering activity. These councils, cabinets, or whatevers tended to cut across or "matrix" the academic units as well as the more traditional administrative units. They typically were headed by an administrator with position power or by a coordinator whose authority tended to be more symbolic or derivative from the campus CEO. It is not clear which model is more effective.

Most of the exemplary institutions also spent hard hours in the policy mines. These efforts helped *align* a very disparate set of elements. These included: the pre-existing rocks and shoals of university rules and legal constraints; the new mission and vision language and goals; the evolving structure of partnering programs and activities; as well as the occasional cowboy activities of individual program managers. This is essential work. In a way, it represents a move from an ad hoc approach to one that is more "routinized," in Yin's terminology. It serves to stabilize and make less vulnerable to attack the new partnering orientation of the institution. Certain policy issues were more frequently mentioned in this context, such as conflict of interest and commitment, as well as intellectual property management. For example, as these cases were being written, a number of universities (sometimes in conjunction with their state legislature) were revisiting the issue of equity ownership of spin-off companies.

STATE AND REGIONAL CONTEXT: POLITICS AND POLICIES

There is another set of policies and programs that are quite pertinent to the story that is being told in this book. It is no coincidence that virtually every university case is located in a state that is currently or recently active in technology-based economic development. For example, Penn State and Carnegie-Mellon must share the historic spotlight with the Ben Franklin partnership, as well as with more recent initiatives under the current administration. Wisconsin is working in close collaboration with state government in the development of initiatives in the biological sciences. Virginia Tech has benefited from the state's Center for Innovative Technologies program. UCSD is a current winner in a huge state of California centers program that has an explicit partnering orientation. And so on.

The enabling context of pro-technology state government goes beyond the benefits of merely a benign policy environment. Many of the universities described here are active partners with state government in fostering a technology-based economy. Several are de facto operators of state programs. These include Penn State, North Carolina State, Purdue, and most notably Georgia Tech. This undoubtedly has had some effect on "routinizing" the partnering agenda in these institutions. For example, the Industrial Extension program at North Carolina State has been in operation for more than 45 years and comparable activities at Penn State and Georgia Tech have been underway for many years as well. Georgia Tech has been, in effect, an operating partner of several of the state-based Georgia Research Alliance initiatives.

These relationships tend to reap other benefits for the involved institutions. While the evidence is not overwhelmingly clear, it does appear that state appropriations discussions are friendlier, there is a greater degree of consultative activity on university-sensitive legislation, and legislators do not see university campuses as hostile territory. These are some of the fringe benefits of university-industry-government partnering.

FUTURE POLICIES AND ROLES OF STATE GOVERNMENT

Although the focus of our analysis and practice descriptions has been the university itself, we feel that there are lessons that state government can derive. We would recommend the following:

Influence the selection of leaders. If the process of selecting university leaders — both administrative and scientific — only involves traditional academic voices, the result will be traditional academic hires. This is not to say that the separation of government and university governance should be overturned, but that technology-focused interests in private and public sectors should have some voice. There are various ways that this can be accomplished. For example, when Georgia Tech hires for endowed positions that have been enabled by funding support provided by the Georgia Research Alliance, this significantly tilts the search toward world-class individuals with industry backgrounds.

Support research funding with partnering incentives. Relatively few federal research-funding programs are oriented toward partnering. However, if state government can somehow "sweeten the pot" with significant funding programs that explicitly call for partnering over a period of time the culture of research will shift. Some additional words of advice are pertinent here. One is to make sure the size of the individual awards and the size of the overall fund are of significant magnitude to attract the attention of star researchers. Second, make sure that there is a longitudinal, preferably nonpartisan, commitment to providing such funding. Programs that wax and wane along with budget politics will not grab the serious attention of faculty. One solution here is to put the source of such funding off the annual appropriations table, so to speak. For example, a number of states have dedicated portions of long-term tobacco settlement money to these purposes, and others have used energy revenues or settlements. Third, make the call for partnering a *requirement*. Some states' programs start with a strong emphasis on industry partnering and financial matching, but then state bureaucrats chicken out when senior university officials whine to governors or powerful legislators. Fourth, create funding mechanisms that emphasize the involvement of smaller, technology-based companies in the state. These are the enterprises that have the hardest time surmounting the university bureaucracy and are also the most likely to be neglected in federally funded partnership initiatives. Among their ranks are some of the fastest growing companies in the country.

> **Recommendations for State Governments:**
> - Influence the Selection of Leaders
> - Support Research Funding with Partnering Incentives
> - Support Research Parks and Incubators
> - Increase Formal Partnerships With Universities
> - Pay Attention to Economic Geography
> - Show the Flag

Support research parks and incubators. There is ample evidence among our cases that universities committed to partnering are also committed to supporting and nurturing entrepreneurial activity. Two types of programs, often interconnected, seem to enable this: research parks and incubators. Regarding the latter, there is now a body of practice knowledgec[5] and evaluation evidence[6] that we know how to nurture technology-based new companies that derive from the commercialization of university technologies. However, to accomplish this demands incubator space and programming to serve this need. Typically, the most difficult financial challenges in establishing and operating an incubator are: (1) initial capital investment for building and facilities (e.g., computers, wet labs); and (2) ongoing staffing of the incubator management and core staff. This is a very meaningful role for state policy and support. The positive experiences in Pennsylvania and Georgia are illustrative.

However, incubators are not enough. Equally important is the presence of research parks that are adjacent to university campuses. These facilities serve several functions. They function as an economic development tool to lure technology-based companies that have technology interests compatible with research strengths of the university. They can provide an opportunity for spillover lab space for the university, at the same time creating venues for mingling of university and industry people. The layout and physical structure of the Centennial Campus at North Carolina State University is a particularly striking example of this trend. Each building is organized around an area of science and technology and has both industry and university tenants. A third focus served by a research park is that it can provide transitional space (particularly in multi-tenant facilities) for graduates of technology business incubation programs. In addition, both a park and an incubator can provide space for essential business service providers such as accountants and lawyers. Finally, some universities have chosen to put their various outreach programs in a cluster of adjacent offices, and place them physically off campus in a research park environment. There are a number of ways in which states and regional units of government can enable the establishment of research parks including zoning practices, bonding authority, capital loans, and the like.

Increase formal partnerships with universities. In our opinion, some of the most notable accomplishments by universities have occurred when there were formal, operational program partnerships in place with state government. The two sectors are running something together, or the university is doing what might be construed as state government work. Examples are many.

Pay attention to economic geography. A wide variety of partnering activities have been described in this book. In that process, we have tried to examine the regional implications of various programs. For example, a university may be quite active in technology transfer and licensing, but if few or none of those deals involve state-based companies then the regional impact is minimal. Similarly, two of the authors have been involved in research on issues of "brain drain," and have documented the huge disparities across states in the retention and attraction of newly minted science and engineering graduates. State policy leaders are deeply concerned about this issue for obvious reasons. If the "best and brightest" leave home and never return, and if the most promising homegrown technologies get commercialized in another state, then the future growth of the state's knowledge economy will be stunted.

A number of universities among our cases have made special efforts in student placement to serve state-based companies, and others have tilted their technology transfer activities to place greater effort on local deals, often start-ups. Some states have launched major scholarship programs to lure promising high school graduates to in-state universities. All of these efforts are going in the right general direction, but they tend to be on the program development back burner. We urge a higher priority.

Show the flag. As described above, the magical language of vision, mission, goals, and objectives plays an important role in enabling partnering universities. In this book, we have focused most of our attention on how these language tools get developed and used by and mostly inside the university. There is a complementary role that should be played by elected and appointed officials. They should get more informed on the potential of universities to contribute to state economic development (by reading this book, for starters), then start using whatever "bully pulpit" they can command to spread that message among their constituents and political allies. Equally important, they need to visit campuses more frequently and make the same kinds of speeches in that setting. A popular governor, extolling the benefits of university partnering and engagement, can make a positive change on the university culture. Despite the cynicism among some academics about some politicians, a well-crafted speech by a sitting governor still has the potential to stir positive spirits in the campus community.

FUTURE POLICIES AND ROLES OF FEDERAL AGENCIES

It would be overoptimistic to conclude that federal agencies — particularly those that provide the bulk of funding for university research — care much about the partnering activities described here. Likewise, those same agencies are only dimly aware of state and regional economic development priorities and concerns. But for a variety of historical reasons, and occasional pressures from the Congress, some of the federal agencies have been involved in the support of partnering activities. For those programs in those agencies, we would recommend the following:

Increased support for university-industry research partnerships. There have been federal programs for a number of years to fund this type of activity, at the level of both individual projects and centers. The National Science Foundation has been a leader in this area, but agencies such as the National Institute of Standards and Technology (NIST), DARPA, and NASA have also played significant roles as well.

Nonetheless, from our perspective there are two problems with the current federal agency role in support of university-industry research partnering. For one, the aggregate money has been relatively low as a fraction of total agency support. Given the leverage provided by industry participation, and the demonstrated role that such partnerships have played in accelerating the movement of research into practice, these would seem to be wise investments. The second issue is a bit subtler. That is, in supporting university-industry partnerships the tilt has tended to be toward the university side of the equation. For example, within the National Science Foundation there are a number of center programs which all have some element of industry involvement. However, the program that has the most industry involvement (financial and substantive) has been the one that has received the least support.[7] In contrast, other programs in which the industry role is more advisory and less financial or agenda-setting focused tend to receive the lion's share of NSF support. The whole issue of benefits, costs, investments, and public policy payoff in supporting industry-university research partnerships needs to be revisited among the cognizant federal research and development funding agencies.

Protect Bayh-Dole. By a wide margin, the Bayh-Dole legislation of 1980 has had the most impact on pushing universities into the world of industry partnering. From time to time, it is reexamined and various tinkering efforts are undertaken. It is important that the basic thrust of Bayh-Dole be protected. Universities and faculty need to be enabled and rewarded for protecting and commercializing their intellectual property. These efforts have had a huge impact on the growth of technology-based industry, and that impact is likely to increase with a burgeoning biotech industry over the next few decades. Do not kill the golden goose.

Champion a new breed of university. As people who have been employed in universities as faculty and staff, struggled with university change processes as consultants, conducted research on universities, and worked in federal agencies that fund university research, our team of authors brings more than 80 years of collective experience and scholarship to this project and the book. We believe that we are on target about this powerful trend among research universities in the United States. That is, an institution that can be national or world class in its research, scholarship, and educational programs, but *also* can be effective at a variety of partnering activities that enhance regional economies and contribute to the growth of technology industry. In short, universities can be smart, do well financially, and do well in a public mission sense, all at the same time.

A ROLE FOR MAJOR NATIONAL FOUNDATIONS

In the Introduction we suggested that officials in major national foundations be readers of this report. Assuming that some of them have done so, what are their potential roles in realizing the action agenda implicit in this book? One obvious answer would be to send money, but we believe that there are other activities that are equally important.

Reconceptualize giving strategies. Support of higher education tends to be a relatively common and valued activity of foundations, as does support of projects and programs to enhance community development and opportunities for disadvantaged groups. Rarely is an explicit link made between the two streams of activity. The case studies in this book have attempted to describe new roles for universities that have significant potential for regional economic development. In turn, the authors subscribe to the notion (which much of the research literature supports) that an excellent route to improving social conditions is via improving economic opportunities. We urge foundations to rethink how their support of higher education can be more directly tied to their social agenda — via new roles for institutions of higher education.

Convene a national dialogue. The development of the case histories in this book has stirred a great deal of excitement among our informant institutions, as well as among leaders of other institutions that have received an early peek at the findings. Many institutions not among our 12 are under significant pressure — external and internal — to make a difference in their state and region. There is a corresponding hunger for innovative and effective practices and policies that others have tried. We believe that the time is ripe for a focused exchange among the leadership of the research institutions of the nation. Based on formal and informal communications, we know that the CEOs and leadership of our study sample would welcome a chance to share their experiences and lessons with their peers. We also know, from the reception that this book has received from readers of early drafts, that there is interest in a dialogue. One role that one or more foundations could play — particularly those with a longstanding interesting in higher education — is as convener of a series of such interactions that could potentially lead to constructive action.

NEXT STEPS

Our team and the observations in the book can be little more than a blip on the vast sea of university life in the country. What would change this? We firmly believe that the leadership of the institutions spotlighted in this book — and their government and industry and partners — have themselves a powerful story to tell. We would strongly urge some federal entity, some national association, or some national foundation — or combinations of all of the above — to take on a 10-year challenge of which this book can be a part. That challenge would be to advocate, educate, champion, and harangue the larger academic community to pay more deliberate and more informed attention to the successes described here and that are occurring at other campuses as well. It is truly the era of the "engaged university," and the policies, practices, and visions of these exemplary institutions should show the way.

ENDNOTES

[1] Blumenthal, D. (1992). Academic-Industry Relationships in the Life Sciences: Extent, Consequences and Management. *Journal of the American Medical Association.* (268: 3344-3349).

[2] Boyer, E.L. (1990). *Scholarship Reconsidered: Priorities for the Professoriate.* Princeton, N.J.: Carnegie Foundation for the Advancement of Teaching.

[3] Armstrong, D. (1992). *Management by Storying Around.* New York, N.Y.: Doubleday, 1992.

[4] Yin, R. (1979). *Changing Urban Bureaucracies.* Lexington, Mass.: Lexington Books.

[5] Tornatzky, L., Batts, Y., McCrea, N., Lewis, M., and Quittman, L. (1996). *The Art and Craft of Technology Business Incubation.* Research Triangle Park, N.C.: Southern Growth Policies Board.

[6] Molnar, L., Grimes, D., Edelstein, J., DePietro, R., Sherman, H., Adkins, D., and Tornatzky, L. (1997). *Impact of Incubator Investments.* Athens, Ohio: National Business Incubation Association.

[7] The Industry-University-Cooperative Research Centers (IUCRC) program within National Science Foundation is an interesting case that has been around for over 20 years. NSF financial support in these centers (over 50 in existence) is dwarfed several times over by the consortia of technology companies that provide most of the backing.